【Voices from the Edge】

NARRATIVES ABOUT THE AMERICANS WITH DISABILITIES ACT

[Voices from the Edge]

EDITED BY
Ruth O'Brien

OXFORD
UNIVERSITY PRESS

2004

OXFORD
UNIVERSITY PRESS

Oxford   New York
Auckland   Bangkok   Buenos Aires   Cape Town   Chennai
Dar es Salaam   Delhi   Hong Kong   Istanbul   Karachi   Kolkata
Kuala Lumpur   Madrid   Melbourne   Mexico City   Mumbai   Nairobi
São Paulo   Shanghai   Taipei   Tokyo   Toronto

Published by Oxford University Press, Inc.
198 Madison Avenue, New York, New York 10016

www.oup.com

Oxford is a registered trademark of Oxford University Press

Library of Congress Cataloging-in-Publication Data
Voices from the edge : narratives about the Americans with Disabilities Act /
edited by Ruth O'Brien.
   p. cm.
Includes bibliographical references and index.
ISBN 0-19-515686-2; 0-19-515687-0 (pbk.)
1. People with disabilities—Legal status, laws, etc.—United States—Popular works.
I. O'Brien, Ruth.
KF480.Z9 V65 2004
342.73'087—dc21   2003004242

9 8 7 6 5 4 3 2 1

Printed in the United States of America
on acid-free paper

 Rogers M. Smith

We made the normal jokes.

At least, they were normal among the teenagers in my hometown of Springfield, Illinois, in the 1960s. It is the state capital, and the biggest employer in town is the state of Illinois. There were certain stereotypes about state employees. If we had to wait impatiently in our cars while a man in a wheelchair crossed the street, someone would be likely to remark, "Looks like a state worker racing to the office." If one of us said something that seemed a bit dim, another might say, "I'm not calling you dumb, boy, but looks like you're headed for a career in state government." And I admit: when in high school I got a summer job in the Illinois secretary of state's office, for the first couple of weeks I used to amuse my friends, when they asked what I was up to, by jerking my arms, slurring my voice, and saying, "I've got a state job."

I stopped that soon, though not soon enough, because I got to know more of my coworkers, who were indeed disproportionately drawn from the ranks of the disabled—some with multiple sclerosis, some with lost limbs, some with mild mental retardation. I learned they were all too vividly and bitterly aware of the bigoted branding of state workers as incompetent "spazzes" and "retards." I learned that, angry and alienated as they were, most worked hard at their jobs, did them well, and knew they did them well. And I learned in grim detail that the reason most of them worked for the state was that, regardless of their capabilities, no place else would hire them.

I also saw other patterns in state employment, though at the time I did not really connect them with the state's hiring of the disabled. In those days, every state elevator had an operator who would ask you what floor you wanted and then push the appropriate button. On the older elevators they then had to pull a heavy lever, but on most of the ones then being used, they just had to push that button. These were obviously make-work jobs, patronage jobs, and we healthy young men with good prospects snickered about them, too. The elevator operators were sometimes people in wheelchairs, but most often they were African Americans; sometimes, they were both.

Eventually, the elevator operators came to be seen as a waste of taxpayer dollars, and they were eliminated. By then, with the impact of the civil rights movement and civil rights laws, more and better jobs were opening up for African Americans, in and out of state government. I was thrilled by those developments. I knew racial discrimination was pervasive and that it was wrong. Blacks had been treated as second-class citizens in both the public and private sectors for far too long.

But though I came to see that many disabled people were also subjected to unfairly limited employment opportunities, I did not think of them as second-class citizens. That just wasn't the category that occurred to me in thinking about their disadvantages (insofar as I thought of them at all). Unlike the case of black Americans, the heart of the problem did not seem to be so much false stereotypes and invidious prejudices against the disabled. It seemed to be their very real physical or mental limitations. Yes, employers and the rest of us probably overestimated how limiting those disabilities actually were, and that was a shame; but the disabilities were genuine, whereas racial inferiority was not.

Those, at least, were my half-conscious assumptions in those days, and similar assumptions seem to have been common among many disabled citizens themselves prior to the politics of the civil rights era and, especially, the politics surrounding the passage of section 504 of the 1973 Rehabilitation Act. That section appears to have catalyzed the emergence of a new understanding of the identities and interests of disabled Americans among many activists on disability issues. As Ruth O'Brien notes in her introduction to this marvelous book, from that point on, many more came to argue that the disabled should not be seen in terms of a medical model, which portrays them as damaged people who need society's help. Instead they should be viewed in terms of a civil rights model, which depicts them as citizens who are often discriminated against in public institutions and practices because of their physical distinctiveness, when it is perfectly possible to construct institutions and practices that would accommodate their differences and enable them to participate and contribute equally with all "normal" citizens. Just as some people were long denied (and are still denied) jobs and equal access to public services and facilities because of others' aversions to their physical pigmentation and accents, other people were being denied (and are still being denied) jobs and equal access to public services and facilities because of aversions to their physical configurations and manner of speech—when they could do those jobs and participate in those public arenas as well as the next guy, if things were set up right.

Though this connection between racial discrimination and disability discrimination was not frequently made prior to the 1970s, O'Brien is right to argue that in fact the two have long been intertwined: in U.S. history, both native blacks and immigrants from anywhere other than Northern Europe were long demeaned as being not only racially inferior but also particularly prone to disease, deformity, and retardation. All of us who analyze the history of U.S. citizenship need to explore further how categories such as "likely to become a public charge" have operated historically to deny access to the United States to many disabled persons and to make others into second-class citizens.

But this book is concerned with yet more pressing matters. It focuses on where we are right now, as government officials at all levels, business managers, and judges are charged with giving life to the greatest victory of the modern disability rights movement, the 1990 Americans with Disabilities Act. Their tasks are not easy, just as they are not easy in the case of measures combating racial discrimination. In both instances, we face questions about how far to give special assistance to the minorities in question, since doing so may help eliminate unjust obstacles but may also foster resentments and perpetuate stigmas. Much of the time, inclusion and accommodation can be achieved in ways that are clearly beneficial even in narrow economic terms, as talented people are added to the workforce at low cost. But sometimes the choices are more difficult; and some of the hard questions concerning disability policies are very different from those concerning racial policies.

Some disabilities can be hidden, in ways that racial identities generally cannot be. Is it right to hide them, or to have to hide them? Some disabilities represent genuine incapacities, in ways that pigmentation does not, even though people are able with great determination and with some special accommodations to overcome those disabilities. If they can overcome them, how much special assistance do they really merit? And if they can overcome them only with rather extensive and expensive accommodations, are they really being unfairly discriminated against when they are denied certain opportunities?

Those are some of the issues with which officials, businesses, and especially courts are now wrestling. Unfortunately, many are doing so in ways that are all too reminiscent of historical and current struggles over racial equality: after laws guaranteeing rights and fair treatment are put on the books and political agitation for action subsides, frequently bureaucrats, businesspeople, and judges look for ways to avoid the costs and disruptions of change by limiting the scope and significance of those apparent legislative victories. Without slighting the genuine complexity of the issues involved, this book shows that such subtle strangulation is being exerted against rights under the Americans with Disabilities Act today. This book does so, in part, through highly perceptive scholarly analyses of the legal and political issues involved. It also does so through stories that take us to the very heart of the profoundly personal, as well as profoundly political, struggles that inevitably arise in both individual and societal efforts to live with disabilities. I believe these stories are essential to serious scholarly inquiry, because intellectual inquiry aims at achieving sharper insights and fuller knowledge, and there are some insights that cannot easily be achieved any other way.

In my case, it was only when I learned the personal stories of my state coworkers that I stopped making the "normal" jokes about the disabled that were common among "normal" people like me. The insight that led me to do so is a vital yet flickering one that must not ever be lost sight of, here and in so many other contexts:

Some things may be "normal," but that does not make them right.

[Preface]

Informed by my own experience, I came to the understanding that living with a physical impairment, even a temporary one, means that you are bound to face humiliation when you present your needs to other people. Your private, personal situation becomes open to public scrutiny, exposing you and making you vulnerable. Having only a minor, invisible disability of bilateral tendonitis in my forearms, I was curious about what other persons with disabilities experienced. Were people who relied on seeing-eye dogs or who used crutches and wheelchairs treated differently? Was it me who was a fraud? Did the temporary nature of my minor impairment account for some of the most unpleasant experiences I had ever had? Or was there something universal about how persons with disabilities are treated in the United States?

Initially, I read memoirs (including some written by some of the contributors to this book) to look for the answers to these questions. I found Stephen Kuusisto's, Leonard Kriegel's, and John Hockenberry's memoirs so compelling that I did not end there. I began talking with people. In 2000–2001 and 2001–2002, I received Professional Staff Congress–City University of New York grants and in 2002 a Diversity Project Development grant, which enabled me to interview some persons with disabilities in Vermont and California. They told me stories that were riveting, sometimes heartbreaking, and always emotionally complex. The power of their stories, however, gave me concern. With my limited creative writing skills, how could I do justice to their experiences?

Having discovered Stephen Kuusisto's whereabouts, then a small town in the Hudson Valley, I found his name in a directory and, almost on a lark, gave him a call. To my delight, Steve was immediately receptive to the idea of writing narratives about the ADA. With his encouragement, I began calling the contributors cold. All of the authors with whom I talked were open to the idea. We would do for disability rights what Derrick Bell, Richard Delgado, and Patricia Williams had done for civil rights. Unlike these law professors, however, our volume was to be divided into two distinct parts: fiction and creative nonfiction and legal commentary. The narratives were picked on the strength of their writing. They were not chosen because of the different disabilities they covered. I reprinted a chapter from John Hockenberry's *Moving Violations* since it fit so well in the book. Nor were they selected because they shared any one point of view about disability rights.

The two years that I have spent with the contributors to this volume have been an eye-opening experience. It was a tremendous pleasure to see how their creative minds work. My contributors have given me an invaluable education, and I am very grateful. I hope this experience will manifest itself in other writing projects.

There are many people I would like to thank for helping me with my part of the project. My friends Susan Martin-Marquez, Martha Campbell, Robin Boyle-Laisure, and Nadine Cohen are well appreciated for reading my contribution to this volume and being so encouraging about the project as a whole. Susan, in particular, had the patience to read through a multitude of drafts. My colleagues Dianne Avery, Peter Blanck, Chai Feldblum, Paul Longmore, David Pfeiffer, Dan Pinello, and Bonnie Tucker were astute critics. I must also thank my colleague Jill Norgren for her insightful criticism. Jill has an innovative eye or approach that I unfailingly benefit from. I appreciate Elliot and Isaac Stryker for lending me their mother, Sharon Miller, for a long weekend while Sharon helped me comb through some of the legal issues in the commentary. Stephen Dodge also provided illuminating information about building codes and accessibility. Anonymous reviewers of the legal commentary were especially generous with their time, giving me insights I failed to see. Rogers Smith deserves special mention for his enthusiasm about writing the foreword. Opening with his own narrative, he sets a wonderful tone for the book. I also valued the help that Jennifer Rappaport gave me with her thoughtful comments about the commentary. As for Dedi Felman, our editor, there is no string of adjectives long enough to capture the role she played. Not only did she spoil me by line editing several versions of the commentary, but in scores of e-mail messages she helped me figure out what form it should take. At the same time, she gave me quite a bit of latitude for experimentation (and I must add that the mistakes are all mine). Dedi was so upbeat and inspiring that I'm sorry the project came to an end.

Finally, I cannot neglect to mention the support of my family. My mother and my sister, Kathleen, helped by reading my creative contribution to the volume. It was fun to watch my mother take such delight in reading the stories as they rolled in. As always, I'm grateful to Rudi for being my in-house skeptic and critic. As a historian, he initially felt uncomfortable mixing law with fiction. But, after he spent a long weekend reading the manuscript from cover to cover, I was happy that we won him over. It is to our sons, Max and Theo, who as small children represent hope and the future, that I dedicate *Voices from the Edge.*

[Contents]

[Contributors]

Joan Aleshire has written numerous books of poetry, including *Litany of Thanks* (2003) and *The Yellow Transparents* (1997). Her work has appeared in the *American Scholar, Poetry, Kenyon Review, Marlboro Review, Nation, Agni,* and other journals. Aleshire has won a Pushcart Prize and other grants. She lives in Cuttingsville, Vermont.

C. G. K. Atkins is a recipient of a Fulbright Award and has published articles on disability rights. She lives in Calgary, Canada.

John Hockenberry is the author of *Moving Violations: A Memoir: War Zones, Wheelchairs, and Declarations of Independence* (1995) and the novel *A River Out of Eden* (2001). He has been a National Book Critics Circle Award nominee, and *Moving Violations* was named an American Library Association notable book of 1996. He lives in Brooklyn, New York.

Leonard Kriegel is the author of many books, including *Flying Solo: Reimaging Manhood, Courage and Loss* (1998). Kriegel's essays and stories have appeared in *Harper's, Nation, Best American Essays,* and *American Scholar,* and he has received many grants and awards, including a Guggenheim fellowship and an O'Henry Award. He lives in New York City.

Stephen Kuusisto is the author of *Planet of the Blind: A Memoir* (1998), which was a *New York Times* notable book of the year, and *Only Bread, Only Light* (2000). His work has appeared in *Antioch Review, Partisan Review, Poetry,* the *New York Times Magazine,* and *Harper's,* among other places. He lives in Worthington, Ohio.

Achim Nowak has published essays and articles in the *James White Review, Washington Review,* and *Gay Travels: A Literary Companion, Men Seeking Men.* He has received a Pen Syndicated Fiction Award, a National Endowment for the Arts fellowship, and other fellowships. He lives in New York City.

Ruth O'Brien is the author of *Workers' Paradox: The Republican Origins of New Deal Labor Policy, 1886–1935* (1998), *Crippled Justice: The History of Modern Disability Policy in the Workplace* (2001), and academic articles on labor and disability. A theory book is also under contract called "Bodies in Revolt: Gender, Disability, and an Alternative Ethic of Care in the Workplace." She lives in Metuchen, New Jersey.

Shawn Casey O'Brien is a voting rights activist in the disability community and a host for KPFK's radio show on disability rights, *Access Unlimited.* He lives in Santa Monica, California.

Jean Stewart is the author of the novel *The Body's Memory* (1989). She is a contributor to *With Wings: An Anthology of Literature by and about Women with Disabilities* (1987) and has published articles on health care and disability rights. She lives in El Sobronte, California.

Joan Tollifson is the author of *Bare-Bones Meditation: Waking Up from the Story of My Life* (1996). She has received a National Endowment for the Arts creative writing fellowship, among other grants. She lives in Chicago, Illinois.

【Voices from the Edge】

INTRODUCTION

[1]

What is it like to use a wheelchair? What happens when you are deaf, hospitalized, and about to undergo surgery? What transpires when you tell your boss you are HIV-positive? How does it feel to tell—or not to tell—your supervisors and colleagues that you have a serious neurological disease? What runs through your mind when, for the umpteenth time, you hear that patronizing "compliment" about how well you appear to cope with your impairment? The stories in this collection reveal what it is like to live in such a world.

The list of impairments included in this collection admittedly is not complete, nor are the narratives themselves comprehensive. This book offers readers a sampling of what happens to someone with a disability who enters the workforce, a hospital, or a subway or who simply tries to park a car. It opens a window onto something that is naturally individual and yet strangely universal.

One theme that all of the stories share is that persons with disabilities confront a nondisabled society and face some form of discrimination. This discrimination may not be legally actionable; a lawyer might not advise the people in the narratives to sue under the Americans with Disabilities Act (ADA). The commentary that accompanies the narratives carries this theme one step further and provides a legal framework to help us understand the ADA's complexities. Organized around the ADA's main themes and titles, the commentary constructs a legal context replete with "what ifs" and what might have happened, which will provide readers with a more complete picture of disability rights. Most significant, the commentary underscores the difficulties of getting the federal courts to enforce the ADA.[1] To that end, most of the Supreme Court's decisions are reviewed.

Read together, the stories and commentary extend the use of legal narration about the civil rights of people of color—first employed so effectively by law professors Patricia Williams, Derrick Bell, and Richard Delgado—to the civil rights of persons with disabilities.[2] These professors started writing stories about racism and civil rights legislation in the 1980s. The stories recounted by Williams, Bell, and Delgado resonated with readers since they themselves had faced discrimination. In praise of Bell's work, one reviewer wrote that he captured the "hope and despair" underlying civil rights, balancing it all "on a knife's edge."[3] The legal narratives draw out not so much the logic of a judge's decision, but rather the bigger problems associated with enforcing civil rights law.

Williams's, Bell's, and Delgado's life experiences as people of color gave them insight into civil rights. Similarly, the contributors to this volume have each lived with a physical impairment and therefore have first-hand knowledge about disability rights. As disability studies scholar Jenny Morris explained, "We are the experts on our experiences."[4]

Yet, not all of the contributors write about their specific physical conditions. Having lived with one type of impairment, some of the contributors describe learning to cope with another one. No one makes the claim that only a deaf person, for instance, can describe what it is like not to hear. While this book suggests that each physical impairment creates an idiosyncratic environment, it also asserts that many of the attitudes and beliefs that the contributors face are universal.

What makes this book's narratives different from those of Williams, Bell, and Delgado is that they do not consciously address legal issues. With a few exceptions, little discussion, let alone analysis, of the ADA appears in the stories. That is the volume's intent. Fiction and creative nonfiction stories were selected to bring to life the issues underlying the ADA without this type of analysis. The purpose of separating the narratives from the commentary was to give readers room to relate to the protagonists without being distracted by the law.

For those readers who prefer placing these stories in a legal framework, the book also provides analysis and commentary. These commentaries were purposefully placed behind the narratives to cast a legal shadow rather than to set a foreground. This shadow shows how large the law looms over the everyday lives of persons with disabilities. The ADA has helped the disabled, and yet its shortcomings have also become a source of frustration. Just as feminists proclaim that "the personal is political," one could also say that for persons with disabilities, all of life is legal—or at least involves bumping up against the law and its boundaries.

[ ] NOT AN OPEN SOCIETY

The stories in this volume give readers a chance to step into the lives of persons with disabilities in the United States, a country that clings tenaciously to the idea of self-reliance. While not everyone has read Horatio Alger's stories about poor and powerless newspaper boys going from rags to riches, most people know of the myth. Given this emphasis on self-reliance, it is not surprising that of the entire industrialized world, the United States has the most robust set of rights designed to maximize the autonomy and independence of persons with disabilities. Indeed, this country has led the world with its passage of the ADA, and forty-odd other nations have emulated it or adopted some of its key elements.[5] That said, it is still very difficult for persons with disabilities to live in the United States. It is the only industrialized nation with no universal health care, and it has the highest poverty rate of all of the industrialized nations.[6] Over 29 percent of persons with disabilities live on $15,000 a year or less, whereas for those with no disability, the number drops to 10 percent.[7]

The United States has been a tough place for persons with disabilities from the earliest days of the republic. Up until the industrial revolution, persons with disabilities depended upon their immediate and extended families. "Wherever possible," writes disability rights law professor Chai Feldblum, "people with disabilities were cared for by their relatives who often hid them out of shame."[8] Members of their communities, most notably those in religious organizations, also helped take care of persons with disabilities.

The early to mid-nineteenth century witnessed the creation of asylums. Institutions were constructed for all those who were unable to compete in the industrial revolution: the deaf, the blind, the insane, the poor, and the "feeble-minded."[9] "The response in the Jacksonian period to the deviant and the dependent," explains historian David Rothman,

> was first and foremost a vigorous attempt to promote the[ir] stability at a moment when traditional ideas and practices appeared outmoded, constricted, and ineffective. The almshouse and the orphan asylum, the penitentiary, the reformatory, and the insane asylum all represented an effort to insure the cohesion of the community in new and changing circumstances.[10]

Warehousing persons with disabilities suited the new economic system of capitalism.

Paradoxically, institutionalism went hand in hand with the new form of participatory democracy described by Alexis de Tocqueville.[11] Putting away persons with disabilities was preferable to having them live with their families and participate in the community, even if that participation only involved being visible in the community. As cultural theorist Rosemarie Garland Thomson explains, "Disability's indisputably random and unpredictable character translates as appalling disorder and persistent menace in a self-order predicated on self-government." Disability undermines the American ideal of liberal individualism. Composed of self-government, self-determination, autonomy, and progress, the American ideal rests on principles that, as Thomson elaborated, "depend upon a body that is a stable, neutral instrument of the individual will. . . . It is this fantasy that the disabled figure troubles."[12]

Finally, disability undermines the morality that underlies the American ideal, as Ralph Waldo Emerson, among other nineteenth-century thinkers, propounded. In his essay "Self-Reliance," Emerson wrote, "And now we are men . . . not minors and invalids in a protected corner."[13] Disability in that era was characterized as an individual's moral problem because it spoiled the American ideal of self-reliance or self-sufficiency. A physical or mental impairment was considered a "preordained fate, a divine stigma incurred at birth, or a result of individual moral flaws and self-destructive habits such as criminality, alcoholism, and sexual promiscuity."[14]

The federal government made one exception to its policy of self-reliance after the Civil War. It awarded pensions to all of the northern families who lost a soldier or lived with an injured veteran. The post-Reconstruction South granted some Confederate soldiers state pensions. "Even poor and socially marginalized veterans," law professor Peter Blanck and historian Michael Millender argue, "seized upon the opportunities granted by pension legislation."[15] Blanck's and Millender's work, however, goes against the conventional grain. The social scientist Theda Skocpol's work returns the reader to the standard interpretation, underscoring attitudinal bias against people with disabilities after the Civil War. This program was for veterans, not for the disabled. "[N]o matter how materially needy," Skocpol writes, "the morally undeserving or less deserving were not the nation's responsibility."[16]

By the late 1890s, the moral perspective about disability began to fade. As the epidemiological studies of Louis Pasteur and Robert Koch became increasingly influential, public health officials and politicians substituted an environmental perspective on disability for the moral one.[17] It was the physical environment not the damaged soul or psyche that explained why people were injured or became ill to live with permanent disabilities. Physical and mental impairments were attributed not just to warfare, but also to infectious diseases, unsanitary health conditions, and a new understanding about the health risks associated with factory work.

After World War I, when the American state and society again recognized a debt of gratitude to veterans, Congress passed the War Risk Insurance Act. This legislation differed from the Civil War pension policy in that it established a program based on an environmental explanation of disability. The War Risk Insurance Act reflected the Progressive movement's argument that industrial capitalism made people dependent upon larger economic forces in society. This policy departed from the American ideal in which, as Thomson observes, the citizen was seen as a "microcosm" of the country. As that story went, it was self-reliant, physically and mentally so-called whole, hard-working persons who helped create an industrious nation. By contrast, the War Risk Insurance Act was part of the Progressive movement's attempt to humanize industrial capitalism. The legislation followed the Progressive belief that no one should be liable for getting injured, be it in battle or in the workplace.[18] It rested on the principle of "no-fault" insurance found in workers' compensation programs, which blamed neither the worker nor the employer for industrial accidents. Built into the newly forming notion of industrial or corporate capitalism as simply part of the so-called cost of doing business, workers' compensation remunerated injured workers or their families if they died.[19] This said, the new no-fault idea only applied to those who worked—the deserving disabled—not to the rest of society.

Equally important, the War Risk Insurance Act departed from the Civil War pensions by medicalizing disability. That is, it put physicians at the center of its operation. Only doctors could determine whom should be covered under this legislation. Injured veterans received their benefits on the basis of medical diagnoses made by doctors.[20]

Although the environmental explanation of disability was gaining validity, immigration inspectors offered what were called "snapshot diagnoses," assessing the health of immigrants. The inspectors checked immigrants on Ellis Island and other points of entry and at times refused them entry because of arthritis, asthma, bunions, deafness, deformities, flat feet, heart disease, hernia, hysteria, poor eyesight, poor physical development, spinal curvature, vascular disease of the heart, or varicose veins.[21] Sometimes, the inspectors simply marked an X for "insane" on a form recommending that someone be deported. Beginning with the first immigration law in 1882, the U.S. Congress and the president ensured the exclusion of any "lunatic, idiot, or any person unable to take care of himself or herself without becoming a public charge."[22]

The behavior of the immigration inspectors tells a story about discrimination against people with disabilities in the guise of protecting public health. What these officials did reflected a deep strain in American political culture, an abiding value coexisting with two other traditions, liberalism and republicanism, which reinforced inequalities of people on the basis of race, gender, ethnicity, and disability, or what Rogers Smith calls "ascriptive Americanism."[23]

The so-called restrictionists sought to limit immigration. Over three decades, the restrictionist definition was broadened. In the Immigration Act of 1891, the term "becoming a public charge" was changed to "likely to become" one. By 1907, amended legislation gave immigration inspectors even more latitude. These inspectors could deny entry to anyone judged "mentally or physically defective, such mental or physical defect being of a nature which may affect the ability of such [an] alien to earn a living." As the commissioner general of immigration reported in 1907, "The exclusion from this country of the morally, mentally, and physically deficient is the principal object to be accomplished by the immigration laws."[24] Thus, a major part of an immigration inspector's job was to detect who had physical and mental impairments.

Although persons with disabilities were singled out, regardless of their country of origin, those in favor of restricting immigration did claim that certain ethnic groups were more susceptible to disability. The justification for discrimination on the basis of disability helped account for the immigration quotas included in the Immigration Act of 1924. The New York Supreme Court, for instance, blamed immigrants for "adding to that appalling number of our inhabitants who handicap us by reason of their mental and physical disabilities." In particular, it was said that Southern and Eastern Europeans were mentally defective. Slavs, for instance, were "slow-witted," whereas Jews were "neurotic" and virtually "the polar opposite of our pioneer breed."[25] The federal immigration policy thus intermingled race, ethnicity, and disability.

Further, some medical officers explained that an "immigrant of poor physique is not able to perform rough labor, and even if he were able, employers of labor would not hire him." It was a circular argument. The "belief that an immigrant was likely to encounter discrimination because of a disability was equally justification for exclusion."[26]

With physicians deciding who qualified for veterans' benefits and immigration officers determining who should be allowed to enter the country, it is not surprising that the idea that people with disabilities could have rights surfaced in the United States only in the 1930s. The first laws were local statutes that permitted the blind to carry white canes.[27] It was not until the late 1960s—after the civil rights movement had won its great legislative victories—that disability rights made it onto any national policymaking agenda.

[ ] THE ADA IN POLITICAL CONTEXT

The first disability rights measures enacted on the federal level were the Architectural Barriers Act of 1968 and the Urban Mass Transportation Act of 1970.[28] Then, almost by accident, five years later Congress enacted the most comprehensive civil rights law—the Rehabilitation Act of 1973—by amending the existing vocational rehabilitation program, which had been established by the Vocational Rehabilitation Act of 1954.[29] This law was named the Rehabilitation Act during the last round of routine amendments formulated to update and fund the vocational rehabilitation program. Most important, the legislation included the commanding section 504, which prohibited discrimination against persons with disabilities by anyone who worked in sectors that received federal funding. "No otherwise handicapped individual in the United States, as defined in section 7(6)," the section established, "shall, solely by reason of his handicap, be excluded from participation in, denied the benefits of, or be subjected to discrimination under, any program or activity receiving federal financial assistance."[30] Surprisingly, section 504 had not been anticipated by lobbyists or politicians during the policymaking process, and it offered no legislative guidance to the executive branch about how to implement it. According to Richard Scotch, staffers from congressional offices included this one-sentence section in the Rehabilitation Act almost as an afterthought, not knowing that it would become the foundation of disability rights.[31]

Section 504 shaped a new field of law. The law was not enforced immediately, however. Given how vague the statute had been about implementation, the executive branch called for regulations to be issued. After announcing its intent in the *Federal Register*, which enabled concerned parties to make comments, the Department of Health, Education, and Welfare (today's Health and Human Services Department) was responsible for drafting the regulations. Three presidential administrations worked on the section 504 regulations, and each one used the regulatory drafting process as a means of delay. When the regulations became stalled under the Nixon, Ford, and Carter administrations, the disability rights movement, angered by the delay and fearing the growing opposition, began to mobilize.[32] It was this mobilization that united disability rights activists and their followers into a full-fledged movement. Not only did the movement stage the longest sit-in demonstration in U.S. history to force the executive branch to issue the regulations to implement section 504, but it immediately pushed for its enactment in key places, like public schools and universities.[33]

In the late 1980s, disability rights activists worked toward extending the rights orientation underlying section 504 to the private sector.[34] "Indeed, one of the best 'selling points' of the ADA," suggests Chai Feldblum, who also helped draft the statute, "was that Congress would simply be extending to the private sector the requirements of an existing law, section 504 of the Rehabilitation Act."[35] As written, the Rehabilitation Act only covered federally financed programs and the private ones that received federal monies. When these activists lobbied for what eventually became the ADA, they hoped to clarify some of the problems they had discovered with section 504 after wrangling with the federal courts. Given the section's hasty inclusion, Congress had not clearly articulated its position on disability rights. It was only when the federal regulations were issued that the need for clarification of some key concepts, for example, who is "otherwise qualified" for antidiscrimination protection in a school or in the workplace, became more evident. Even then, the Supreme Court muddied some waters with its interpretations of key terms, such as *reasonable accommodations*.[36] Disability rights activists therefore lobbied to make the legislative intent more clear. They hoped that such clarity would give the federal courts, most notably the Supreme Court, more direction when they enforced disability rights.[37]

In 1990, the disability activists succeeded in their public campaign when Congress and President George H. W. Bush enacted the ADA, legislation that many of them had had a hand in drafting.[38] The law passed easily in both houses with a marked absence of dissension and debate.[39] It also "received little public discussion," observed disability rights activist Mary Johnson.[40] Along with the disability rights activists, an almost unprecedented number of senators and members of the House of Representatives claimed credit for its passage.

Nonetheless, the ADA's passage remains a great puzzle. Some scholars have noted that it was the key sponsors from both parties who had personal experiences with disability who helped generate bipartisan support.[41] These sponsors included Kansas Republican Robert Dole and Utah conservative Republican Orrin Hatch along with Massachusetts Democrat Edward Kennedy. Other scholars have argued that while this personal connection might well be true, Congress was more interested in the ADA's rhetorical value than in its effectiveness. The Republicans, moreover, appreciated a civil rights law that might reduce the number of people on Social Security. Getting persons with disabilities to work constituted "free market civil rights," as Marta Russell, a disability rights activist, put it wryly.[42] Also, some of the primary sponsors, such as Dole, had insisted that the measure, particularly Titles II and III, contain a weak enforcement apparatus.[43]

[ ] FOUR TITLES: HEAVY OR NOT?

The ADA has five titles, four of which constitute the substantive parts of the statute. It also contains a section that defines the key terms used throughout the statute.[44] Appearing in a definitions section, which precedes the five titles, the definition of *disability* is the most critical, and it cuts across all of the substantive titles.[45]

Title I, the employment provisions, offers antidiscrimination protection to persons with disabilities who seek employment. Making a workplace free from discrimination often involves having an employer accommodate an employee with a disability who has requested an accommodation. To do so, the employment provisions provide that employers and employees participate in what is referred to as an "interactive process." Does the person with a disability need a piece of equipment or a change in a work rule or condition?

Part of the assessment process under Title I requires determining whether the accommodation interferes with the essential tasks associated with a specific job. While an employee must be qualified to perform all of the essential duties, she could be released from performing the nonessential ones. No hard and fast rules exist, however, that distinguish what are the essential and nonessential functions of a job. The nature of the functions rests on the structure of the particular company and the job itself. For instance, if a receptionist who sustained a severe neck injury, who works with three other receptionists, asks that he no longer answer the telephones, this accommodation could be granted. The number of receptionists in combination with a low volume of calls might make answering telephones a nonessential task. The receptionist's primary duty would be greeting walk-in customers. But, if he worked in an office alone, answering the telephone would be an essential part of his position. And while the receptionist could be accommodated by being reassigned to a different position, if this move interferes with the office's seniority system and there are no special circumstances justifying a departure from the system, an employer could let him go.[46]

The final step before an employer would be bound to furnish an accommodation requires determining whether it would cause a business hardship. While cost is taken into account, this does not simply mean that a particular piece of equipment might be deemed to be too expensive. Undue hardship is defined as significant difficulty or expense in the context of the company's overall operation and its financial resources.[47]

Clearing the same hurdles, prospective employees can also sue employers for discriminatory treatment during the hiring process. Yet, the same receptionist with the neck injury will face more difficulties convincing someone to hire him who knows in advance that he cannot answer telephones. Proving discrimination during the hiring process is problematic for all people in the protected classes. Title I is no exception. An employer could offer a myriad of reasons other than the issue of accommodation to justify why he did not hire the receptionist.

Title II extends civil rights to persons with disabilities who seek or receive state and local governmental services, such as mass transit or public education. The governmental services provisions are broken into two subtitles. First, a general provision outlaws the exclusion of people in places that provide governmental benefits and services. This includes students in public schools, people at polling places or who apply for federal assistance, patients in state hospitals, or patrons of town parks. Title II mandates that all services and programs handled by the state and local governments be accessible. In theory, the actual facility—the bricks and mortar—of the building need not be physically accessible. It is the services and programs offered in a state office like a department of motor vehicles, for example, that must be accessible to persons with disabilities. Nonetheless, in practice, the services and programs are usually housed in facilities that are compliant with Title II.

Second, a subtitle of Title II specifically outlaws the exclusion of persons with disabilities who use public transportation.[48] A public bus company, for instance, must provide a wheelchair lift or require that a bus driver announce the name of the streets at each stop. This subtitle imposes an affirmative obligation on all states and municipalities to make mass transit accessible. If a person with a disability needs the bus company to make another accommodation, this accommodation faces one limiting caveat. The state or local government can demonstrate that accommodating this individual request imposes an "undue financial burden."[49]

The suits that have the greatest success rate under Title II are those that challenge agencies that do not provide services to persons with disabilities. For the most part, the federal courts have interpreted "qualifying" for a service to mean otherwise eligible to "benefit" from one.[50] That is, every person with a disability does not necessarily benefit from a governmental service. He might not qualify for a service. Yet, no signs can be posted that exclude all people who have the use of one arm, for instance, from applying for drivers' licenses. Whether the persons with this disability receive their licenses depends on if they pass the written and driving tests, just like everybody else. No matter what the outcome, a person cannot be excluded from applying for a governmental service. It should also be added that many services, like using a public park, for instance, require no entrance examinations or qualifications.

While persons with disabilities have succeeded with the suits that exclude their participation, they have been frustrated when it comes to gaining compliance. Title II contains the same enforcement procedures that were included in section 505 of the Rehabilitation Act of 1973.[51] This title permits compensatory damages and attorneys' fees, and it also includes preventative relief. That is, a plaintiff can seek an injunction to prevent a builder, for instance, from excluding a ramp on an office building.[52]

The third substantive title—the private entities provisions in Title III—charts new territory in antidiscrimination legislation. The difference between Title II and Title III stems from the fact that the latter affects only privately owned businesses. Modeled after the public accommodations provisions in the Civil Rights Act of 1964, these provisions go much further in that they cover public accommodations by private entities and establishments that are large *and* small. What these provisions primarily do is require businesses to provide their regular goods and services in a nondiscriminatory fashion. For example, if a store is not accessible to someone using a wheelchair, it can provide this person with curbside service. Existing facilities must make modifications wherever they are "readily achievable." Usually, the parking facility would first need to be made accessible, then the entrance to the building, and then the bathrooms. Unlike existing facilities, all new construction projects are required to be accessible.

The types of facilities covered under Title III include transportation systems, hotels, restaurants, theaters, auditoriums, retail stores, service establishments, museums, parks, zoos, social service centers, like daycares, and gyms or places of exercise. The Title III provisions, however, do not mandate that the modifications place persons with disabilities in the same situation as persons without them. For instance, a restaurant need not provide a menu written in Braille as long as a waiter will read it aloud to a person with vision problems.

To enforce this title, private citizens can file suits against a business or establishment. They can also seek injunctive relief.[53] Yet, neither compensatory nor punitive damages can be awarded.[54] While the first piece of disability rights legislation contained these types of damages, "the damages section," as Johnson described, "was gone" from what became law.[55] Historically, one of the plaintiff's legal strategies for compliance has been to request punitive damages. Compensatory damages, or financial settlements that are paid to the plaintiff bringing the suit for any harms she has suffered, also make lawsuits viable for private citizens. If a plaintiff cannot collect any damages, most attorneys will not accept these cases since very few people with disabilities can pay their fees.[56] The one exception is that the ADA gave the Justice Department the authority to seek these damages against facilities that do not comply with the federal courts' rulings.[57]

Finally, Title IV mandates that all common carriers that provide interstate or intrastate telephone services give hearing and speech-impaired individuals the ability to communicate with hearing people. These carriers must supply telephone relay services either individually or in concert with other carriers.

[ ] GUIDING THE COURTS

Courts often employ legislative history when they review statutes like the ADA. The Supreme Court renders the final interpretation about the constitutionality of the law. When doing so, it also offers definitions of key legislative terms, such as *reasonable accommodations*, that will guide the lower federal courts, which enforce the ADA.

Given the section's spontaneous inclusion in the Rehabilitation Act, Congress provided the federal courts with little legislative history when it enacted section 504. This left the courts with room for interpretation. Believing that the federal courts had sometimes misinterpreted section 504, disability rights activists who helped draft the ADA thought this new piece of legislation should have a detailed legislative history.[58] Three reports outlined almost all of the sticky terms, such as what is meant by being *qualified* for a job or governmental services.[59]

One of the most important pieces of legislative history that Congress supplied was the extensive explanation of what constitutes a disability; there are many examples offered, including cancer, diabetes, scars, hearing aids, HIV/AIDS, and epilepsy. According to the Senate report, a *disability* is "a physical or mental impairment that substantially limits one or more of the major life activities."[60] This definition also includes someone who has a record of such an impairment, like a cancer survivor, since this person might encounter discrimination from an employer who might worry about insurance premiums being increased. Finally, the definition covers people who are regarded as having an impairment, like a person with a burn scar.

Realizing that a legislative history, no matter how elaborate, could not anticipate all of the eventualities, the authors of the ADA called for extensive regulations. These regulations, however, were not to be drafted by a single administrative agency. Rather, the task was divided among three agencies. First, the Equal Employment Opportunity Commission (EEOC) had responsibility for creating regulations for implementing disability rights in the workplace. Congress specified that the EEOC, for instance, should develop regulations that would define what the terms *essential functions* and *reasonable accommodations* meant.[61] The EEOC was also given the authority to issue guidelines and to bring cases to court, seeking injunctions and other remedies. Second, the Department of Transportation was given the responsibility of outlining the modifications necessary to make mass transit and public buildings accessible to people with disabilities. The ADA already contained specific sections instructing mass transit systems how to maintain lifts and what type of paratransit systems were acceptable.[62] Finally, the Justice Department was given the authority to get involved with enforcing public accommodations by public and private entities by issuing guidelines, seeking injunctions, and taking its own suits to court.

[ ] A ROLE FOR THE COURTS

While different departments and administrative agencies issue regulations, it is always the federal courts that render all of the binding decisions. Proponents of the legislation concluded that a fixed standard could not be applied with any consistency.[63] The federal courts, members of Congress decided, would do better applying the law on a case-by-case basis. The statute called for an individualized assessment of each person's impairment.

During the debate on the House and Senate floors, members of Congress from both sides of the aisle repeatedly claimed that the federal judiciary had interpreted disability law appropriately. As a result, the federal courts ended up enforcing the ADA.[64] Congress instructed the EEOC, the

Department of Transportation, and the Department of Justice to write mandates and guidelines, but it did so knowing that federal courts are not obliged to follow them. Rather, they need only give deference to the authority that Congress has granted and the regulations that the different administrative agencies issue, which they view as consistent with the statutory language. When the Supreme Court rendered its first opinion about the employment provisions, Justice Sandra Day O'Connor did just that. In *Sutton v. United Airlines,* where twin sisters claimed that United Airlines had discriminatory eligibility criteria that excluded them from becoming national airline pilots, O'Connor rejected the EEOC's interpretation of a "disability," which meant that the twins were not covered under the ADA.[65]

[ ] THE COURTS CRIPPLE THE ADA

A decade after the ADA's enactment in 1992, persons with disabilities who thought the new law would protect them from discrimination became disenchanted with the federal courts' interpretation of certain aspects of this civil rights law. As disability rights lawyer Arlene Mayerson said, the Supreme Court renders "hyper-technical, often illogical interpretations of the ADA." Robert Burgdorf, a disability rights activists who helped draft the statute, explained that "legal analysis has proceeded quite a way down the wrong road."[66] Or as Feldblum explained, "The courts have carefully parsed every word and every term in the definition, and have concluded that individuals with a range of impairments—from epilepsy to diabetes to manic-depression—do not have disabilities under the ADA."[67] The greatest cause of disappointment has been the federal courts' interpretation of Title I, the employment provisions, which is the most heavily litigated section of the law. Between 80 and 90 percent of all suits have been decided in the employer's favor.[68]

The disability rights extended under Titles II and III have been more successful in protecting persons with disabilities from discrimination than have the employment provisions of Title I. Particular reform has been achieved in the cases contesting physical barriers in public places, transportation, and deinstitutionalization. Approximately 46 percent of all of the rulings under Title II have favored persons with disabilities.[69] When suits reached the appellate level, moreover, the rate of success for these complainants rises to 71 percent.[70] Suits against discrimination in welfare and the public schools have been the most successful. The plaintiffs who protested rules and regulations surrounding professional credentials or the education leading to these credentials have proved less successful in litigation.

People in prison constitute the second largest group of litigants under Title II of the ADA (employees are the largest group). They too have had little success challenging the rules.[71] Judges tend to agree with prison officials that they should have "leeway" because of concerns about security. The other category of cases that has fared poorly is those suits that had plaintiffs who requested accommodations that interfered with the discretion or expertise of policymakers.[72] When persons with disabilities questioned the rules or regulations underlying a public policy, they ran into more difficulties than when they faced physical architectural obstacles.[73]

Litigants have had little success collecting damages under Title II.[74] Most federal court judges have issued a new standard, which maintains that unless an establishment did not comply because of malicious intent, it should not have to pay punitive damages. Judges have arrived at this conclusion despite the language within the ADA that indicates that malicious intent is not required. In 2002, the Supreme Court ruled unanimously in *Barnes v. Gorman* that a city would not have to pay punitive damages. The Court overturned the lower federal court's decision to compensate Gorman, a paraplegic who suffered serious injuries when he fell in a police van. Picked up for trespassing after having an altercation with the bouncer at a bar," Jeffrey Gorman had protested when two officers took him out of his wheelchair to load him into a van that was not accessible. When Gorman's seat belt came undone on the way to the station, he fell; his urine bag broke; and he was injured so severely that surgery was necessary. After this incident, Gorman could not return to his work full time as a dental supplies salesperson. Gorman sued the city, and a jury awarded him $1 million in compensatory damages and $1.2 million in punitive damages.

The Supreme Court upheld Gorman's right to sue a municipality for compensatory damages but not punitive damages because the former did not affect the state's coffers and therefore need not be immune from such a suit under the Eleventh Amendment. Nonetheless, there is some question as to whether an earlier ruling, *University of Alabama v. Garrett,* which had been rendered by a 5–4 majority a year earlier, would gut Title II. One of the plaintiffs, who was a director of nursing services at the University of Alabama Hospital in Birmingham, sued when she was demoted after undergoing breast cancer treatment. The other plaintiff was a security officer at Alabama's youth services department who had chronic asthma and suspected that his substandard work performance evaluations could be correlated with his request for accommodations. Both plaintiffs sued the state for monetary damages. The district court dismissed the case on summary judgment because of state sovereignty. The Eleventh Circuit Court of Appeals reversed this ruling and awarded them damages. Then, the majority on the Supreme Court reversed these damages, arguing that the state agencies—a public university and the youth services department—had no obligation to pay them because the state enjoyed immunity from the federal government. The ADA, a federal piece of legislation, should not dictate what a state could do. The Court found that although Congress had compiled a lengthy legislative history that showed discrimination against persons with disabilities in the states, history did not warrant federal intrusion into an area of state governance. As Sharon Miller, who litigated the most suits against the airlines for discrimination in the 1990s, said, this is a highly unusual use of the Supreme Court's power.[75] The Court rarely questions such a history.

Federalism, or how state and federal agencies should divide and share governmental power and authority, is an enduring, yet ever-changing concept in U.S. constitutional law. Since the New Deal, most constitutional scholars have maintained that the federal government's reach has become so expansive that it could legislate just about anything. The idea that the states should be in charge of all health, welfare, and morality issues had changed during the 1930s as the federal government expanded its jurisdiction beyond issues about interstate commerce and international relations.

Reversing this trend toward nationalization, the Supreme Court began creating the "new federalism" doctrine in the mid-1990s. Led by Chief Justice William Rehnquist, who has been a states' rights proponent throughout his long career, an almost constant 5–4 Court started limiting Congress's power and authority to create federal statutes that undermined state policymaking in non-economic issues involving health, welfare, and morality.[76] The five Supreme Court justices—Rehnquist, O'Connor, Anthony Kennedy, Antonin Scalia, and Clarence Thomas—who ruled in favor of the University of Alabama have supported expanding the Eleventh Amendment immunity doctrine.[77] This means that the states can operate free from private damage suits, for instance, in violations of the federal minimum wage and maximum hours law, age discrimination, patent law, and trademark infringements.[78] Meanwhile, the remaining four justices—Stephen Breyer, Ruth Bader Ginsburg, David Souter, and John Paul Stevens—have vowed that they will remain in the dissent and "never surrender" to the majority's position on new federalism. This is unusual, writes *New York Times* Supreme Court reporter Linda Greenhouse. Supreme Court justices do not usually "confront an entire precedent, openly denounce it, and publicly vow to keep on dissenting."[79]

In *Garrett*, the majority held that when Congress conducted public hearings during the legislative process that led to the ADA, it had not sufficiently demonstrated the constitutional abuses by state actors encountered by people with disabilities. The operative word here was "sufficient." The majority ruled that the record of employment discrimination by state and local governmental officials was not strong enough to warrant the remedy of a private damage suit. This finding, as a lawyer who has litigated extensively under the ADA argued, is unusual.[80] The Supreme Court rarely questions the substance or the extent of public hearings. Supreme Court justices takes Congress's findings at face value.

While this challenge had been raised under the employment provisions rather than under the governmental services provision, disability activists were concerned that it would undermine the latter, particularly those suits that involved states rather than municipalities.[81] Public law experts who have analyzed post-*Garrett* decisions argue that this is a reasonable expectation.[82] They conclude that the "greatest threat to the success of Title II lawsuits stems from an external source: the Supreme Court's preference for state sovereign immunity over individual rights."[83] Law professor Jaclyn Okin goes so far as to speculate that section 504 may be in jeopardy.[84]

Most significant, the Supreme Court decided in late 2002 to hear another Title II case that addresses federalism. In this case, *Hason v. Medical Board of California*, a physician is suing for discrimination because he was denied a medical license because of his depression.[85] The plaintiff argued that he is qualified to practice medicine since he is being treated for depression. While the district court dismissed the complaint on the basis of state sovereignty, the Ninth Circuit overturned it. The Supreme Court pulled the case from its docket just before oral argument.[86] As a reporter explained, the case "had been briefed by both sides and was all set for an oral argument March 25. But on March 3, California Attorney General Bill Lockyer sent the court a one-sentence letter telling the justices, in effect, "never mind."[87] The fact that *California v. Hason* was dismissed was different. "Plenty of cases have been dismissed on the eve of oral argument because the parties reached a last-minute settlement," this reporter elaborated, "but in this settlement, talks had failed."[88]

Before the disability activists, who had lobbied for this outcome, could celebrate and just before the end of the term, the Supreme Court agreed to hear another case about whether states can be sued under the ADA.[89] This case, *Tennseesse v. Lane and Jones*, involves two plaintiffs who use wheelchairs and could not enter their state courthouses. George Lane brought suit after crawling up two flights of stairs in a failed attempt to make his arraignment, whereas Beverly Jones is a court reporter who had difficulty getting into county courthouses with too few elevators. "It is a sad day in America," explained their attorney, when these two individuals have to sue the state "for money damages to get them to obey the law."[90]

Ruth Colker has analyzed a study of the public accommodations provisions in privately owned businesses under Title III. The number of cases remains too small, with 25 before the federal court of appeals as opposed to 475 under Title I, to paint a comprehensive picture. Nonetheless, over 70 percent of the decisions in those cases favored those defending themselves against allegations of discrimination.[91] In other words, the private places of businesses had a greater chance of success than the persons with disabilities.

The small number of cases underscores another problem with the public accommodations provisions. With no punitive or compensatory damages possible, few people can afford to take those who violate the provisions to court. As a result, the public accommodations provisions, as one law professor concluded, are largely voluntary.[92]

[ ] AN EFFECTIVE LAW?

Will the ADA become a more effective statute over time? On one hand, persons with disabilities have become part of the public landscape. People know for whom blue parking spots are reserved. The symbol that shows a person using a wheelchair is ubiquitous. Most buildings—public and private—have had ramps installed, and buttons with Braille letters and numbers grace many elevators. A large number of lawsuits against places of public and private accommodation have been settled, making different modes of transportation and buildings, large and small, accessible. Persons with disabilities have become so well integrated into the public view that Mattel Toys introduced a Barbie doll who uses a wheelchair. (Ironically, this Barbie cannot enter her dollhouse since Mattel did not make the doorways wide enough for her wheelchair.)

On the other hand, disability rights activists and lawyers have written opinion pieces in newspapers around the country and expressed their outrage about the federal courts' interpretation of the ADA. Mary Johnson writes that *Toyota v. Williams*, a Supreme Court opinion that narrowed the definition of a disability, was "wrongheaded, and wrong."[93] Justice O'Connor, who wrote some of the pivotal decisions, has gone so far as to condemn the legislation while cases were still pending before the Supreme Court. At a conference of business lawyers early in 2002, O'Connor said that the ADA had been drafted too quickly, leaving the Supreme Court with a "heavy load" of disability rights cases.[94]

Has this significant piece of civil rights legislation helped persons with disabilities become fully accepted members in society? Are they, and disability rights lawyers and activists who speak on behalf of them, unjustly "complaining" about the federal courts' interpretation of civil rights in a time when these courts no longer reflect the civil rights era? Were the disability rights established by the ADA enacted in an era characterized by how collectively tired the public has become of litigation, especially civil

rights litigation? Will the federal courts' narrow interpretation of the definition of a disability and the high rate of cases dismissed on summary
judgment have an effect on how many lawsuits are brought or settled in
the future?

The stories that follow give readers a chance to visualize and perhaps
resolve some of these questions for themselves. Writing either fiction or
creative nonfiction that builds upon experiences in their own lives, the
contributors in this volume bring the problems that persons with disabilities face to life—everyday life. The stories are not courtroom dramas. Nor
do they contain many references to the ADA itself. Instead, the stories offer
readers a chance to identify with what someone who uses a wheelchair,
someone with a hearing impairment, or someone living with a debilitating disease or injury encounters in his daily life. They show how the ADA
affects the most mundane and routine aspects of each person's existence
without bogging down readers with legal concepts and cases. The legal
commentary that shadows the narratives is then organized analytically to
reflect the ADA's main provisions.

Joan Aleshire's story about growing up without a fully developed arm
and hand addresses the overall question of what *is* a disability. She
poignantly discusses her own identity and raises questions about normalcy. The legal commentary that follows then discusses this issue.

The next three stories—by Achim Nowak, C. G. K. Atkins, and
Stephen Kuusisto, each of whom write about a debilitating disease—are
addressed in a commentary about the federal courts' interpretation of
Title I, the ADA's employment provisions. Nowak and Atkins reveal what
their characters encounter when they disclose their illnesses to their
respective employers and prospective employers, while Kuusisto tells a
story about the dismissal of the protagonist in his story, Henry, who has
multiple sclerosis.

Commentaries about mass transit and the public transportation subtitle of Title II follow Leonard Kriegel's essay and John Hockenberry's
autobiographical story about the problems they encounter getting around
New York City in wheelchairs. In moving accounts, both authors capture
the frustration they face using public transportation. Hockenberry's experience with taxicab drivers and in the subway underscores how the ADA
can remedy some situations, but not others. While the ADA may mandate

that subway systems include elevators to help Hockenberry navigate the subway, can the ADA convince or compel cab drivers to pick him up?

An essay about the public services provisions in Title II follows Joan Tollifson's nonfictional narrative about getting a driver's license at the Chicago Department of Motor Vehicles. Tollifson aptly conveys the fear she faces, knowing the power that the official handling the paperwork has over her everyday life.

Jean Stewart's fictional account of taking her deaf daughter to a public hospital and my own autobiographical story about asking for help photocopying documents at the Library of Congress when I had bilateral tendonitis in both forearms and hands are followed by a commentary that examines the new federalism under Title II. Both stories revolve around the frustration that the protagonists encounter seeking reasonable modifications from state entities, which the ADA requires but which are frequently unavailable in the real world. Stewart's character Zoe seeks a sign-language interpreter in a state hospital, which means that it is a state agent and therefore not necessarily under federal jurisdiction. Meanwhile, in my story, I ask for services in a federal archive, which is not covered under the ADA. Some archivists understand my situation and help accommodate me, whereas others do not.

Finally, Shawn Casey O'Brien's story about trying to park at a fast food restaurant in Venice Beach, California, is followed by legal analysis about how Title III, which regulates public accommodations in private places, has been enforced in the federal courts. Coming up against a businessman who refuses to comply, O'Brien's character faces great difficulties trying to enforce the ADA.

Offering a whole array of perspectives, given the different physical disabilities the authors have experienced, this book gives readers a glimpse of what happens when the protagonists seek their rights.

WHAT IS A DISABILITY?

EYE OF THE BEHOLDER

 by Joan Aleshire

There is a photograph in a family album of my mother in the late summer of 1938, when she is a few months' pregnant with me. She's at the beach, leaning back on her elbows, wearing stylish sunglasses with bottle lenses and thick plastic frames. She's smiling with an unusual carefree abandon, it seems to me; she and my father, a hard-working intern at Johns Hopkins, must have gotten away for a few days at Ocean City or Cape May, at the end of a long stretch of hot city weather. She has the beauty of the quieter, more genteel movie stars of the period, like Joan Bennett or, even more, Joan Fontaine, and—for all her modesty, and though she'd never admit to an interest in popular culture—may have acknowledged the resemblance by breaking family tradition and giving me "Joan" as a middle name.

Her obvious pleasure and relaxation may indicate that the medicine she's been taking for morning sickness has been working; it's something new, something that must have been akin to Thalidomide or Benedictin.

At the point when my forearms and hands were forming, something began to go wrong; I was born with malformations below my elbows, three fingers on my left hand, two on my right. My right arm is shaped like a wing, forearm and upper arm connected by skin; my left arm twists strangely, bunched at the elbow but mobile and, in fact, strong.

It would be easy to say that this photograph is the last evidence of her happiness, but, in fact, the scenes of her holding, carrying, and caring for me as a baby are full of an unmistakable sense of accomplishment and joy. I have no record of her reaction to my birth, except for two other photographs in the old album. I'm probably only a few days old, and I'm bundled in a blanket, so that only my face is visible. Strangely, in these photographs, I've been placed on the floor in a swath of sunlight surrounded by long shadows; from one side, a young woman in a nurse's uniform looks down at me with what seems, at this distance, to be a fond concern.

I must still be in the hospital with my mother, whose cesarean then required three weeks of bed rest. What's strange is the way I've been placed on the floor, utterly alone, and those shadows that provide a frame. Because I'm swaddled tightly, it's impossible to see the brace that supports my right wrist, which was thin as a stalk, unable to support the two-fingered hand that drooped from it like an asymmetrical flower. I only learned about the brace from my mother's casual mention of how much I hated it; it had to be removed for baths, I guess, and I resisted having it strapped on.

I tend to attribute my instinctive revolt against any kind of restraint to this early experience, but may be overreaching. I don't have any conscious memory of this one mark of my difference from most children and have no knowledge of my mother's reaction to my birth. If I asked her now what she felt, I doubt that she'd answer honestly; so much of her accomplishment as a parent was to make me feel that I was loved intensely and unconditionally. I draw on her most spontaneous remarks, like the one she made recently, when my own daughter's first child, my first grandchild, was born (with, like my daughter, the usual arms and hands). I had been saying how responsive the baby is to people, how alert, when my mother said, "The first time I saw you, you looked at me with such a wise look that I knew everything was going to be all right."

My mother's memory is faulty now, riddled by dementia, and her sense of time is slippery. She tends to make up what she can't recall, but sometimes—as in this instance—there's a compelling certainty in her tone that makes me trust the memory, and at the same time I wonder when she *did* first see me. Babies can't focus their eyes until they're at least three weeks old; unconscious during delivery, was she kept from seeing me until she was deemed strong enough to withstand the shock? I've wondered—and never asked—how they told her, what they said in describing me, how she reacted in those first moments of knowing I was different from other children. The only documentary evidence from that time is a telegram in an album from her sister Betty, who was skiing in Sun Valley and who wired to say that she was delighted that I'd finally been born—I was several weeks overdue—on her own birthday.

The early photographs of my mother with me and the ones she took of me as a baby and small child—she was more gifted as a photographer than she realized—confirm my sense of being cared for and appreciated in my individuality. Often, family photographs conflict with memories and adult perceptions; here, they confirm what I believe. My childhood was almost embarrassingly happy, which used to make me doubt that I'd ever become a serious writer, or to think I must be missing or denying a dark truth. One of my favorite photographs—probably taken by my father— shows my mother, with her fresh face and tweeds, holding me so that I'm seated on the top rail of the fence that separated our rented country house from the road. I'm about one year old, with cheeks like pumpkins and a delighted smile. I look not at my mother or the camera, but out at the road I'll eventually take with scarcely a backward look. My mother smiles fondly at me, not at the camera, and covers my right, and most vulnerable, hand with her own.

There were only a few children in the neighborhood, and their parents were friends of my own; my playmates were their children. When I was three, our neighbor's granddaughter came from Argentina to live with her, at least until the war was over. It was 1942; the Allies were struggling; no one knew when the end would come, or what it would be like. Diana and I were inseparable for the next five years: best friends, although I was the older, dominant one who invented all the games we would play in the gardens and woods of the adjoining houses. At first we were equals, but as time went on, I sensed the power of my will and bossed her to a degree that was unhealthy for both of us. When her mother decided to go back to Latin America and her marriage, it seemed like a tragedy; I resolved never to have a best friend again. I was forced to find friends among my classmates and realized that I could bend none of them to my own wishes, but had to negotiate and compromise. I had a conscious sense of learning and growing.

My childhood was normal for that time and place, interrupted only by yearly trips to an orthopedic specialist, who measured my arms and ordered X rays. If I were to have surgery, it would be when I had stopped growing, and then it would be my choice, an extraordinary amount of latitude for a child of that time. The degree of protection I was afforded, and the degree of access, may have been possible only in those circumstances; I was fortunate in my family's security and in their love.

Denial was one of my mother's strategies of psychic survival; she was able to appreciate my cuteness—the chubby, smiling face and curly hair—and ignore the oddly shaped arms—which actually seem in the early photographs to be appealing rather than grotesque. It helped that her own mother—the strong-willed doyenne of the family—thought that I was "the smartest baby" she had ever seen, and that I became one of her favorites. Her own disability—she suffered from chronic asthma, which was hard to treat at that time—and, later, her love of language gave us an emotional affinity that made me feel privileged. My mother's sisters and brother and their children made a close and supportive environment. She and her siblings had largely raised themselves during my grandmother's frequent hospitalizations and trips; my grandfather was charming, but undeniably alcoholic. My aunts, uncles, and cousins were constant presences in my early life and adolescence, providing a buffer of normalcy against a possibly uncomprehending outside world.

Money and social position unquestionably made the challenge of raising me much easier. I had the best care, but more important, I had a sense of possibility: that I could do whatever I chose to. My parents were secure in their community and remarkably lucky in their friends, whose children became my playmates in an atmosphere of acceptance and support. Luckiest of all for me, two of my parents' friends were pediatricians, a husband and wife of warmth and wisdom, who counseled that I should be treated like my peers—that is, raised by nursemaids, who would tie my shoes and wash my hair for me until I figured out how to do those things myself; sent to private school; enrolled in tennis lessons and dancing classes. My parents did the "right thing" quite instinctively—not because they were told to, but by inclination. That I should be treated as normal, that I *was* normal, was a form of denial, but it was also powerfully enabling. In our social world, my difference was never mentioned; the gentility that would seem so narrow to me as an adolescent and adult was also a protection that allowed me to *feel* normal, not malformed. If I hadn't been born into such ease and indulgence, my life might easily have gone another way.

Visiting my daughter and newborn granddaughter last fall, when I moved to sign my name in the maternity floor register, I was startled when the woman behind the desk said—at the moment when I had most completely entered the mainstream—"Oh, you write so well! Most people, if they were born like you, would have just given up." Insulted to be reminded that I look as if I might not be able to hold a pen, I snapped that giving up wasn't my style. What I didn't say was that, in the atmosphere of encouragement and optimism that surrounded me from birth, "giving up" has never crossed my mind.

If the definition of disability is the inability to do the common daily tasks of life—getting out of bed, washing, dressing, eating, going to the bathroom—and working at one's age level in school, I've never been disabled. My mother says that she once took a class in occupational therapy at the local Children's Hospital to see if she could help me when I was a child, but I can't remember being shown anything. Rather, I watched to see what needed to be done and adapted my own way of working—using my teeth on a shoelace or bending strangely—to accomplish the job. Of course, when I was very small, everything was done for me, as they would be for any child of my background. There was someone paid to dress and wash me, to brush my hair and teeth, someone else to cook and serve the food, and someone else to attend to every need. Affluence protected me from struggle, gave me an ease I never would have known in a poor family.

When I was four, I could read from the headlines of the morning paper propped in front of my father's plate. By five, I was able to write and to play the teacher in games of school I invented for Diana and, later, my brother David, the hapless pupils. By the time I was ready to enter first grade at six, I was well prepared.

The choice of school was obvious; a friend of my parents was the principal of the private school my mother and her siblings had attended. It was considered the best in Baltimore and had a program of home instruction for students in remote places around the world. Presumably, I could have been taught at home if school proved too difficult. I'm not sure whether there were questions about my ability, or who encouraged my parents to mainstream me, but I took the tests for admission and passed easily. I don't remember being asked to prove my abilities in any unusual way and never doubted, or sensed doubt on my parents' part, that it was the most natural thing in the world for me to enter first grade at Calvert School.

The first day, when my father drove me to school, as he would all my years there, I felt no nervousness or pangs of separation, but stood on the sidewalk outside the building, staring at the other children. I had never seen so many people in one place in my life and was purely fascinated by how they looked and moved. My father, alarmed, got out of the car and urged me up the broad staircase, where the principal was waiting—as he waited every morning—to shake every student's hand. He took my left hand gracefully, tactfully, in his left. Harder than shaking hands—sometimes an awkward maneuver now that handshakes are an instant and forceful form of communication—was the curtsey that the girls had to make at the same time as they shook Mr. Brown's hand. But everyone found that a little strange—and then it became a mark of gentility that many of us would scorn later.

Gifted children, as I was said to be, are easily bored in school, but I loved the repetitions of what I already knew, or grasped quickly. I had a sense of constant accomplishment, and my doing well in class contributed to my fitting in. Brains and talent were not then despised; the brightest students were the leaders, and I made some friends whom I have to this day. I fell in love, too, in first grade and had difficulty deciding where to place my affections. Should I love N., with his perfectly pressed gray flannel shorts and knee socks, his right answers and straight stance? Or was it really F. whom I loved—F. with his deep blue eyes, seven-year-old's sweetness, and failure to read? I invited both to my seventh birthday party and placed F. beside me, where we told first-graders' jokes in perfect harmony. The great sadness at the end of a year in which by all measures I'd triumphed, with all 1's and gold seals for the year's marks, was that F. had to stay back and repeat the grade. The teacher—who had been my mother's teacher too, and whose gentleness and patience were legend—had found that words appeared to F. backward and upside down. He was the first of many dyslexics with whom I'd find an affinity, in an interesting mesh of visible and invisible handicaps.

If I hadn't excelled in schoolwork and been able to keep up in sports—at least in kickball and the relay races we ran on the gravel playground, which lacerated our knees when we fell—I wouldn't have felt so well integrated at school. If I stood out, it was for academic excellence and for the ability to memorize long parts and to feel at ease on stage. We were encouraged to perform in public—the school had a reputation for educating the area's leaders—and I loved having starring roles in school plays so much that I often overran other children's parts. I had an immense self-confidence, which was shaken only at the end of fifth grade (or eleventh age, as it was more precisely known there) by a teacher who tried to coach me to inflect words in a way unnatural to my own cadence, which left me with a case of stage fright that lasted for twenty-five years. This sudden affliction had nothing to do with my appearance, which was accepted without comment by my peers, and everything to do with my individuality, which that narrow-minded and tyrannical teacher tried to suppress.

The only times when I was reminded that I wasn't indeed quite like everyone else was during softball, since I couldn't really catch, but stood in the outfield, hoping that the ball would never come my way, and at gym meets, when I was embarrassed to move the wing of my right arm in the group exercises we had to perform for an audience of parents. I never said anything about my discomfort, though, and never thought of being excused. I was thoroughly in the mainstream—of Baltimore in the late 1940s—and thought anything I wanted was possible to have.

Because my mother's family, except for my grandmother, was un- or even anti-intellectual, I felt under no pressure to excel. No women in my family had gone to college; I would be the first. I did well because it pleased me to; I liked following directions, staying within the lines, because I could prove to myself that I could, and because it was easier to do so than not. If

I were under unconscious stress as a child to "pass," to be normal, perhaps—as a dentist later suggested—the evidence was my terrible teeth, which relentlessly decayed despite all efforts at cleaning and a rationing of sweets. Consciously, I moved easily in my world of plenty, rarely meeting mockery or harsh questions.

A child I tutored in a school volunteer program in Brooklyn years later once asked me if other kids had made fun of me when I was in school, and clearly had difficulty believing me when I answered honestly, "No." Sometimes there were questions, though not from children in my own class or neighborhood—whose parents and teachers, I'm sure, had prepared my way—but from younger children or ones who had never seen me. Sometimes, when the children were (or are) very young, the questions were (or are) innocent and concerned; at other times, there is an edge of hostility, a distancing, that made (or makes) me defiant and guarded, though I always answer airily, dismissively, that "I was born that way." This has mostly worked because it's simply true, and because there's nothing more I would add, unless I sense true care rather than mere curiosity.

Recently, when my mother was visiting me in Vermont, I asked my elderly neighbor over for a cup of tea. His wife had died the fall before, and he'd asked me to check on my daily walk to see if his window shades were up, which I did, and I took in his mail when he was gone. We'd never talked about anything but the weather and daily tasks, but as soon as he was seated in the kitchen, as if somehow the location gave him permission, he said, "I've always wanted to ask you about your handicap. Do you mind?" He couldn't have known that it's a topic—among others now, like sex, religion, and popular culture—that I never discuss with my mother, and I cut him off rudely, abruptly, by saying, "I *do* mind," which embarrassed my mother, more for my bluntness than for the sentiment. She changed the subject, as she's always been teased for doing, by remarking on the weather or the flowers on the table. She seemed protective of me, soothing, thinking that I would always be resistant to the topic, not realizing that, for me, time, place, and interlocutor count for everything.

She has, as I've said, always been an adroit denier of difficulty in her immediate vicinity, but a fearless critic of the failings of others. My grandfather told my aunt he was afraid of her: the only person who would confront him about his drinking. About unkempt appearances—personal or domestic—she can be ruthless, noticing cobwebs and flaws everyone else has ignored. At the same time, she has never mentioned my anomaly, but praises my hair and "sweet expression."

Denial, defiance, and trust in her own judgment (she can be fierce and blunt in her dislikes) have given my mother the power to withstand the stares, questions, and unsolicited opinions that attend a disabled child's existence. Her view of how women should look and behave, however, has always been entirely traditional; when I began to be overweight at nine, wore "chubby" sizes and looked matronly at eleven, she insisted that I go on a diet. The appearance of my arms could only be changed by plastic surgery when I stopped growing. Weight, my parents believed, could be controlled by will, and they took me to a nutritionist at Hopkins, who put me on a strict high-protein diet, which I followed faithfully for a year, keeping a diary of everything I'd eaten. The nutritionist was direct and impossible to fool; I lost probably twenty pounds over nine months, learned food values, grew taller, matured, pleased myself as well as my parents. I continued to do well in the all-girls school I attended after elementary and played field hockey and basketball—always defense, but using my ability to run well.

I "came out" with my classmates at eighteen—not in the contemporary sense, but in the old-fashioned, classic custom of introducing eligible young women to eligible young men in "society," in the narrowest definition of that term. "Coming out" was really an excuse to have parties. Its main challenge was learning to make conversation of the least promising material—the weather, the party the night before—and to keep the talk flowing easily until an avenue of escape arrived. Never during that year or in my time at college was my anomalous appearance mentioned, nor did it seem to matter. Whether or not the young men at the dances were bribed to cut in on me—to give me a "good time," as I learned happened with well-connected wallflowers—I never knew, but I found friends: young men with humor and intelligence, who were also kind. I was blessed with unself-consciousness—a prized quality in that world, which meant being at ease with oneself, belonging completely, but also being oblivious, unquestioning.

To make my debut, I had to leave college to attend the Monday party, the Bachelors' Cotillion, as it was called, though most of the men there were married, or "Monday German," which was a kind of patterned dance always held on a Monday. Young women weren't expected to have conflicts with that schedule, were not expected to be attending college or working. I was embarrassed to explain to my dorm mates where I was going in my new fur coat, and after the event, I wrote to the cotillion committee and asked to be taken off the list of invitees. I had had a good time—my family was well liked, my partners numerous—but the discrimination inherent in the custom made me guilty, and I refused my part in it after the fact and for the future. I would love to reread that expression of my disdain—I didn't keep a copy—and wonder what the committee of my father's friends must have thought. They probably had some discussion about whether to invite me in the first place; even though my family was well placed, well respected, they may have been making allowances for my unusual appearance and felt magnanimous in doing so.

If my parents had doubts about whether it was appropriate for me to come out, they kept them to themselves. The only time I can remember my mother ever referring to my difference was when I must have been about three, when my aunt Betty was about to get married. My mother and I were walking down the road past our house; I remember sticky blue buds on a bush whose name I don't recall. We must have been talking about the wedding, in which my mother was to be a bridesmaid, when my mother said to the air, "I wonder if you'll ever get married," and I wondered myself after that, thinking there must be some reason why I might not. Much later, when I married, she said that I had "such a good sense of humor, [she] knew I'd get married"—as if marriage were an endorsement of a pleasing personality. Unfortunately, I would marry a man with no sense of humor, though that is another story, irrelevant here. I became through that difficult time more like other women than not: through raising a child, through betrayal and divorce, I became more human, less superior in my sense of being unique.

For all their benevolent denial, my parents weren't naive about the outside world's perceptions of disability. Not long ago, I found in an old file a letter from the Maryland Department of Motor Vehicles to my parents in response to one from them, evidently describing my appearance and abilities. I'd taken and passed a course in drivers' education—although my mother couldn't ride in the care with me without loudly sucking in her breath in horror at every turn—but they were writing in anticipation of resistance, to pave the way for my acceptance. The official at the DMV was naturally puzzled, saying that all I had to do was pass the written and road tests, and there would be no problem in giving me a license. What interests me is that they felt the need to ask for special consideration, and I wonder if they would have pursued an appeal if I'd failed the tests. There was a certain Canadian modesty to their approach (my father was born there and became a U.S. citizen in his thirties), as well as the decorum of my parents' social milieu. It was as if one had no right to question authority or assert one's own rights, but must accept convention—and yet they practiced a quiet form of resistance to the accepted treatment of the disabled at that time. And, for all their wish to protect my life, the choice not to have plastic surgery was mine, of college, and to move out into the world.

[3]

Aleshire's story raises *the* pivotal issue in both disability studies and disability rights: what is a disability? Scholars in disability studies address the subject by exploring questions of the self and identity. How does a physical or mental impairment affect one's development? What influence does it have on other people's view of this person? Are persons with disabilities normal, abnormal, aberrant, deviant, or just different?[1] Aleshire's story reveals just how fortunate she feels about being raised by a loving and caring family that appreciated her individuality.

Disability rights law addresses individuality and normalcy. The Americans with Disabilities Act (ADA) takes into account the individuality of persons with physical or mental impairments without basing it solely on a medical diagnosis. To determine if someone has an impairment that, as Justice Sandra Day O'Connor suggests, "rises to the level of a disability," the ADA's definition requires a case-by-case assessment.[2] The statute requires what is called an "individualized assessment" so that persons with disabilities are not labeled, stigmatized, or stereotyped.

Ironically, the federal courts' interpretation of what should be taken into account during this individual assessment has meant that few persons with substantial impairments are what I call "legally disabled," particularly under the ADA's employment provisions.[3] The functional definition of a disability has worked against many persons with disabilities and prevented them from having access to remedies under this antidiscrimination statute. "For the high court . . . some people are not disabled enough; some people are too disabled," Charles Lindner, a disability rights advocate and a past president of the Los Angeles Criminal Bar Association wrote, "but, so far, nobody has been disabled 'just right.'"[4] That Aleshire never needed help tying her shoes or writing means that she might well not receive the label "legally disabled," which would make her eligible for protection under the ADA.

The problems associated with this restrictive definition, however, are less acute under Titles II and III of the ADA. Building modifications take into account all types of impairments. No fit among an individual, her impairment, and a job must be made as is necessary for a reasonable accommodation in the workplace. Also, the type of individualized assessment required is not conducted as rigorously as it has been under the employment provisions. Under Title II, someone may sue for discrimination because she could have "benefited" from a state or local government's service.

The difficulty that people with impairments have faced in the courtroom under the employment provisions stems, in part, from the question of normalcy that underlies what constitutes an individual assessment. Federal courts have based their determinations on all sorts of factors. Someone can compensate for an impairment—and therefore not be considered disabled—if medical equipment, medicine, her lifestyle, or her education are taken into account. Some federal courts go so far as to link worldly success and disability. A successful person, several federal courts have ruled, cannot be a disabled person and therefore is not protected under the statute.[5]

Aleshire is one of these "successful" people. There is no question that she can function as a writer without any reasonable accommodations.

Nonetheless, Aleshire and many other persons with disabilities reject this interpretation of the ADA. The ADA was not drafted to protect the "losers." It establishes disability *rights*. To differentiate between persons with disabilities on the basis of their backgrounds and their lifestyles suggests that the ADA is not based on rights but on an assessment of need, which turns it into yet another disability law that extends charity. Life's "losers" need and get help, whereas the "winners" do not.

Aleshire realizes that her nurturing family, a strong will and intellect, and a first-rate education help account for her success. Where Aleshire departs from her parents is her idea about disability rights. She demands rights for the disabled, not legal protection based on moral judgments. Aleshire compares her parents' "quiet form of resistance" with her own resistance, which she purposefully strips of any bourgeois decorum. The disabled should not receive rights, she implies, because of their politeness. Still, what both Aleshire and her parents share is a belief that she must always challenge the boundaries of normalcy.

[ ] FUNCTION AND APPEARANCE

According to Lennard Davis, disability presents itself to "normal" people through two modalities: function and appearance.[6] The functional modality involves standards of movement, sight, hearing, and any other type of physical or mental activity. Simply put, this modality means that someone *does* things differently. This person might move from one place to another by wheeling in a chair rather than by putting one foot in front of the other.

For Aleshire, the question of her ability to function as a writer is not germane. A court would categorize her with the many people whom the ADA recognizes as "regarded as" having a disability. That is, she falls under the second modality: disability on the basis of appearance.[7] Since she "looks" like a person with a disability, she sometimes faces discrimination when people make assumptions, often uninformed ones, about her ability or inability to do things. "It is through our sense of sight," Erving Goffman explains, "that the stigma of others most frequently becomes evident."[8]

Scholars in disability studies recognize that stigma is culturally bound.[9] Cultures change and contexts change and so does normalcy, carrying with it the definition of disability. The anthropologist Robert Murphy underscores how the treatment of disability as unspeakable and unsightly is a phenomenon of middle-class culture. Children are taught not to point at those who are unfortunate. This said, "unfortunate" does not mean without culpability, he argues, since the same middle-class culture lumps disabled people into the same category as criminals.[10] People who commit crimes or who look and act differently depart from societal norms and are therefore considered "deviant."

Drawing an even more comprehensive picture, anthropologists and cultural theorists argue that disability reflects the classic divide between nature and culture.[11] To Claude Levi-Strauss, persons with disabilities represent an infringement upon nature as they make those without disabilities come face to face with their biological needs. Persons with disabilities, he submits, undermine those who consider themselves the "bearer of culture."[12] "Cultural dichotomies do their evaluative work: this body is inferior and that one is superior; this one is beautiful or perfect and that one is grotesque or ugly. In this economy of visual difference," writes cultural theorist Rosemarie Garland Thomson, "those bodies deemed inferior become spectacles of otherness while the unmarked are sheltered in the neutral space of normalcy."[13] Or as Henri-Jacques Stiker put it, "People have never felt comfortable with what appears deformed, spoiled, broken."[14]

Aleshire echoes the thoughts of these disability studies experts, anthropologists, and cultural theorists when she asks about her mother's first thought in facing her. "Was she kept from seeing me," Aleshire wonders, "until she was deemed strong enough to withstand the shock?" Although she harbors these concerns, Aleshire also tells us that her parents spurned the verities of their time. While she was still a child, they gave her the room to decide if she would like an operation that would presumably make her "look more normal." Recognizing how unusual this was, Aleshire observes that this, among other things, gave her the strength to accept herself. And indeed, she defines her identity, in part, by her rejection of any surgery.

Aleshire is adamant that physical differences may reflect what society perceives as "normal," but that these differences must not be transformed into a judgment about the inferiority of all those who supposedly are not normal. "That I should be treated as normal, that I *was* normal," she writes, "was a form of denial, but it was also powerfully enabling." What Aleshire suggests is that denial kept her from internalizing the bias against persons with disabilities that existed in the larger world. Hence, Aleshire could assert her rights and make her way more freely in the world.

[ ] INDIVIDUALITY, LEGAL CATEGORIES, AND COUCH POTATOES

The individuality that Aleshire describes in her story started to become codified in disability rights law in the 1970s. Issuing enforcement regulations for section 504, the Department of Health, Education, and Welfare first drafted what would become the definition of a disability in the ADA. Divided into three parts, the definition first stipulates that a person has a disability if he or she has a "physical or mental impairment that substantially limits one or more of the major life activities."[15] The major life activities include "functions such as caring for one's self, performing manual tasks, walking, seeing, hearing, speaking, breathing, learning, and working." Also, a person should be recognized as disabled if she has "a record of such an impairment." Finally, people have disabilities for the purpose of this statute if they are "regarded as" having such an impairment.[16]

The disability rights movement endorses this definition of an impairment for two interrelated reasons. First, it associates individuality with an impairment. Although physicians and other rehabilitation experts often provide evidence that someone has a substantial limitation of a major life activity, the definition is not dependent on the determinations of these experts.[17] Second, the statute and the regulations define a disability by virtue of what a person cannot do, rather than in terms of a specific medical condition or disease.[18] Put differently, disability studies expert Simi Linton explains that the ADA's definition of disability is consistent with the sociopolitical model, not the medical model. The last two parts of this definition, she emphasizes, acknowledge that even "in the absence of substantially limiting impairment, people can be discriminated against." Moreover, the ADA recognizes that "social forces, such as myths and fears regarding disability, function to substantially limit opportunity."[19]

Basing the definition of a disability on functionalism makes disability rights different from other types of rights. In the absence of a medical diagnosis or expert opinion from a vocational rehabilitation counselor, it is the federal courts that end up conducting individual assessments to determine if someone has a disability. Further, these courts sometimes reject the expert opinions and make their own assessment. This is different from other civil rights since, unlike race or gender, persons with disabilities must prove that they have one. What is more, these courts have made it extremely difficult for someone with impairments to show that they are disabled enough to receive protection from employment discrimination.[20]

The difficulty lies in that individuality has not been separated from the dominant conception of normalcy. It is one thing for Aleshire to realize that she is different and quite another for her to accept the difference. This is precisely what the judiciary is not doing. During the individual assessment, federal judges, most notably the majority of Supreme Court justices, have suggested that an impairment can be mitigated.[21] In the workforce, the personal attributes of someone—whether it be access to equipment, education, or lifestyle—offset the person's disability. So, ironically, someone with a severe impairment might not be recognized as disabled, whereas someone with less of one could be.[22] The Supreme Court did not arrive at this conclusion overnight. In 1998, the justices first attempted to define a disability in *Bragdon v. Abbott*. The case involved Sidney Abbott, who had asymptomatic HIV. When she sought routine dental treatment, her dentist insisted that he would only treat her in a hospital two hours away, not in his office. In a 5–4 decision, the majority concluded that an asymptomatic disease can be considered a disability because it impedes the major life activity of reproduction.[23]

That Abbott could not procreate, the majority concluded, without a 20 percent risk that this disease would be passed on to anyone who tried to conceive a child with her, meant that she was limited in the major life activity of reproduction. Also contributing to this conclusion was the evidence that the child conceived would have a 25 percent chance of contracting HIV. With medical evidence showing that HIV only impeded, rather than foreclosed, the major life activity of reproduction, the majority emphasized that the ADA took into account "substantial limitations, not utter inabilities."[24]

Contesting exactly this point about Abbott's life, Supreme Court Chief Justice William Rehnquist argued in his dissenting opinion that her limitation in reproduction did not substantially limit *her* life. "There was no evidence," he wrote, that she "would have had or was even considering having children."[25] The minority argued that since the definition of a disability was written "with respect to the individual," Abbott's individual goals and desires must be taken into account.[26] Not having expressed any desire for procreation, Abbott had not lost anything.[27] Unlike the majority, the four dissenters took Abbott's personal lifestyle into account when determining what constituted a disability. Though Abbott won her case, the personal lifestyle question that was raised became increasingly important in lower federal court cases.

[ ] MITIGATING FACTORS

The idea of weighing a variety of factors—medical, technical, educational, and even lifestyle choices—became part of the majority opinion in the lead decision, *Sutton v. United Airlines*, about the ADA's employment provisions. In 1999, the Supreme Court rendered this decision and two others, which delineated how someone could mitigate her impairment and therefore not be considered disabled and protected under the statute's employment provisions.[28]

Most important, the Supreme Court decided in *Sutton* that twin sisters, who had severe myopia that was corrected by glasses, were not "legally disabled." While the twins had an impairment that only 2 percent of the population shared, it "did not rise to the level of a disability" since it could be mitigated by glasses. The medical equipment—the glasses—helped them compensate for their impairment.

Examining the next plank of the definition, the Supreme Court ruled that United Airlines, the twins' employer, had not "regarded" them as disabled people. The employer must "mistakenly" believe, the majority argued, that the twins had a substantial impairment. It "must be based upon a myth," whereas in this case, the employer was correct in believing that the twins had poor eyesight, which the glasses corrected.[29]

The majority knew that using the idea that someone could compensate for her impairment and therefore not be considered to be disabled had been recognized by few lower federal courts. Most of these courts had followed the lead of the administrative agencies, like the Equal Employment Opportunity Commission (EEOC), which had rejected this interpretation.[30] But, as the majority opinion explained, the Court had no obligation to follow these agencies.[31]

While this decision represented a departure from the definition developed by the administrative agencies that help to enforce the ADA, the majority's opinion was not unprecedented. In addition to the minority opinion in *Bragdon*, the Court had previously depended on the idea of compensation in *Hendrick Hudson District Board of Education v. Rowley*. The majority's opinion was reminiscent of the *de minimus* doctrine that then Justice Rehnquist had established for disabled schoolchildren.[32] If a child with a disability could compensate for having a physical impairment, she was not entitled to help in the classroom simply because of it. This is where the idea of normalcy comes into play. If the twins could mitigate their impairment by wearing glasses, they could enter the mainstream and should not qualify for statutory protection. The twins were "normal," the Court concluded. After all, both twins were already regional airline pilots. To the majority of the justices, the ADA is not about protecting this type of person from employment discrimination.

Realizing that the majority had created a new functional interpretation so that few people would qualify for protection under the ADA, Justice John Paul Stevens wrote a stinging dissent. The majority's functional definition was so broadly cast, he argued, that it penalized those who could compensate for their deficiencies more than those without them. "With the aid of prostheses, coupled with courageous determination and physical therapy, many of these hardy individuals can perform all of their major life activities just as efficiently as an average couch potato."[33]

Most important, Stevens's dissenting opinion explored how the Court's action, in general, would affect disabled people in the future. Presenting such a narrow interpretation of what constitutes a disability, he maintained, made the Court a stern gatekeeper, which would exclude most persons with disabilities. To Stevens, this was puzzling since it represented such a significant departure from earlier precedents. No other antidiscrimination legislation, let alone other pieces of legislation, kept people out of the courtroom. The Civil Rights Act of 1964 was written for African Americans, but other minority groups, like Latinos, could use it. Someone can file for discrimination based on race, gender, age, or religion, as Stevens explained, thereby making it "hard to believe that providing individuals with one more antidiscrimination protection will make any more of them file baseless or vexatious lawsuits."[34] Stevens went so far as to underscore how federal courts had recognized that the Racketeer Influenced and Corrupt Organization Act (RICO) could be used against organized *and* nonorganized criminals alike.[35]

[ ] DAILY DUTIES

In 2002, the Supreme Court turned the functionalist definition of a disability under the employment provisions on its head again. In *Toyota v. Williams*, Williams had developed carpal tunnel syndrome and other repetitive motion impairments in a factory, and nothing could mitigate her condition.[36] She could not take any medicine nor rely on any equipment to control her injury. When Williams used her arms and forearms in the same repetitive way that had caused her initial injury, she would re-injure herself. Her muscles, nerves, and tendons would be re-inflamed. The manual tasks that caused this re-injury, the tasks that she had to perform to keep her position, the unanimous Court decided, however, were not central enough in her daily life to make her disabled. Here too, the Court, in effect, extended the Catch-22 that applied to the twin pilots.[37] Williams was so disabled that she could not work without accommodations, but she was not sufficiently disabled to receive protection under the ADA.

Writing for a unanimous Court, Justice Sandra Day O'Connor argued that people with impairments that restrict them from performing manual tasks at work but not at home may not be legally defined as disabled. Not heeding her own ruling about an individualized assessment, O'Connor added another caveat. Under the ADA, she wrote, an impairment must limit the ability to perform tasks that "are of *central* importance to people's daily lives."[38] That is, their private lives. It is the judiciary, moreover, that decides what is centrally important in someone's daily life. O'Connor reprimanded the lower federal court for not assessing whether Williams could sweep the floor or play with her children as opposed to her ability to brush her teeth or wash her face. Only after weighing *these* tasks could the judges decide that this plaintiff had a "central, substantial, or major" impairment that rose to the "level of a disability."[39]

What seems to concern the majority on the Supreme Court is that too many persons with disabilities, particularly those with nontraditional disabilities like carpal tunnel syndrome, will be able to use the ADA, and it will open the flood gates. The Court also recognizes how unique the ADA is in employment. Providing reasonable accommodations gives employees the power to undermine an employer's right to manage a workplace. Therefore, the majority on the Supreme Court has been very conservative in assessing who should qualify for this antidiscrimination protection and has ruled against all six employment plaintiffs.[40]

[ ] ENDLESS MITIGATION AND LITIGATION

The impact of the Court's decision in *Toyota v. Williams* remains to be seen. Given the *Sutton* decision, many lower federal courts had already adopted the Supreme Court's doctrine that someone can mitigate an impairment and therefore not be disabled in the workplace. Nevertheless, the doctrine continues to generate litigation. As one law professor maintained, "The debate about mitigating measures may prove to be endless."[41]

Overall, the federal courts have cultivated a functional definition of disability that is elastic. The definition is pulled and stretched, changing in accordance with whatever court applies it. Few governmental officials or disability activists lobbying from the outside have opposed the functionalist approach to defining disability. Indeed, it was the EEOC that clarified the functional definition by suggesting that a disability is determined by what a worker or an employee can and cannot do in comparison with the average person in the general population. But neither the EEOC nor disability activists anticipated that the federal courts' doctrine of functionalism would become so expansive and take into account not just medical and scientific evidence of what the person can do, but also personal and societal considerations. A person with a debilitating impairment with more education than the "average person," like a pharmacist, can do more than a person without this education. The courts, in other words, look at how a person functions *generally* and essentially compare disabled people with "normal" ones.

Evaluating each person with a disability on a case-by-case basis, the federal courts have ignored the EEOC's expansive guidelines about what constitutes a substantial impairment, like a missing extremity, epilepsy, or diabetes. They have used this case-by-case basis not to avoid stereotyping people, as the disability rights activists had hoped. Rather, the federal courts have scrutinized personal, societal, medical, and technological ways that disabled people use to mitigate their conditions.

The federal judiciary's interpretation of a disability has had unexpected punitive results. Courts have not simply failed to protect people from employment discrimination. Filing a suit against an employer for disability discrimination has given some employers cause to fire employees. This strategy is problematic for an employer, however. If the employee were legally disabled, terminating her would be considered a retaliatory action. Nonetheless, this does not alter the larger point that the federal courts have ruled that if a person does not have a severe enough disability to warrant protection under Title I, this disability still can be considered limiting enough to provide grounds against hiring or, further, for dismissal if she already has the job. Justice Stevens, one of the two dissenters in the *Sutton* decision, has described this as "especially ironic." The Supreme Court's interpretation denies "protection for persons with substantially limiting impairments that, when corrected, render them fully able and employable."[42]

[ ] IS ALESHIRE LEGALLY DISABLED?

If scrutinized by the federal judiciary, would Aleshire's impairment rise to the level of being a disability? What major life activity is hindered by her disability? What can't Aleshire do? Does Aleshire's physical agility or her ability to use her partial right arm and her left arm compensate for the loss of her right hand? Should she be covered under the first definition of a disability?

Under the ADA's employment provisions, relief would depend on the type of position she sought. If the major life activity being asserted was working at any job, however, then Aleshire would have to show that she is substantially limited in a class or broad range of jobs. Would this mean that if Aleshire applied for a position that required no use of both hands, like being a teacher or a writer, she would not be considered legally disabled? Does Aleshire's intellect mitigate her impairment? Having won prestigious awards for her writing and having raised a child, judged against the average person, should Aleshire be considered "successful"? Should Aleshire's intelligence or success mitigate the loss of her hand and part of her arm? Should she be considered legally disabled?

What if Aleshire applied for a position that required the use of her right hand and while she could perform the position adequately, she could do an even better job if her employer provided her with a piece of equipment—should she receive a reasonable accommodation? In a lower federal court, there was a case that involved a janitor who only had one hand. Although he had not received complaints about his work performance, when he asked for an accommodation, his employer terminated him.[43] The federal judge listening to the case ruled in favor of the employer, finding that the janitor's termination was lawful. No reasonable accommodations could be made that could compensate for the loss of his hand. Would Aleshire's situation be the same? If she is adequately compensating for the loss of her hand, should she receive an accommodation that could enhance her performance? Or could her employer argue that no piece of equipment can fully compensate for the loss of her hand and be justified in terminating her?

Aleshire might find relief under the third part of the statute, where an employer would "regard" her as disabled. An employer or a prospective employer might think she is disabled, just as the nurse did when she praised Aleshire for her ability to write so clearly. Yet, how would Aleshire prove this? Was the nurse's "compliment" malicious? Was it based on a false myth? Only if an employer has made an egregious error or substantiated a stereotype about people who do not have the full use of their arms and hands and therefore are substantially limited in a specific major life activity could Aleshire seek redress in the courtroom from a jury of her peers. But, do many employers feel comfortable enough to tell Aleshire what they are thinking about her "abnormal" appearance during a hiring process? Do they even know what major life activities she is limited in doing? Have disability rights become so accepted that employers might want to hide their motivation for not hiring someone who looks different? Or have disability rights been so well integrated into the American ideal that Aleshire would be hired despite her appearance?

This legal question about an employer's attitude toward Aleshire should be extended to the rest of the society. The ADA mandates that employers provide accommodations in the workplace and that managers of public buildings and owners of private establishments make their facilities accessible. But, how much has this law changed attitudes? Will bias and discrimination diminish over time as the ADA becomes entrenched in the legal landscape? Will the federal courts' narrow interpretation of this law affect societal attitudes toward persons with disabilities?

Arguably, the history of the Civil Rights Act of 1964 and different affirmative action policies in the 1970s shows that no single law can alter prejudice against a group of people. It takes a public policy to have an impact on the state and society. Civil rights legislation did form public policy and helped change societal attitudes, whereas affirmative action laws did much less to alter these attitudes.[44] What path toward dampening discrimination will the ADA take? While Aleshire may still encounter some prying neighbors and patronizing nurses, will the number of these comments diminish over time? Will the ADA's path resemble that of U.S. antidiscrimination policy or of affirmative action?

WORKING

(TITLE I)

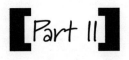

DISCLOSURES

[4] by Achim Nowak

It is a gray afternoon in New York, the sort of gray that I know so well from the afternoons of my childhood in Germany, but a gray December sky in New York has a bleakness all its own, a steely cool that magnifies all that is charmless about the East Village, where I live. I'm walking down Fourth Street toward Avenue A, alongside an impossibly handsome man named Miguel. He has the smooth, chiseled profile of an upper-class Filipino, tipped by a lean, imperial nose, and he walks with the cocky stride of one who hasn't been troubled by adversity. I have met Miguel only once before, inside the video booth of a gay bookstore, where we locked the door and tore off our clothes with the sort of surrender that seems so easy with a total stranger.

Miguel chatters away with a quick and steady stream of words, but I don't seem to hear a single sound he utters. I just see the gray of the pavement on East Fourth Street as it races past my feet, the gray of naked tree trunks that whir past my shoulder, and I feel the icy breeze that whips my cheeks. It is December 29, 1988, two days after I received my official HIV diagnosis at the Beth Israel Medical Center. I am thirty-three years old. I told myself I wouldn't tell him, this man who happens to be my first date after D-day. Diagnosis Day. Because I look healthy, I have no symptoms of any sort of disease, and there really is no reason to tell. Or so I told myself. But here, as we walk toward the bar that my friend Maria mischievously calls the Betty Ford Clinic, I feel the fear grip my chest. I'm about to violate the code of the evening, the tacit understanding that this will be a breezy post-Christmas dinner date. I stop before we reach the corner of Avenue A.

"I have to tell you something," I say to Miguel. He looks at me with his penetrating eyes and the easy charm that seems so permanently wedged into his dimples. Only the tiny quizzical frown that rises between his eyebrows lets me know that he understands I'm no longer making small talk.

"I found out two days ago that I'm HIV-positive."

I find it impossible to add another word, any further explanation for why I'm telling him, here and now, before we reach our destination. Standing on the sidewalk on East Fourth Street, I notice my heart pump inside me, hard and fast, as if to remind me that I am, indeed, still very much alive. My skin feels cool and numb, but it must show in my eyes, all of this terror that I feel inside.

"You don't really want to go and have dinner, do you?" Miguel asks after a mere second's pause, and he asks with the same ease with which he has managed the entire conversation so far. As if I had not just disclosed, for the very first time, my new medical status. As if I had simply told him that, today, I will have vanilla ice cream and not pistachio.

"Let's go back to your apartment," he suggests, and without waiting for a response he grabs my arm, quite forcefully, and turns me around. "Let's go and make love."

The moment we shut the doors of my studio on East Seventh Street, that is what we do. It is different from the love we made in the bookstore booth. But we are naked, and the moment is graced with the sense of whimsy and quick attack that I expect from Miguel. I watch him closely, watch if he is holding back, if anything has changed for him, because everything has changed for me. I have never made love to anyone knowing that I was HIV-positive and might infect the person. But I don't know Miguel well enough, and I certainly don't know him well enough to tell the difference. Only after he has gotten dressed again and is about to leave does he give himself away.

"Just one warning," he says with the same charm that has bubbled forth so effortlessly all evening. "Don't fall in love with me."

And as he pulls the door shut I wonder: Was this a mercy fuck?

I tell myself again and again that there is no reason to tell anyone, really. I am still having tests done, tests that will indicate the relative status of my health and the strength of my immune system. After all, I'm not sick and I don't look sick, and any announcement of my HIV status will just worry folks. I am now in the early weeks of January 1989. These are the dark ages of HIV treatment. The only legal drug available is AZT. Its side effects are toxic, and no one is sure of AZT's long-term impact. The prophylactic treatment of the moment for PCP, the severe pneumonia that incapacitates the bodies of many persons with AIDS, is a poisonous inhalant called aerosol pentamedine, which is sucked in through the nostrils with the help of a gigantic, tarantula-like apparatus. Each inhalation feels like an invasion by a creature from outer space.

As I sit in the plush Upper East Side office of my first doctor, one of the city's new crop of AIDS specialists, I'm struck by the fact that he is the one who looks unhealthy. When he leans forward from his gold-studded leather armchair, his prominent stomach spills onto a desk that is littered with too many mounds of paper and a stack of empty styrofoam containers that tell of long-devoured meals. His shirt is soiled with food stains, and I watch him shuffle one more piece of New York cheesecake into his mouth as he faces me. "You have two years before you get hospitalized," he declares matter-of-factly. "If you're lucky."

I drop him after that visit. But then my next doctor, another of the new crop, tells me the very same thing. This, after all, is 1989. My T-4 cell counts, it turns out, are below the 200 mark. And they're dropping with every new round of bloodwork. A level of 200 is considered the cut-off line between an impaired and a severely impaired immune system. "Below

200" puts me in the immediate danger zone for every opportunistic infection associated with AIDS. Instant hospitalization.

Maybe it was because of Miguel's charm and the fact that during my first coming out I wasn't rejected, but it only takes another couple of months before I come out at work. I'm one of the directors of the Creative Arts Team, a well-established New York theater company that produces plays about social issues for youth. The late 1980s have been a heady time for this company. A recent play about the death of a basketball star from a drug overdose has garnered national attention, and our current play, which is based on the Howard Beach racial attacks in New York City, is receiving international recognition. Each production has been an intensely personal collaboration between the playwright, Jim Mirrione, and me, his director.

I haven't planned to tell him; there has been no master strategy on how to go about this. Jim and I are sitting on an Amtrak train, heading up the Hudson River to a theater conference in Albany. It is a day not unlike the day of my first confession, a day swathed in the color gray. But today it is the choppy charcoal of a river lumbering toward the Atlantic, the olive-gray of a landscape of trees and meadows preparing for spring. As we race through commuter town after commuter town, we rehash the latest theater company gossip of which there always seems to be an endless supply. Jim is resolutely heterosexual, a macho Italian pussycat from the Bensonhurst section of Brooklyn. *Saturday Night Fever* country. We spend much time together at work, hanging out in coffee shops and rehearsal rooms, script meetings and actor auditions. It is a jovial and often passionate relationship, but Jim is a colleague and collaborator, not a close personal friend. Jim founded this theater company with Lynda Zimmerman, the executive director. By confiding in Jim, I go right to the source, the heart and soul of my work.

"I have to tell you something," I say to him, and I can tell that he can tell by my tone that this is a shift in conversation, a different kind of announcement.

"I found out a couple of months ago that I'm HIV-positive."

Waves of emotion ride up my chest. I don't know why I said it, and I also know that there is no turning back now. Jim stares at me for a quick moment, and then I notice his eyes well up, and almost instantly he starts to sob. Fast and hard, his tears are coming. I'm surprised and moved by the sight of his tears. It is a clear and uncensored response, and it speaks of Jim's deep affection for me. This is the first time I have seen a straight man cry for me. But I'm already learning that every time I announce my medical status, the person that receives my announcement hears something else. I state that I'm HIV-positive, and the person hears that I'm dying. My disclosure of my status, spoken by someone who is healthy and with no symptoms of disease, precipitates a dive into memories of personal loss and disease and deep-seated fears of death. I say one thing, and I unleash a stream of complex and uncontrollable currents. I see the power of this confession. I begin to understand how no relationship will be the same after this moment of disclosure.

"Don't tell anyone else at the Creative Arts Team," I say to Jim, as the emotion of the moment starts to drift away. It is the first time I ask a colleague to hold this professional secret, the first of many more such moments to come. Here, on this Amtrak train, I begin to separate my work world into two camps: those who know and those who don't. Jim agrees to my request at once. And, just as quickly, I think to myself, no, he'll have to tell Lynda, he won't be able to keep this one to himself.

Six weeks later, I sit on the frayed Danish sofa in Lynda Zimmerman's office at 715 Broadway, and I tell her too. Sitting with her is Mark Riherd, the Creative Arts Team's program director and my immediate supervisor. I'm no longer just confessing to my best buddy in the company. I'm confessing to the two individuals who run this company. The bosses. And this time it is not an unexpected burst of information, a moment born of my impetuous desire to tell the truth. I requested this meeting. I am telling because I want something that these two individuals have never granted anybody else in the company. In the fall—to be precise, in the months of November and December, at the start of our theater season—I wish to take six weeks off to go to the Golden Phoenix, an alternative healing center for people with AIDS in the Arizona desert. This is our busiest time of the year; leaving during those months will be like pulling the emergency brake as the express train lurches out of the station. I have a plan for who will take over in my absence. In addition, I wish to cut my workload down to four days a week to help reduce the stress of my job. I don't call it a medical leave, and I don't call it a change in my job description. But that is, in fact, what I'm requesting.

Lynda and Mark listen with silence and compassion. I receive the politically correct response, the one I thought I would receive. They will make every effort to accommodate my request. I wonder if either of them senses the heat that is rushing through my body, the heat of revealing information that is way too personal for a business meeting. I wonder what Mark, who is gay, really thinks and feels about HIV. Does he have friends who are positive? Has he ever slept with a positive man? Or is he, like me, one of the positive ones?

Even in this act of disclosure, there are things I disclose—and things I withhold. I don't tell Mark and Lynda just how low my T-cell counts are. I certainly don't tell them that, according to statistics, I'm one of the ones who could be in a hospital bed anytime soon with an opportunistic infection. The only other experience in my life that approximates this act of disclosure is the experience of my brother's suicide. I remember the phone call from my crying mother, one Friday afternoon, sobbing on the telephone with my best friend Ellen, delivering a eulogy for him in German inside the little chapel on the Heiderhof in Bonn. Every moment is vivid, and yet every step of the way it feels like I am caught inside a dream—not a good dream or a bad dream, just a dream that is entirely surreal. I cannot control the dream and I cannot end it; all I can do is stay inside it and persist. Every conversation such as the one with Lynda and Mark is a death, a death of the Achim who is carefree and healthy, the one who can get by with charm and wit without being second-guessed. I am no longer just another employee. I am the one whose medical history they know.

At the end of the meeting, Lynda requests a moment alone with me. "Do you have a good doctor?" she asks after Mark has left the room.

I appreciate the question, and I resent it at the same time. Is Lynda expressing her sincere concern for my well-being, or is she afraid that I will die on them one day, here in the office? Lynda is a smooth and polished manager, and she carries this part of the conversation with her usual aplomb. Maybe it is my paranoia setting in. Am I simply imagining it, because I know less and less what is real, or is Lynda really suddenly lowering her voice, as other people do now when they inquire about my health?

As if we were speaking about a shameful secret that dare not be mentioned aloud? My whispered condition.

"Make sure you know what you're doing," Lynda replies with a doubting frown when I explain to her that I'm pursuing alternative treatments. There is a fine line between judgment and concern, and just this moment I'm not sure which side of the line Lynda is on. And I resent the fact that because she, my boss, knows about my medical condition, I feel I must indulge this conversation and listen to Lynda's unasked-for advice, no matter what her intent. I don't wish to discuss my medical choices at work. And yet, this is the unspoken agreement: We'll give you what you ask for, and you'll give us what we ask for.

I leave the room relieved that my request was heard, but I don't feel happy or elated. Revealing my status makes me more vulnerable than I like to be. Every moment of disclosure makes me subject to rejection, and it also opens the way to possible privilege. I am just beginning to understand to what degree each revelation gives me power over others. And I begin to see the price I pay for this power. I can't go back to being one of the gang again. Ever.

On January 1, 1992, I become a person with AIDS. It is another of the invisible transitions in my life. The condition of my body is unchanged, healthy and holding, with bloodwork indicators that continue to hover deep down in the emergency zone, but as of January 1, the Centers for Disease Control's classification of a person with AIDS has been broadened to include HIV-positive individuals like me who have not manifested any of the AIDS-related opportunistic infections but whose T-4 cell counts have dropped below the 200 mark. This is an odd reclassification. Its intent is to make healthy folks like me who are considered at "high risk" for infection eligible for the benefits available to individuals with AIDS, and yet to receive any of those benefits, I have to document that I have been ill with an opportunistic infection. It is the classic Catch-22. I now carry the label of the person with AIDS, the heightened stigma of one who has already moved a little closer to death than a mere HIV-positive individual, without being any closer to receiving disability benefits. All stigma, no perks.

This is also the year that I switch jobs, after having taken some months off to hang out in the Caribbean. I end up being hired as a mediation trainer for the Victim Services Agency, a sizable social services provider in New York City. This agency serves runaway youth, homeless people, battered women, and, yes, people with AIDS. My new boss, Lynne Hurdle-Price, is a wonderfully big-hearted and gregarious manager. My instincts tells me that I can confide in Lynne about pretty much anything, including my HIV status, but I have already made my decisions:

> I don't tell on the job.
>
> I no longer wish to deal with people's responses to my act of disclosure.
>
> I don't tell when I fill out the medical questions on the application form at my new fitness center.
>
> I don't tell when I receive my membership card at the municipal baths.
>
> I don't tell when I fill out the medical emergency report forms at the various artist colonies where I go to write—even though each colony clearly states that it doesn't discriminate against persons with AIDS.
>
> I don't tell every time I enter a foreign country that does not allow people with AIDS.
>
> I don't tell when I'm asked about my medical history at Seeds of Peace, an international camp for teenagers where I work for several summers—even though one July afternoon, I'm rushed to the emergency room because I have pains from a kidney stone. The kidney stone is a reaction to Crixivan, a medication I am taking to help contain the spread of HIV in my body.
>
> I do tell on the medical history forms at my dental clinic, and I tell every new AIDS specialist I see for help.

I tell only when it suits me, and when it gives me power. I certainly tell when I am on the phone talking to a creditor. In the mid-1990s, I'm paying off a debt to Optima. It is a credit card that I have long ago returned and no longer use, and I have managed to negotiate repayment terms that include no further accrual of interest. I am committed to paying off this debt, but I have no interest in paying it off quickly. Every six months, an individual from Optima, invariably a male, calls to attempt to negotiate new repayment terms with me, and we engage in a soon-familiar dance. It is his job to get me to increase my monthly payments. It is my desire to keep my monthly payments as low as possible. Sometimes the negotiations with this stranger on the other end of the line are simple. At other times, however, the caller decides to confront me. When he challenges me about why I don't earn more income or get a second job to increase my earnings so I can honor my commitment to repay this debt to Optima in a timely fashion, when he persists and persists and doesn't back off, I take a big, long breath and say it.

"Look, I'm a person living with AIDS."

It stops the conversation, every time. I know the triggers, the images, the fears that are unleashed in his brain and in his heart by my simple declaration. Whatever the particulars may be for him, I know that this is a battle I have won. For the moment.

On June 1, 1999, I start work as a corporate trainer for a large international company that trains other corporate trainers. It is a Canadian company, and there are many things that appeal to me about this job. I'm working for the industry leader in this niche of the corporate train-the-trainer market. I'm nearly doubling my income, and, better yet, I will be working on a 1099 status and can therefore maintain my role as an independent contractor, with all the perks of tax deductions that this arrangement entails. I'm currently insured by Blue Cross/Blue Shield, an insurance plan with which I'm very happy and which I have been paying for out-of-pocket. My new employer does not put American staff on a company health plan. Instead, it will give me up to $4,000 a year to purchase my own insurance. This is ideal for someone with my medical background. There will be no switching of doctors, no waiting period for preexisting conditions on a new plan, or worse yet, no rejection by a health plan that verifies my health status.

Or so I think.

On my first visit to the company's headquarters in Ottawa, I meet with Olga, the head of human resources, who also happens to be the sister of the company's owner. I like her instantly. Olga is a portly and bubbly, no-nonsense kind of dynamo, a former nurse who left that profession to join her brother's thriving training business. We joke and laugh as I sit down in her tiny office and fill out the remaining paperwork for my new job.

"What about the check for my health insurance?" I ask as we both leave the room. "Oh," she says nonchalantly. "Just send me a copy of your latest health insurance payment, and make sure that you purchase short-term disability and send me a copy of that contract, and then I'll send you a check." I don't know if she can tell, but I feel the heat rise up inside me again, suddenly and sharply, the heat of the one who has been found out. I have the health insurance stub Olga is asking for, but I cannot comply with her second request. I don't have any disability insurance, and I'm marked in the big invisible "system" as a person with AIDS. No insurer will sell me disability insurance. No one.

For several months, I avoid the issue altogether. I do what other folks in my condition have done: I continue to pay my health insurance out of my own pocket instead of collecting the monies to which I'm entitled from my new employer. I make telephone calls to find out if there is a New York state fund that offers individual disability insurance for self-employed people like me. I get caught in hours of voice-mail hell with several state agencies and never receive an answer. I talk to Eileen, a colleague in my company whose brother sells insurance in Boston. He was able to find her an individual disability insurance plan. I call the brother, and he sends me papers for an insurance plan. I fill out the papers, and all the while I think to myself, if I fill this out, I will be rejected and then Eileen will know.

I never send in the forms. I avoid the issue again.

Two months later, I finally call the legal department at GMHC, the Gay Men's Health Crisis here in New York. I leave a voice-mail message, as I have done for weeks now whenever I had to call anywhere to receive information about purchasing individual disability insurance. Jeannette, a lawyer who works for GMHC, promptly calls me back and listens patiently to what I tell her.

"I've never heard of any such thing," Jeannette says firmly but without much sense of reassurance. "They cannot by law ask you to buy your own disability insurance." She pauses, and then she says, with firm conviction. "Whatever you do, don't tell them you have AIDS."

I end this conversation more confused than I was before. I'm now in my third month on this new job. I love the work, and clients are responding to me with great enthusiasm. I'm receiving rave reviews. I don't want to go back to Olga and tell her that, by law, she can't ask me to buy my own disability insurance. I will immediately be branded a troublemaker. I certainly don't wish to contemplate the possibility of legal action. My gut instinct is to disclose my status. It was, after all, not so difficult to do this at the Creative Arts Team. But at the Creative Arts Team, I had already been an employee for seven years. I can't imagine that Olga, who was a nurse and seems like such a compassionate woman, won't be sympathetic if I disclose. And then I remember what Jeannette from GMHC said so firmly: "Don't tell them." The truth is, I don't want to tell. I don't know if it's because I'm simply so tired of the conversation, or if I'm tired of, again, being the person with AIDS. Or if I'm just really, really afraid.

When I finally have my telephone conversation with Olga, my personal script is well-rehearsed. "Olga," I say to her after a round of schmoozy banter. "I have a problem with getting this disability insurance."

Olga pauses and then replies, in the direct tone that I so like, "So tell me."

That, of course, is exactly what I have decided not to do. "Olga, I have a chronic medical condition for which I regularly take medication. I'm completely healthy, but because of this condition, I cannot purchase disability insurance."

There is a quick but unmistakable pause, and then Olga presses ahead. "May I ask what the nature of your medical condition is?"

"I don't believe that the particulars of my condition are important."

These are the words I have rehearsed, over and over, and yet I don't know how I will respond if Olga decides to press ahead. It is the moment I have feared the most—the moment where an employer presses me to reveal.

Olga pauses again, and then says simply, "OK." A week later, I receive my first company check to pay for my health insurance.

A year into my work with this employer, I have moved into the ranks of senior instructor. Part of my new responsibilities involves coaching, via telephone, some of the new trainers who are being hired for this rapidly growing company. My first assignment is to help prepare a perky new trainer from Miami, Jaime. During my initial phone call, I do the sort of reading between the lines that one gay person does with another. I assume he is gay, and I'm sure he must guess that I am as well. But this is our first business contact. He's the new employee; I'm the senior trainer. We don't tell. Instead, we make an appointment for our first official telephone coaching session.

"I'm not feeling so well," Jaime says at the start of our coaching call, when I ask how he's doing. I am surprised by this response, as I thought I was just engaging in harmless small talk.

"I'm waiting to hear from my doctor," he explains. "So if the other phone rings, please know that I will have to talk to him."

I'm even more surprised by this statement. I wonder what can be so serious about Jaime's health that he will have to interrupt an important business call to have a chat with his physician. Twenty minutes later, his phone rings, and Jaime excuses himself. "Call you right back," he says.

Two hours later, I hear back from Jaime. I'm quite angry now, because his delays are throwing my entire day off track.

"I suppose I owe you an explanation," Jaime says sheepishly when he finally speaks. "I'm on an experimental treatment procedure for chronic fatigue syndrome. Each treatment lasts a whole week, and it really knocks me out when I take it. And I need to be in touch with my doctor every day during these periods. And I just feel very weak today."

"How long have you had this?" I ask Jaime, and I immediately have the eerie sense that, with this question, I'm becoming Olga and Lynda and all the others who have interrogated me about my medical status. Jaime chatters on a bit about his medical history, and I notice that he is as vague as I was when I disclosed at the Creative Arts Team. At one point, he mentions T-cells, and then I suddenly understand that this must be about AIDS and not about chronic fatigue syndrome. Jaime has invented his own cover, and at the same time he has already revealed more than I ever have. He, or so I assume, must actually be sick whereas I haven't been.

"Are you strong enough to do this work?" I ask Jaime, and I immediately want to take this question back, because I know I have just put into words what all of my bosses must have thought when I disclosed my status.

"I only do my treatments during those weeks when I don't train," Jaime replies dutifully, and at this point I no longer know what I can and cannot believe. I want to be compassionate toward my brother with AIDS, and at the same time I resent that I'm in on a secret that nobody else in the company knows. And I'm annoyed that because of his treatments, I will not be able to complete my coaching with him today. We will have to continue the following morning, and I will lose a precious day that I had set aside for personal projects.

"Does anyone in the company know about your treatments?" I inquire, just to be clear about this matter. When Jaime explains to me that, just as expected, I'm the only one who knows, I urge him to call the company's senior vice president.

"You may want to call Victor. I think he should know about this."

As we hang up, I realize that while I played the part of the sympathetic senior trainer in this phone call, I did not reveal my own medical history to Jaime. And even though I asked colleague after colleague to do it on my behalf, I also know that this is true for me today: I don't wish to be the carrier of another's secret. Even if only half-truths have been revealed.

"Watch what you say to people in the company," says Andrea, the new vice president to whom I now report on a weekly basis, in the middle of a telephone call. "There's a witch hunt going on. They're after everyone who they think has a bad attitude. They're on Jaime's case right now."

It is February 2001, and for the first time since I was hired, this booming company is encountering a slump in enrollment for its seminars. Jaime, like me, has become one of the top performers in this competitive business, where clients are constantly scoring our performance. Jaime is one of the company's new stars. I also know that he has disclosed his health situation to Victor, the senior vice president, after I urged him to do so. What he said, and how much he revealed, I don't know. I certainly don't know whether he chose to use the word AIDS.

I call Jaime after my conversation with Andrea to simply say hello, but also because I'm a bit alarmed after her witch hunt remark. When Jaime picks up the phone, he speaks with a harsh, raspy voice, and then he immediately starts to cough.

"What's wrong?" I ask him, surprised that Andrea didn't tell me that Jaime was sick.

"I have a slight pneumonia," Jaime says, and in my mind I immediately wonder, is this the basic old pneumonia that everyone gets once in a while, or is it the PCP pneumonia that ravages people with AIDS? I have seen friend after friend perish in a hospital ward. Many have never recovered from the impact that this severe pneumonia has on an already weakened body, or from the impact of the drugs that are poured into their bodies as the required treatment.

"You didn't have to get hospitalized?" I ask Jaime, and I think to myself, he must realize that I know he has AIDS, because no one would contemplate hospitalization for basic pneumonia.

"No," Jaime says. "My doctor and I caught it just in time. It was in the right lung and hadn't spread yet."

"How has the company handled all of this?" I press on.

"Well," Jaime replies, and his tone is suddenly a bit dour. "I'm on a two-week sick leave. I don't know if they understand, but they have pretty much left me alone, which I guess is good."

When he mentions the sick leave, I realize that his situation is, indeed, serious; as he elaborates, I realize just how grave it really is.

"What I feel bad about is that they had to fly me home from a training in Vegas. I simply couldn't go on for one more day," Jaime says, and I hear the sting of defeat in his voice. Having to break off a training in midstream is a trainer's worst fear. I can't imagine what it must feel like when you also suspect that what is happening may be an AIDS-related condition.

"They had to fly in someone else to take over for me. I called Victor at home over the weekend because I wanted to talk to him in person, and I wanted him to hear how rough my cough is. I think that's when they finally realized that this is real."

After a pause, during which the despair seems to suddenly magnify the distance between us, Jaime adds, "Last summer, after I first talked to Victor, he sent me a brochure about safety precautions in the workplace and being careful with blood." Jaime lets out an exasperated sigh. "Like I'm gonna wear some fucking surgical gloves while I train."

"They're so clueless," I say to Jaime.

"Yeah, they're clueless," he replies.

I offer a few words of generic paternal advice about how our health always comes first, and then we hang up. The word AIDS was never mentioned in this conversation, but I think again of what Andrea had said to me earlier in the day. "Beware. They're on a witch hunt."

And just what witch is being hunted, Jaime and I will never know.

A CHAIR UNSEEN

[5] by C. G. K. Atkins

It is the morning prior to Gretta and Felix's housewarming party. Within hours, dozens of colleagues from both of their workplaces will be ringing the front doorbell. The festivities are an attempt to christen their new house and to make social connections with a select group of people they know from the office. Framed pictures lean against the walls in all four corners of the living room. Sunlight filters through partially drawn curtains as the couple leafs through photo albums. Gretta holds up three photos. "What about these ones? They are of your graduation—this is a such a good one of you and the kids."

Felix quickly scans the images lying across her palms. "I don't know—I don't know whether I am prepared to go that far yet."

"OK."

He settles back into the sofa, stretching his arms along its high, ridged back. "Why is this so bloody difficult? We're sitting here censoring family photographs as though we have something to hide!"

Gretta speaks quietly and evenly to him. "It's your decision really—we'll do whatever you want. It doesn't really affect me. You have to decide how much you want them to know."

He stands up with irritation, slapping his thigh with one hand. "Let me think about it for a bit longer. We've got plenty of other things to do before they arrive. I'm going to get ice cubes at the store."

"They're going to be here in a couple of hours," she warns.

"I know, I know. Let me think."

As he puts on his coat and rustles through the pockets for his car keys, he can hear the gentle clinking of dishes as Gretta lays platters of finger foods on various surfaces in the dining room. He calls out to her, "All the wheelchairs—they're in the garage, right?"

"Don't worry," she reassures him through a partially closed door, "the children and I put them there yesterday."

"OK, I'll be back in a few minutes."

In the car, as Felix waits for the engine to warm in the cold of the winter afternoon, his anxiety builds and his face flushes self-consciously as he thinks back to the previous spring, when he accepted this new job in this alien city halfway across the continent.

He had flown out to meet with the university administrators and with faculty members to talk about his research and to negotiate his salary. Gretta had come with him, but they had left the children at home. As the two toured city neighborhoods with a realtor, they were plagued by the familiar worries of most families: they fretted about the proximity of good schools and transit, as well as about the cost of housing. But they also scanned houses with a sharp and hidden critical eye. They needed a wheelchair-accessible house—something they dared not admit even to the realtor because he had been referred by the dean. They vetted houses quickly. Within minutes, both silently assessed the possibilities for installing a ramp or an accessible bathroom. With mute gestures and obscure comments such as "I don't think that hallway is wide enough, do you?" they inspected a dozen properties. The speed of their assessment astonished the realtor. At one point he stuttered, "I like your style. There's no point in lingering in a house you don't like." He smiled, "There's no point in that. But I thought that last house was pretty nice and," he coughed, "fairly priced."

"We realize we're particular." Gretta and Felix had smiled at him sympathetically. "It's just the type of people we are. We have to live in the house, after all."

Despite their misgivings, by the end of the day, two houses looked as though they might do. They were within the appropriate price range and had potential for a quick and not-too-obvious adaptation for a wheelchair.

That night, in the hours prior to meeting with the dean, they had dined alone in their hotel room. Felix lay on one of the beds as Gretta unwrapped the sandwiches and salads from room service. "You all right?" she queried.

"Yeah, I have a bit of pain though, which feels as though it might explode, so I'm going to take some pain medication."

"Are you up to eating?"

"Yeah, I think so. I should if I can. I have that early appointment tomorrow at the university." He propped himself up on an elbow. "Can you hand me the med bag?"

"Here." She tossed a small duffel bag at him. "Do you want to eat on the bed or at the table?"

"Bed."

"You're sure you're OK?"

"Yeah. I'm sure." But he wasn't. When he had stayed in this very same room for his interview a few weeks prior, the ten-hour day of lecturing and conferences had worn down his mind and body. When he returned to the hotel that night, somewhat elated and hopeful at his performances, a small nervy ache held part of his head and arm. By two or three in the morning, the ache had grown so large that it had engulfed him in sickening, wretched flames of nausea and pain. He had limped to the bathroom and crouched naked under the spray of the shower, letting the warm, water spatter him numb—crouching there until dawn, and then until full morning, and then finally pulling himself from its fluid embrace to dress himself, pack and gather his bags, and go downstairs to hail a cab to the plane.

Now, as they contemplated the houses, the job offer, and an imagined future, they were both aware that his pain might take off again, muffling his capacity to think and speak clearly. His now-invisible "disability" haunted them as they ate with the television tuned mutely to an all-news channel.

Felix played with the soup in his spoon, pouring it back into the bowl and then lifting it out again. "So, what did you think of the yellow house— you know, the second to last one?"

"It's a possibility."

"It's pretty ugly."

"That's irrelevant. We can deal with ugliness. We always make the places we live in look all right. It's the accessibility that counts. And it's close to the school we liked."

"Hmm." Felix continued to dribble his soup and then looked up at his wife. He watched her knowingly as she ate by the blue, flickering light of the TV. Her gestures were overfamiliar to him and yet he still loved her terribly. His passion for her sometimes felt as sharp and as painful as a wound. They had been together for over a decade, and this feeling oscillated but always held. Their life together was a narrative of extremes: of tenderness and woe, of happiness and ruin.

They had met when he had been dying. He had been paralyzed by an unknown demon of an illness. And as doctors declared him incurable, his body had sunk closer and closer to death. The muscles of his chest walls became so weak that he often struggled to breathe. The day that he was first put on life support in intensive care, Gretta became sure she was in love with him. That he survived that ordeal was in large part due to her presence by his bed for endless hours, day and night. Her severe and grievous love held him suspended in a dreadful netherworld of psychological and physical consciousness. He had never had anyone cry out for him before. It buoyed him. And so, he had climbed, inexplicably, still paralyzed, back toward life. Within days of leaving the ICU, his body still immobile, they had made love in the cold hardness of a hospital room.

Months later, when he came home, he still couldn't walk, but they moved into an accessible apartment together. Her children became his children. His health undulated like an unpredictable tide—reasonably stable and then perilously bad. She had watched him being resuscitated at least three times. His crises had ruined holidays and weddings and, it seemed, any chance of a career. Even as his body faltered, his physicians puzzled over why he was ill. The uncertainty left everyone feeling powerless.

Five years later, his health miraculously improved. An aloof physician suggested a rare cause for Felix's afflictions and then promptly dismissed it. But Gretta and Felix had gone home and read encyclopedias, articles, and books. They became convinced that the doctor's suggestion had been right. One night, as Felix lay dying again in an emergency room with tubes being shoved down his throat, Gretta uttered the words of this mystical, dismissed disease. In desperation, because Felix was fiercely clinging to life, the ER doctor agreed to try the diagnosis. He prescribed the appropriate medication and procedures. Disagreement and disputes raged over Felix's prone body in the ICU, but the ordered therapies remained and Felix gradually got better.

Within a year, he was on a complex assortment of medications and, to his great delight and confusion, he walked out of his wheelchair. Both Gretta and he felt as though a great hand had reached out of the abyss and yanked them all onto some hallowed shore. The drugs often made him sick to his stomach—but this was nothing when compared to the torment of the previous years. He had pain, but it no longer required morphine to be calmed. He tired easily and often tripped when trying to climb stairs. On some days, the paralysis reared up in his body and his face became partially immobile and he had trouble swallowing, talking, or walking. On those days, he took to his bed. But overall, Felix reveled in the fact that he was restored, alive, and loved. Gretta, he, and the children left their wheelchair-accessible apartment and moved to a cheaper and more vertical abode.

He finished his doctoral degree and began to apply for university positions all over North America. The first year, he sent out thirty-five applications and received only two inquiries of interest. One had come as a phone call as he worked at his desk on a dark February afternoon. A gravelly, static-ridden voice had expressed a keen interest in his letter and resume—would he be interested in coming for an interview? The snaps and fizzles crackled sharply in the receiver. Felix restrained himself from shouting with elation and solemnly answered, "Yes."

"We'll send you an air ticket. Are you free on the tenth?"

When he hung up the phone, Felix joyfully shouted for Gretta. But the airline ticket never arrived. As the interview date loomed, Felix telephoned the professor three or four times. The assistant took messages, but no one returned his calls. The date passed. Four months later, one of a mass of rejection letters fell through the front mail slot and onto the floor. In the interim, another university on the Pacific coast expressed interest in him. But again, the travel ticket never appeared.

Felix asked friends and colleagues what they thought had happened. He had begun to suspect that his reference letters were scuttling his efforts. His former thesis supervisor tried to reassure him. "The job market is tight. It's been tight for years. You have good references. It's just hard for even the very well qualified. I don't know what to say. You just need to have patience."

The telephone rang one morning as he was getting out of the shower. A woman's voice asked, "Is Felix Gardner there?"

"Speaking."

"This is uncomfortable." The voice hesitated. "I shouldn't be doing this."

Felix swatted a towel at the rivulets of water running down his calves. "Excuse me?" He groped for the T-shirt lying on the bed. With one hand, he levered it over his damp head and over one arm. He quickly rotated the phone to his other shoulder and yanked the shirt down over the rest of his torso. "Excuse me?" he said again.

"You applied for a job recently at a university, didn't you?"

"Yes." He swept the towel around his waist and then sat down on the side of the bed.

"Well, you'll be getting a rejection letter soon."

"Oh."

"I just thought I'd tell you. You've got to change your reference letters."

A heat of shame swept through Felix's body—so his letters *were* bad. The thought that his advisors had lied to him—that they had said that they had given him good references but had in fact privately skewered him—made him feel instantly and simultaneously humiliated and enraged.

The voice went on. "It's not that they're bad. They are actually very good. They are glowing. It's just that *all* of them talk about your illness."

Felix grasped at his forehead in disbelief. "You're kidding." He massaged his temples with apprehensive vigor.

"No, I'm not. One of them even talks about the fact that you have been on life support."

A wave of anxiety tore into him. He couldn't speak.

"You made the final pile, and you would have been interviewed but those letters got you tossed out. There's no way a committee can bring you to interview with those letters. There's too much risk."

"Well, it makes it sound as though I'm dying." He interrupted her.

"Well that, and the fact that if we don't like you in the interview stage and don't give you the job, you may try to launch a discrimination suit. It's just safer to toss you out before there's any paper trail."

The bedroom seemed to throb and skid away from him as Felix pushed down panic and an urge to weep.

"Look, that's all I can say. You need to get your references to change their letters." And she hung up the phone before he could say anything more.

The following week, he visited each of his professors and opaquely asked them to rewrite their letters and ensure that they made no mention of his ailments. One of them, a philosophy professor, objected, "Are you sure?"

"Yes," he said flatly. "I am very sure."

"But, I think it is dishonest of you to hide it."

"I don't think honesty has anything to do with it. At this point, I need a job."

"My letter speaks well of you—and what you've accomplished is even more remarkable given your circumstances. It reflects well on you." She resisted. "I don't want to take it out."

"I really think you should. It creates a problem. No one is going to knowingly hire someone who can become ill."

"I think you are overreacting. You might even fit a minority profile," she tried to placate him. "But if you insist, I will take all mention of it out."

"I insist," Felix said simply.

She leaned forward. "But they will find out eventually, you know. You have difficulty speaking when you tire, and that could happen in an interview," she cautioned.

"Let me worry about that once I am *actually at an interview*," he exclaimed.

"All right, I will do it—but under protest."

All of the letters were changed. Within a year or so, he received several invitations to interview at universities, and the plane tickets all arrived.

In the car, Felix's mind careens over the various convolutions of his job search. The engine protests as he shifts the car into first and releases the clutch. He cranks the steering wheel hard over and as he inches out of the parking spot, he ponders the morning of negotiations in the dean's office the previous May. He and Gretta had fretted endlessly in preparation for that meeting.

A year before the interview, paralysis had overwhelmed him once again. Exhausted from travel and from speaking engagements, it had crept swiftly and stealthily through his body, stifling his movement and breathing until once again he lay precipitously in a hospital bed. It took months, with the help of therapies and medication, for him to slowly recover his movement and strength. He, Gretta, and the children felt bereft by the disease's surges and wizened and gladdened by its repeated retreat. Their lives together glistened more keenly with his return to health. But they became more vigilant. They finally agreed to borrow money and purchase a motorized wheelchair. They sold the vertical house and vowed to always live in an accessible environment regardless of Felix's physical state. The illness had always stalked them, but now they openly turned to face it and acknowledge its presence. They applied for and received a disabled parking permit. Even as Felix grew more robust, they reminded themselves daily of the looming possibility of his incapacity. Nothing—no salary, no bonus, no form of prestige—was worth a collapse back into illness.

It was this new ethos that dogged him as he walked into the dean's office that spring morning. He wanted the job—even craved it. Years of ill health had forged an iron weight of longing for the normalcy of employment and routine. But the memory of infirmity lingered in his consciousness, admonishing him that no job was worth a descent into the crucible of suffering that composed the very worst of his sickness. He and Gretta had paid a labor lawyer to investigate the university's benefits package— they both worried about prohibitions against preexisting conditions. Surprisingly, he reported that the benefits package contained no such wording. Gretta had asked him to go back and review his information. Again, he informed them that no prohibitions were included, and it seemed as though Felix's therapies might be covered. Nonetheless, Felix and Gretta remained wary.

As he sat with the dean that morning, he knew he could not overly scrutinize the benefits folder that lay open before him on the low table. Too much inspection might create suspicion. He pushed for more salary, aware that the new monstrous wheelchair in their living room was, as yet, unpaid. He couldn't sign the contract without knowing that their income could service the loans they had taken to cover the exorbitant expenses of his illness of the past year. His income had to be large enough to cover the cost of his medications as well as the monthly obligation to the line of credit. Gretta's income, they hoped, would handle all the rest of the household expenses. If it turned out that the university's health insurance covered him, they would be that much better off—but they couldn't rely on it.

The sunlight beamed across the formal study in columns of dust-ridden light. Felix watched it settle gently on the table and chairs. He felt plagued by internal dilemmas which he could not share with the benevolent-looking man seated before him. After forty minutes, the dean leaned forward in his green herringbone jacket, arranging the pages of the contract in a neat fan. "So, do you think you're ready to sign?"

Felix fingered the papers and asked, "Do you think I could bring this back to the hotel and look at it tonight?"

"Well . . . yes. But we would prefer to know as soon as possible whether you are interested or not."

"I understand." Felix wanted more time. He yearned for some sort of external confirmation that everything would be all right—that his disease would not flare, that he could work full time without physically failing, that his prescriptions would be covered by the insurance policy, that his family's income would be high enough, that his children would be happy—that, in short, what he was about to do was right and that they would all be safe. "I'd like to take it back to talk over with Gretta. I guarantee that I'll have made a decision by tomorrow morning. Do you think you can live with that?"

"I think that we can live with that." The dean pressed his hands into his knees and stood up. He held out a hand. "We'll talk tomorrow then."

He called to his assistant in the outer office, "Terry, can you get Dr. Gardner's coat and tell Amanda that he is ready to go to lunch."

In itself, the terminology of the contract was simple. They did not linger over its wording for long. It was the unspeakable burden of the decision that made them falter. Felix's disability was obscure but ruthless. They wanted to protect themselves from it but also knew that no true defense was possible—in the end, living well and fully was the best remedy to his mortal shadow. They spoke little that evening. They slumped in chairs and flopped on the bed, surfing TV channels. Occasionally, worries percolated to the surface. Before they finally turned out the light, Felix leaned over the small bedside table and signed and dated the final page of the university's contract. "I guess we're doing it. We're moving." He put the pen down. "Tomorrow, I will send them a fax with a copy of my permit and formally request a disabled parking space."

"That's a good idea," Gretta responded and reached to turn out the light.

As the car crunched across the frozen streets, Felix debated the pictures his wife had just shown him. He had graduated with his final degree while he was confined to a power wheelchair. In the photographs, his face droops on one side and his head is supported by a conspicuous headrest. The children dance merrily around his chair. He decides in the instant he stops in front of the corner store that he will not put those photographs on display in front of his new colleagues at the party. He does not want to frighten them, nor does he want to provide an invisible but potentially camouflaged reason to refuse to renew his contract in three years' time.

But, as he picks up the collapsing bag of ice in his arms and carries it to the car, he is reminded of an invidious curiosity that flows through his workplace. On several occasions, wry and resentful comments have surfaced about his privileged parking space. He stanches the questions by saying that he sometimes has difficulty walking. When he senses that paralysis is creeping into his face, he wears sunglasses and leaves work early. He schedules classes and appointments in the most consistent part of his week. When a fever or cold rises up, he always goes to work, fearful that any sign of weakness might condemn him. Nonetheless, the queries continue, and he knows that he should perhaps provide evidence of his disability in the least threatening manner possible—if only to quell the growing belief of his fellow professors that he does not need his parking space.

Felix returns home, clutching the ice to his chest and kicking the front door open. He calls for his son and deposits the cold plastic bag into his arms. As he is leaning down to take off his boots, he mouths quietly to himself, "This sucks."

His son questions him, "What?"

"Nothing."

"Yeah, whatever."

"No, really, it's nothing." Felix stands up and straightens the waistband of his trousers. "Tell your mother that I've decided what we should do."

"OK."

Gretta comes out in the hall with a dishrag over one arm. "They're going to be here soon."

"I know. I've decided that we should put out the picture of us at the beach, you know, the one in Mexico on our honeymoon. The rest, except head shots, should go away."

"The one in your 'off-road' chair?"

"Yeah, that one. It's nicely framed. And despite the fact that I'm in a chair, I look healthy in it. It's about all the disclosure I can handle at the moment."

"You're sure?"

"Yeah, I'm sure." He looks at his watch and says, "I'm going to go take my next round of pills before they arrive."

[6] by Stephen Kuusisto

It was August and hot when Henry Cole fell down the stairs of his apartment building. His legs weren't working correctly—and, as if that weren't enough, he had no words for his state of affairs. He wasn't ready for his new life—a life with multiple sclerosis and no job. He lay at the bottom of the stairs and thought he might stay for a while on the linoleum. Tall windows flanked the stairs. The building had once been a high school. He looked up at a rectangle of sunlight and heard starlings in the ivy and thought about getting to his feet. He would think his way through it by issuing commands to his arms and legs. "It's like sending telegrams over a mountain," he'd told his sister on the phone. "You send messages to outlying districts and wait for word to come back."

Getting to his feet, he saw construction workers climbing a scaffold. Inch forward, fall back—but keep something moving. He remembered Leadbelly, "king of the twelve-string guitar," who said that if you want to play the blues, "you got to keep something moving all the time." And then

Henry was on his feet. And then he was working his way back to his apartment, having changed his mind about going out. He went straight to the freezer, got a cold pack, and lay down on the couch.

Henry had recently lost his job as an adjunct professor and part-time dean at a small college. He'd been a good—some said outstanding—professor of religious studies and had been repeatedly promised a permanent appointment, if not as a full-time professor, then as an administrator and half-time teacher. The thinking of the administration was that he'd make a good dean or director of disability services and could teach part time as well. Although the college had no tenure-track faculty slot for Henry, they wanted him to stay. That's what they said. They said it in memos. They said it in conversation. They said it over dinners and drinks. He believed everything. He was earnest and full of loyalty. He was only thirty-eight. He was an optimist with a mild version of multiple sclerosis so far. He was a popular teacher. Students walked beside him in the campus gardens, talking of the sacred and profane, of Eros and Thanatos.

One morning, while bookworming with his cat, he received a call from the dean of women, a scholar of the English Renaissance named Marilyn De Quincy, a woman whose integrity was uncompromising. She was also celebrated for running marathons. She was a sight as she ran about town with her owlish glasses and graying, pageboy haircut. Students said she recited *A Mirror for Magistrates* as she ran. Henry couldn't imagine her reciting anything while running: she couldn't be more than 5'2" and couldn't weigh more than 95 pounds. But she was good at getting to the point.

"Jack Minton and I would like you to head a committee on disabilities for the college," she had said. (Jack Minton was the dean of men, a reticent Episcopal minister now pastured in administration.)

"You know," said Marilyn, "sometimes teaching goes on in spite of administration." They laughed. Then she added: "And sometimes the college gets ahead in spite of its faculty."

Henry and Marilyn had a good rapport. She knew he had recently been diagnosed with M.S. She shared his concern that their provincial North Carolina College had no program for disabled students or staff. He'd said yes without a moment's hesitation. "*Esse quam videri*," he'd said, for both he and the dean had a love of lingo in common. "To be rather than to seem." They had even laughed a little; this was the official motto of North Carolina and they wondered if Senator Jesse Helms would understand it.

It was November and unseasonably hot. Henry listened to Marilyn while watching red squirrels fight over acorns in the grass under his balcony. She said they'd need a solid committee made up of the best-known faculty on campus.

"I've got five people in mind," she said. "Danielle MacPherson in art history, Carolyn Dishman in poli. sci., Joseph Younker in chemistry, Martin Kroll in the English department, and Vern Saunders from history."

He could see the group, a stylish assembly, subscribers to *Bon Appetit*. Martin Kroll wore Italian suits; Carolyn Dishman summered in France and wrote about pop culture and politics. It was hard to imagine them worrying about attention deficit disorder. It would be a sea change for the college. Just months before, Henry had overheard the director of admissions tell the dean's committee: "We don't want a reputation for helping these people."

Henry had assumed a Roman tone of weary summation: "Just last month, the Americans with Disabilities Act was signed into law by President Bush. It mandates that all institutions receiving federal funding must ensure that their programs and services are open and available to people with disabilities. And learning disabilities are specifically part of the law."

The speech had been greeted with ceremonious silence. Henry remembered there was a hornet in the room. He thought of the poet Theodore Roethke, who said, "Plain speech is inaccurate but not plain words." He knew no one was listening.

Now Marilyn De Quincy wanted him to take the reins. Henry was no cynic. But a nontenured, disabled faculty member directing the disabilities focus of a college stuck in reverse—it was a risky plan.

But it *was* a plan. The assignment would mark the way for the college to create a full-time position for Henry Cole. Saying yes was easier than saying no.

Besides, there was so much else to think about: his legs were taking on their own lives. They felt hollow. Then, by turns, it felt like they were filled with hot or cold water. He first noticed it while teaching and thought with horror that he'd wet his pants. But he was simply on fire and then ice cold. His legs were like plumb weights. He continued talking about *The Imitation of Christ*, but he sat down—a thing he never did when teaching.

M.S. was capricious, alternately terrifying and familiar. His body had become unfamiliar terrain. The psyche—his mind—well, it was racing in the trenches searching for a map. From now on, it was mind over matter. There would, after all, be only a small decline. He could count on this. Sometimes he thought of it as a romantic education. A string quintet, intimate, frightening, relentless. You had to think like Schubert or Mozart—sketch a story while the moon fell behind clouds. Meanwhile, the body would sail through its unforeseen and private weather.

The disability committee proved more difficult to assemble than Marilyn De Quincy had imagined. One by one, the chosen faculty explained their longstanding commitments. Danielle MacPherson had a leave coming up that would take her to Florence. For the others, there were tenure committees, hiring committees, and curriculum committees. None of this surprised Henry. Committee assignments were *de rigueur* for faculty seeking tenure and promotion. The powerful committees were the plum assignments.

"Here's what we do," said Henry. He and Marilyn were eating chili in the student union. The chili came in edible bowls made from pastry shells. He fingered a piece of baked shell. "We put together a blue-ribbon panel, as they call it in the private sector. We'll ask the emeritus faculty to study the disability issue. This approach has two virtues: we acquire prominent local voices, and we capitalize on the natural connection between disability and what everyone calls the senior years."

"You realize," said Marilyn, "that the emeritus faculty at this college have almost no standing. They spent their entire careers making enemies and now that they're retired, they celebrate by talking to no one."

She poured a whopping amount of sugar into her iced tea. "I mean, they don't even talk to each other."

Henry laughed. "It's a Monty Python skit," he said. "Hello, Dr. Livingston, Stanley here! What brings you to the National Archives? I say, cat got your tongue?"

"The trouble," said Marilyn, "is that the college sees itself as a grade-B institution. And the faculty believes they're mediocre at best. Though, of course, no professor would say this about himself."

She stared out the long picture window at a group of college women feeding ducks beside the reflecting pond. "Therefore," she continued, "any initiative—whether it's curricular or administrative—all proposals for change have always been greeted with condescension."

"OK, but Marilyn, this isn't a contest. We're not picking books for a desert island. The ADA puts a blueprint on the table. I mean, we could use inflatable faculty on the committee—like those blow-up dolls that women have in their cars."

"Think of it!" Henry continued. "An inflatable faculty at commencement! It would be just like Macy's Thanksgiving Parade!"

They pictured a department of "levitation studies"—books on "gravity and the construction of normative behavior"—which would make the school famous at last.

"In the end," said Henry, "it doesn't matter who's on the committee. We're reviewing federal law, not the general curriculum."

"True," said Marilyn, "but I'd hoped for an influential group. The new president comes on board in the spring. From what I've heard, he's opinionated. We really need a jump-start with disability. That's why I thought the most visible faculty should be part of this."

Alone in his office, Henry opened a book on the ADA edited by Frederick Harris, a Washington attorney specializing in disability law. Henry needed to do some homework. His college was a small, private, liberal arts school built with railroad money. The campus, with its loosening bricks and fading whitewash, conveyed a genteel shabbiness. The buildings smelled of vulcanized rubber. The stairwells had an odor of glue where the linoleum had been replaced. Only one building on campus had an elevator and ironically it was the home of the maintenance department.

The problem had come into focus when a college senior, a kid named Toby Emerich, had flipped his motorcycle while attempting to jump a pile of bricks behind the gymnasium. Toby returned to campus six months later with a spinal cord injury, a motorized wheelchair, and a companion dog. The campus had proved to be a nightmare. Not one building had a ramp. There were no elevators in the administrative or instructional buildings. No one was in charge of accommodations for people with disabilities. The college administration had hoped that, following his injury, Toby wouldn't come back.

It was a rural farce, as there was a fund for disabled students. The parents of a blind coed who had graduated forty years ago had donated it. But the physical education department had raided the fund to install handicapped bathrooms at the football field. No one could recall who had authorized this. *Ipse dixit*, thought Henry. The college had always been run this way.

Maybe that was the charm of the place. Problems could be solved by familiarity and consensus. But nothing had gone well for Toby Emerich and his wheelchair. When it snowed, the maintenance department would forget to shovel the walk outside his door. The hastily erected ramps were never up to code, and his chair would lurch or stop altogether. The doors at the top of the ramps often remained locked even after Toby called the dean's office.

By this time, Henry was walking with the aid of a support cane. He would likely need a wheelchair himself in the foreseeable future. He thought of William of Occam. Rely on what you know to be true. Maybe he'd never need a chair. What else? Maybe he was turning into Dale Carnegie? Positive thinking! He felt guilty about this. What else? He felt guilty because he was just as ineffectual as everyone else. He had tried to take a leading role in helping Toby and his parents, but the bureaucracies and the finger pointing had plenty of staying power.

Toby Emerich survived his last semester and received a standing ovation at commencement when he rolled across the stage with his golden retriever, Ulysses. And now Henry was being asked to repair the desultory machinery that had reduced Toby and his parents to such depths of humiliation. He decided to call Frederick Harris in Washington. The dust jacket of his book said he was a consultant on disability compliance.

After a few words with a receptionist, he was surprised to find himself talking directly to Harris. Henry felt the familiar urge to talk fast and tried to introduce bonhomie into his voice by saying that he taught "at the little college that time forgot and that the decades cannot improve." He explained his assignment.

Harris listened. When he spoke, he was considerate, almost avuncular. He sounded like Jimmy Stewart.

"Let me ask you a couple of questions," he said. "First, do you have tenure? You shouldn't be in a weakened position if you're handling such a delicate assignment. In general, private colleges are far worse than public institutions when it comes to providing programs and services for students with disabilities."

Harris summarized the federal law and the ways in which private schools sidestepped accessibility by declaring that they received no government money. "Nowadays, no one in higher education can say that they don't receive government money. Even after years of shrinking federal spending under Reagan and Bush. Think of the Pell grants, the federally guaranteed financial aid packages—these are particularly significant for private colleges."

"The amazing thing," continued Harris, "is that so many of these schools are willing to lay on their oars and drift. In effect, they're just waiting to be sued. They'd rather keep their heads in the sand than retrofit their buildings or provide support services for kids with learning disabilities."

Henry told the truth. How could he lie to Jimmy Stewart? "I don't have tenure," he said, "and I'm not being considered for it. The idea is that I'd ultimately have a new job—teaching part time and developing disability services the rest of the time."

"But," said Harris, "that's only if your committee recommends that you develop a disability program. And then, of course, they have to actually hire you for an unpopular job that you are in the odd position of proposing. I don't like it."

Henry felt momentarily as if he were talking to an astrologer, or a psychic. In his passion, he hadn't considered the weakness of his situation. Or, more correctly, he hadn't allowed any reservations to enter his head. He was working with good people. Oh sure, the place seemed at times to be a harried hive of intensities—and there were ill-fitting proposals and insufficient funds—but he wasn't being set up. Not on this issue. Not with the Toby Emerich story still fresh in everyone's mind and his own diagnosis a matter of record.

Good teaching requires fanaticism. Poetry calls on its believers. Perhaps Henry couldn't see much beyond this. But he would take a chance. The college was inundated with what the Reagan crowd derisively called "political correctness"—gay studies, women's studies, global studies. There was a passion on campus for diversity. The timing was right for a modest nod toward the disability community.

He said none of this. Not everything required argument. Henry figured there were some advantages to middle age. He left the humanities building and entered the botanical gardens. It was a clear day, and there were hundreds of birds in the oak trees. It simply wouldn't happen. Not the way Harris said it would. Marilyn had everyone's attention. And Henry had marched for all the campus causes. He sat on a bench under a trellis woven with red carnations and put his fingers to his temples. He was now experiencing headaches on a daily basis. He sat alone in a bower and massaged his head.

Afterward, Henry saw that time, the ally of progress and hope, had turned feverish—as though something astrological had occurred. He knew of rabbinical scholars who, with just a little wine, would analyze a community's change of fortune and explain it for hours. The marriage of numerology and bad luck was always a fit topic for divinity scholars. But whatever Henry might say, time had turned on him.

The disability committee met only once. The faculty who participated turned out to be junior people—none of them were on tenure tracks. Marilyn De Quincy had spoken with feeling about the timing of the committee. "We have delayed doing something for far too long," she'd said, adding: "If we are to become a top-tier institution of higher learning, we must open our doors to people with disabilities."

She'd gotten them off to a rousing start, but the group lacked authority and everyone knew it. Jack Minton, the former Episcopal minister who served as the dean of men, said laconically, "Mankind can be divided into three principal groups: those who write, those who read, and those who go fox hunting. I'm afraid that with the new president coming in, we're just fox hunting. He's notorious for slashing budgets wherever he goes, and I'm not at all optimistic about what's ahead."

Minton resembled a vastly aged version of Oscar Wilde. He was half dandy, half vicar. The faculty despised him for his fussiness. Students despised him for his high-toned irony. "Surely, Joseph," he'd say to a cowed undergrad, "surely you meant only to plagiarize the plagiarist and not Thomas Carlyle."

"Budget cuts may well be in our future," said Marilyn, "but we're in a new era with disability. The new president will certainly be attentive."

They would be pushing from below. Henry saw that they were at the base of the pyramid.

It was agreed that Henry would write a report outlining the features of programs for disabled students at other colleges. The committee would review the report and endorse it. Finally, the statement would be sent to the college's new president.

All this came to pass. The final document was succinct: the college must assure that students with disabilities could participate in the life of the campus. The school should adopt both academic support services and a long-range architectural plan. Everyone signed.

The new president, a short Connecticut Yankee named Gibson Meese, was an enigma even to his senior staff. Trained as an educator with a doctorate in social psychology, he was by turns charming and phlegmatic. He arrived on campus in March and quickly fired his vice president for academic affairs, a scholarly and well-liked figure. Both traits were of course invaluable for directing faculty initiatives. No one understood what had happened. Then, within weeks, he fired old Jack Minton, who announced with dignity that he was retiring to write a book about the liberalizing influence of the church in South America. No one had known of his interest in this particular area.

Poisonous rumors were all over the place. The president was cutting the size of the faculty by 15 percent. The president had spent over $300,000 remodeling his campus residence. He was said to have screamed at a senior professor of political science behind closed doors: "If you don't like it, then I suggest you take early retirement!" In public, he was all charm. He announced that he would soon be taking the tenured faculty on a three-day retreat to a resort in the Blue Ridge Mountains of Tennessee. "Just so we can plan the future in a place of inspiration," he said. It was clear that the nontenured faculty and the part-time teachers wouldn't be included in the "vision thing," as Marilyn was now calling it.

Henry drove to Raleigh, where he bought a motorized scooter. He'd fallen three times in a single day while walking from class to class. His mother, who lived in New York, cashed some of her mutual funds to help him. A good scooter was almost as expensive as a motorcycle. He decided to stick a Harley-Davidson decal on the snub-nosed hood of the new machine. When he took it out on campus, students commended him for the Harley motif, and one of the student associations bought him a Harley hat. Soon, there was an article in the student newspaper praising the college's "easy rider" for his work to improve services for people with disabilities. In the interview with an enthusiastic journalism major, Henry had alluded to the disability committee and had mentioned that the report was on the new president's desk. He had worried when he'd said it. But then, he worried about everything. And then again, he remembered the words of George Santayana: "An artist is a dreamer consenting to dream of the actual world." *That's one reliable definition of idealism*, Henry thought. He decided that he wouldn't worry. He arranged to have his classes meet in the only building on campus that he could access with the scooter. He would be Dale Carnegie: clean, pragmatic, and idealistic in a public-minded and fraternal way. That's how to get things done.

By now, it was late spring. Nothing had been heard from the president's office about the disability committee's report. Henry wondered if he should call Marilyn and discuss the matter. If something were going to be done for disabled students, this was the time to acknowledge it since the administration was planning the budget for the next academic year. Rumors were seeping through the windowpanes that the president was cutting salaries across the board. At the same time, he'd just furnished his office with Thomas Moser cabinets and desks—the expensive American colonial furnishings one always saw advertised in the *New Yorker*. This was the furniture of Park Avenue attorneys. Marilyn had called the Moser cabinet company and had learned that a suite of offices would cost roughly $30,000. The sum was equivalent to the salary of a full-time faculty member. Some had taken to calling the new president "Doctor Nero."

Henry got the call from the president's secretary as he was preparing to go home. It was twilight and warm, and he'd been planning to sit on his porch with a glass of wine and watch the mulberry tree in his yard. It's funny how you remember these incidental things. He certainly hadn't been thinking of the president or the report on disability services. Mrs. Gleason, the president's secretary, asked if he could meet with Gibson Meese in about a half hour. "Sure," said Henry, "but we can't meet in his office because there's no elevator and I can't climb stairs very easily." "Hold on," said Mrs. Gleason. The line went silent for about two minutes. Then she was back. "The president can meet you on the first floor of the administration building because there's a wheelchair ramp by the back door of the student theater. He'll meet you in the theater. No one's using it now."

Henry rolled up the ramp behind the theater. He saw Gibson Meese holding open the steel fire door that served as the emergency exit and the wheelchair entrance to the building. When he got to the top of the ramp, Gibson said, "Hello, Easy Rider!" The familiarity put Henry at ease. He looked at Gibson Meese and joked, "I lost the rest of the motorcycle gang back by the dining hall." But Meese was already striding toward a row of green theater seats and gesturing that they should sit down. Henry climbed off the scooter and slid into a seat. Gibson grabbed a folding chair and sat down in front of him. It was odd, two men in a darkened theater and not a soul around. You could see blue twilight at the high windows on either side of the auditorium.

"As you know," Meese began, "we are at present experiencing financial constraints. The board of trustees has asked me to cut our operating budget by 15 percent across the board. I am working to assure that the quality of our programs and services remains high while complying with this directive."

The president stopped then and pulled a single gray hair from his left eyebrow. Henry remembered that Marilyn had told him of Meese's compulsive hair pulling. "He'll pull a hair from an eyebrow, or pluck one from an ear," she said, "and he'll keep on talking while twisting the hair between his fingers. It's repulsive!"

Gibson Meese looked at the hair as if Henry wasn't there and then continued. "I've been told by my colleagues in the administration that you are a person whose nontenure-track adjunct employment eligibility is about to run out."

He stopped again and tilted his head slightly as though listening to a far-off freight train. It was clear to Henry that this was a high-strung man. He was obviously insecure and peculiarly electric.

"As you know," he continued, "you've been hired here in a series of one-year appointments for a full seven years. We simply cannot employ you as an adjunct faculty member for another year. To do so would constitute giving you tenure. We cannot afford another tenure-track faculty appointment. Nor do we at present have the resources to develop a disabilities program, although your report on the matter is a persuasive document, and I hope that we will have the resources to address this in the future."

Then Meese inched his chair a little closer and stared at Henry as though he might be staring at an orphan. There was an unctuous look in his dark eyes. Henry remembered thinking how strange the look was. Later he told a friend, "I felt like Prokofiev sitting before Stalin." Meese said something about what might be done in recognition of Henry's service to the institution. What he said next was very strange indeed.

"I've decided to put you in charge of our summer programs. As you know, I'm looking for ways that we can attract outside groups to our campus in the summer months when we're not having classes. I would like you to direct sports camps for children. Can you negotiate grassy fields in your scooter?"

Henry listened as though he wasn't really sitting there. What Gibson Meese was saying was so foreign that he might as well be a Welsh poet or a sorcerer from Lapland.

"Of course," Meese continued, "this will be a full-time job for you, a year-round job. And of course we might be able to let you teach a religious studies course from time to time."

The theater was now completely dark. There was a row of small lights behind the proscenium of the stage. They cast a faint glow on the scene. He could see Gibson Meese toying with the hairs of his eyebrow.

Henry said, "Look, I'm not going to be able to pilot a motorized scooter across the campus soccer fields, and I'm probably not the best candidate for that kind of administrative role." He stopped for a second and cleared his throat. "I find it hard to believe that you can't find an administrative assignment for me that would entail working with disabled students."

Gibson Meese looked at him as if he were a novelty—a ballroom dancer from the Czech republic or a man in a suit of armor.

"Don't tell me what you can and can't do," he said suddenly with a fervor that seemed almost violent. "I had a roommate in college who was a disabled Olympic rower. If you're not competitive, then maybe you can't do the job."

Henry remembered the Stockholm Complex—the concept that people being tortured grow to love their torturers. He wondered who could love this man. He slid himself out of the theater seat and back onto the scooter. He moved as gracefully as he could, thinking consciously that he must not appear flustered. He looked at the president in the yellow, submarine-like light of the theater and said, "I can't believe that the only employment option for me at this college entails my driving about the soccer fields in my scooter and handing out towels to kids in a soccer camp."

"Believe what you want," said Meese. "But the offer is still on the table."

The faculty with whom Henry tried to share this story looked nervously at their watches. Barbara Ruggles, a feminist professor in the English department who had served on the committee that had hired the new president, told him that such a story "just couldn't be true." When Henry told the campus ombudsman, the faculty member responsible for handling employment problems, he simply said, "Well, you know, Henry, it's your word against his. It's just a pissing contest. And you as a nontenure-track faculty member have very little clout in the community."

He wondered about "clout," sensing that a hopeless "lifeboat mentality" had fallen over the faculty. One had to fight for a place in the lifeboat. You got in the boat according to your influence. And influence meant tenure. According to the college faculty handbook, no one hired in a series of yearly appointments could teach at the college beyond six years. A seventh year would constitute what was called de facto tenure. When he mentioned this to his department chair, a religious studies professor whose specialty was Buddhism, the man had said, "That's true as far as the printed word might go, but no one ever gets de facto tenure. And it looks to me as if they've offered you a job. So take it. You can teach a religion course once in a while."

About navigating the thick, grassy fields in a motorized scooter, no one had an opinion. It was as though he had ceased to exist. People looked past him—people who had formerly congratulated him heartily when the senior class had voted him Professor of the Year. Now, he was "dead meat," as the students would say. He was actually starting to get frightened.

At home, he opened a bottle and poured himself three fingers of Johnnie Walker Red. Then he called Marilyn. When he told her the story, she was silent for a time. He pushed the ice cubes in his glass with his index finger and waited for her to speak. Then she said, "You were right, we needed greater influence on the committee. I'm so sorry, Henry. I told Gibson Meese flat out that we should make you the director of services for students with disabilities. I really did."

He could hear starlings rooting about in the ivy outside his apartment. Sometimes it looked as if the birds were coming to raise the building aloft. He remembered how they used to call the jazz club where Charlie Parker performed Bird Land—he was living in bird land. He thought he might put some Charlie Parker on the stereo.

A week later, while he was grading his last exams of the academic year, Henry received a letter on college stationery signed by the treasurer, informing him that they could not retain his services. The letter indicated that he could apply for unemployment compensation if he should so choose, and it gave him a number to call.

He put Charlie Parker on the stereo. He remembered that Evelyn Waugh said of Dylan Thomas, "He's exactly what I would have been had I not been a Catholic." He listened to the urgent popping of Charlie Parker's horn. "He's exactly what I would have been," Henry thought, "if I hadn't been a green and believing man."

He lay on his sofa in the deep August heat and thought that surely tomorrow the mail would bring him something—some news of a place that would have him. The right side of his body felt like it was full of shorted wires. He remembered a cartoon from some place—maybe it was the *New Yorker*—that showed a desert landscape. Nothing but sand as far as the eye could see. There was a single cactus in the foreground and beneath it a discarded tire and a rusty can. The caption under the drawing said: "Life without Mozart."

Henry thought of Time, that unrevealed figure. It dominated the cartoon. He remembered Auden, who wrote: "If we should weep when clowns put on their show, / If we should stumble when musicians play, / Time will say nothing but I told you so."

He spoke to his cat then. "Without Mozart, there is no world at all."

REVEALING WORKPLACES

[7]

All three of these stories reveal how much their protagonists want to work. Most persons with disabilities have the same aspiration. Indeed, Title I of the Americans with Disabilities Act (ADA) was passed to protect persons with disabilities from employment discrimination. Democrats and Republicans alike supported its passage. As disability rights activist Marta Russell explains, "We got our civil 'rights' in exchange for getting disabled people off entitlements."[1] One of the best tests of the ADA's effectiveness is whether people with invisible disabilities rely on it. Nowak's and Atkins's stories explore this issue.

Many of Nowak's and Felix's employers and prospective employers remain unaware of their illnesses. As a result, they have many job opportunities. That they do not disclose their illnesses, however, means that Nowak and Felix both have decided against seeking the ADA's shelter. From experience, they each learned that, whenever possible, it is best to hide their disabilities. Nowak and Felix forgo workplace accommodations that might possibly reveal their illnesses, instead of assuming that the ADA would protect them from employment discrimination. Nowak's and Atkins's stories therefore underscore the limits of the ADA's employment provisions.

Meanwhile, Kuusisto's character Henry does not share the same fate as Nowak or Felix. With his multiple sclerosis (M.S.) exposed, a big change in the college's administration, and restrictive rules about adjunct college professors, he's thrown out of work. To be reinstated, he would have to seek redress under the ADA. But, what accounts for his termination? Is Henry's M.S. being used as an excuse to let him go since he would have to be hired on a tenure-track line, which the college supposedly cannot afford? Or, is Henry laid off because he has M.S.? Highlighting the complexity involved in interpreting the ADA's employment provisions, Kuusisto's story brings out questions about the essential and nonessential functions of a position and reasonable accommodations. Does it matter why Henry was laid off? Can an employer, like the college president described, shift Henry from one position to another, making him no longer qualified for the job?

[ ] NO IDLENESS

The idea that persons with disabilities should work has been a powerful theme in the United States since the nineteenth century.[2] In the United States, sheltered workshops were first established for the blind in the first half of the nineteenth century.[3] It was not until after World War II, however, that work became explicitly associated with rehabilitation and healing for everyone with disabilities. Hoping that these workshops would serve only as part of a transition, vocational rehabilitation trained people for employment with the hope that disabled people would become tax-payers, not "tax-eaters," as Mary Switzer, a long-time head of vocational rehabilitation, was fond of saying.[4] For those who could not find paying work, a job in a sheltered workshop represented a better option than being idle.

While this emphasis on work and productivity had great resonance during the twentieth century, another value of longer standing carried still greater weight. That was the belief that under capitalism, employers must remain unfettered. Chipping away at this belief in Europe, however, was the idea that capitalists must accept some collective responsibility for their workforce. In fact, a system of compensation for workers was put in place for those who were injured at work. As Henri-Jacques Stiker argues, it made business "liable for the accident" and obligated it "to compensate the injury."[5]

While some scholars have argued that vocational rehabilitation was an outgrowth of workers' compensation, which represents one of the earliest social programs in the United States, it should be noted that this latter policy was instituted to relieve a business of liability for its workforce.[6] Without a legislative scheme, members of the business community worried that they would suffer more at the hands of the judiciary.[7] The business community knew that the judiciary staunchly defended private property rights. Nevertheless, many employers feared that it would hold them liable for workplace injuries, particularly those that could have been prevented. Many employers therefore thought it best to make their losses routine by accepting a progressive program for workers' compensation.[8]

Workers' compensation operates like a no-fault insurance program. An employer pays premiums to an insurance company, which covers all of its employees. Neither the employer nor the employee is blamed for an accident. As the story goes, compensating employees for accidents became part of "the cost of doing business." A side effect of the program, however, is that conflicts between workers' compensation and vocational rehabilitation have stymied the latter program. Only 6 percent of all candidates for vocational rehabilitation have received workers' compensation.[9]

Most scholars recognize that American capitalism has been more virulent than its European counterpart.[10] Yet, both variants of liberalism—which led to the strong and the weak social welfare states—created a gap between the social and the economic causes and conditions that gave rise to the concept of disability. According to Stiker, the inherent naturalism of liberal thought consists of regarding all forms of impairment as accidents. It is no one's fault when someone "inadvertently falls from a ladder"; "these things happen" with no real means of prevention.[11]

Disassociating the injury from the workplace helps explain why both employers and coworkers regard persons with disabilities with suspicion when they ask for accommodations. The onus is on the individual. The idea that people should work to be productive balanced with the lack of control over workplace injuries places the adjustment burden on the disabled person. Naturally, only a small portion of all disabled working people were injured on the job. Nonetheless, this helps explain why a person who requests accommodations from an employer is met with great suspicion. Are they asking for too much? Coworkers also wonder if their employers are giving them too much. Nowak's and Atkins's protagonists learned this lesson early in their careers. Whenever possible, they conclude that it is better to protect their privacy than to receive reasonable accommodations.

[ ] QUALIFYING FOR LEGAL PROTECTION FROM DISCRIMINATION IN THE WORKPLACE

To what kind of accommodations, and thus legal protection, are Nowak, Felix, and Henry entitled? And how do they qualify for these protections? The employment provisions are the ADA's most litigated ones. Although the Supreme Court's most important case, *Sutton v. United Airlines*, involves the hiring process, the majority of those who bring suits already have a job.[12] They file for relief from discrimination after being fired when their employers discover that they have a disability; they request an accommodation for a disability; or they return to work after a debilitating injury or illness.

To successfully sue for discrimination in the workplace, people must satisfy four criteria. First, and most important, they must prove that they have a disability, which is to say that they have an impairment that limits a substantial life activity, like hearing, seeing, or walking. (Providing proof that you belong in a protected class is one of the primary points of distinction between civil rights for persons with disabilities and those for women and minorities.) Second, disabled people must be viewed as qualified to perform the so-called essential duties of a position either with or without an accommodation. Third, the accommodations that employees or potential employees request must be deemed "reasonable." Finally, accommodations cannot cause any employer undue hardship.

Given the four criteria, most ADA cases never get heard by a jury. Instead, a study by Ruth Colker, a law professor, shows that over 80 percent of the cases are dismissed by federal judges on summary judgment.[13] The primary reason judges give for dismissing these suits is that the person challenging an employer's discriminatory action has an impairment that is not *substantially* limiting, and therefore not a disability. To warrant protection under the ADA, someone must have a physical or mental impairment that rises to the level of being a disability. Raising the threshold for this definition further, the Supreme Court ruled in a trio of employment decisions that an impairment that can be mitigated by medicine or equipment, like insulin for a diabetic, a hearing aid for a person with hearing problems, or a prosthesis for a person without an arm, is not a disability.[14] (These rulings are in direct opposition to the guidelines issued by the EEOC, which the federal courts are not obliged to follow.) The second most common reason for case dismissal is that a federal judge decides that a person with a recognized disability is not qualified to perform her job. Few cases make it to the stage of determining whether an accommodation is reasonable or if it causes an employer undue hardship.

Essentially, the federal courts' rulings have put disabled people in a Catch-22 position. Either you are not impaired enough to have a disability or your impairment impedes you from doing the job. This interpretation of the ADA has caught both the disability rights activists in support of the ADA and the business lobbies in opposition by surprise.[15] During the legislative battle, they fought not over the definition of a disability, but rather over what the statute meant by a reasonable accommodation and what constituted undue hardship for an employer.

In 1999, the Supreme Court handed down three decisions that created this Catch-22 position for two pilots with vision problems, a truck driver with monocular vision, and a mechanic with high blood pressure. The lead case involved Karen Sutton and Kimberly Hinton, twin sisters who not only had the same career as regional airline pilots, but they shared a vision problem, a severe myopia that only 2 percent of people in the United States have. It was fully corrected by their glasses, but without their glasses, the twins' vision fell well below United Airlines' standard of 20/40, which is required of all pilots. Applying this rule to the twins, United Airlines claimed that while these women could fly regional airline routes, they could not be hired to fly global ones.

The *Sutton* decision, as explained earlier, helped to define what constituted a disability. Writing for the seven-person majority, Justice Sandra Day O'Connor argued that the glasses mitigated the twins' seeing problems, hence they could not be considered "legally" disabled. Relying on the same logic about mitigating equipment and medicine, O'Connor wrote in *Vaughn L. Murphy v. United Parcel Service* that Murphy, a mechanic with very high blood pressure, could not be considered legally disabled.[16] While the sisters put on glasses that "mitigated" their vision problem, Murphy took medication that "mitigated" his disease. None of these plaintiffs were therefore legally disabled and could therefore not protest any discriminatory treatment under the ADA's Title I.

Falling outside of the statute's coverage, moreover, O'Connor wrote in *Sutton*, meant that the twins could be dismissed for being people who have physical or mental impairments that an employer preferred not to have in the workplace. O'Connor concluded that an impairment was like "one's height, build, or singing voice." These are legitimate distinctions. Employers, she maintained, can hire employees on the basis of them. As long as this impairment does not "rise to the level" of a disability, an employer can exhibit her preference for able-bodied employees.[17]

On one hand, O'Connor ruled that the twins' eye problems could not be considered a disability because if all people with mitigating equipment like eyeglasses were taken into account, the definition would be too inclusive. On the other hand, she insisted that each employee must be given an individualized assessment. A "diagnosis" was not enough.[18]

In *Sutton*, O'Connor also laid out the Court's interpretation of what it meant to be "regarded as" having a disability. She maintained that United Airlines had not "regarded" the twins as disabled because this definition can be taken into account only if an employer "mistakenly believes" that an employee is limited. To O'Connor, an employer must base this mistake on a "myth."[19] That is, the employer relies on some stereotype or stigma that has no truth to it. Since United Airlines never claimed that all people with correctable vision problems could not fly, O'Connor held that this employer had made no such mistake.

Finally, O'Connor examined the issue of what it meant to have a physical impairment that substantially affected the "major life activity" of working. The lower federal courts had been divided about this issue. While O'Connor did not suggest that working could not be counted as a major life activity, her ruling made it difficult to claim that this activity had been limited. Following the EEOC guidelines here, O'Connor decided that someone's impairment must apply to a whole array of positions, not just to one particular position. Since Sutton and Hinton could work as regional pilots, but not global ones, this meant that their vision problem had not hindered their ability to work. After all, they could still fly.

[ ] DEFINING DISABILITY: AN INCENTIVE TO HIDE

Would the Supreme Court consider that Nowak, Felix (Atkins's character), and Henry (Kuusisto's character) have illnesses that rise to the level of a disability? The Supreme Court's decision in *Bragdon v. Abbott*, discussed in the previous commentary, makes it likely that Nowak would be viewed as legally disabled.[20] While his disease may be asymptomatic, the fact that Nowak's virus is contagious makes it substantially limiting. Asymptomatic HIV limited Abbott's capacity for reproduction, according to Justice Anthony Kennedy, because attempting procreation endangered her partner. A child born would also have a significant chance of having the HIV infection. Kennedy therefore concluded that reproduction was a major life activity that the HIV infection impeded substantially.[21]

By contrast, Felix's illness might not be considered a disability. Unlike Nowak, Felix's neurological disorder is not contagious. The medication that Felix takes mitigates his condition, though he still experiences plateaus and valleys. At times, he can walk, yet at other times, he must use a wheelchair. A lawyer might advise Felix to claim statutory protection when he is back in his chair since there would be little argument that he is substantially limited in the major life activity of walking. From what Atkins describes, Felix would find this frustrating. The idea that the ADA works best when he cannot hide his disability is perverse; it hinders his ability to maintain his health. In a world without prejudice, or where the law has been more effective, would Felix be more likely to request accommodations despite the invisibility of his disability?

There is little doubt that Kuusisto's character Henry would be considered legally disabled under the ADA. For Henry, the fact that the medication neither cures nor stops the course of his disease would place him in this category. Yet, the degenerative nature of M.S. presents Henry with a different set of problems. As Henry describes, "time has turned on him." With the college administration well aware of this fact, Henry might have to show that he remains qualified to teach and advise students despite the deterioration of his health. At trial, Henry might need medical experts, for instance, to testify that he has gone into remission.

[ ] ESSENTIAL DUTIES

While Nowak's and Atkins's stories involve the issue of disclosure, Kuusisto's story goes into detail about what can happen once disabled people disclose that they have severe illnesses. In the opening, Kuusisto indicates that the college already knows about Henry's M.S. In fact, the administration uses this to put him in the awkward position of fighting for reasonable accommodations for others. As the lawyer he consults explains, they would "have to actually hire you for an unpopular job that you are in the odd position of proposing. I don't like it."

Kuusisto's story addresses three other legal issues: job qualifications, defining the essential functions of a position, and reasonable accommodations. Now that Henry's health has changed as the M.S. has progressed, can the college president transfer him to a position that he cannot handle and then fire him? What the president has done in disability law is to move him to a position where he cannot perform the essential functions of the job—which in this case would be getting around the lawn on a motorized scooter—and then using this as grounds for his termination.

Part of Henry's predicament of being placed in a job he cannot perform has been explored in a unanimous Supreme Court opinion, *Toyota v. Williams*.[22] In the case at bar, the Court explored what it meant to be disabled in the workplace. In this story, Kuusisto demonstrates that Henry clearly was not qualified for the new position the president gave him.

Henry's situation is similar to Ella Williams's, not in the facts of the case (which involve defining disability) but in the logic underlying the Court's opinion.

For two years, Toyota had honored the limitations that Williams's physician had imposed on the company so that she would not re-injure herself. Williams had sustained a myriad of repetitive motion injuries on the job. She then took medical leave, filed, and settled a workers' compensation case with Toyota. After filing an ADA case, Toyota put Williams on the Quality Control Inspections Operations Team. Still on the assembly line, this team performed much lighter manual labor. Williams, moreover, only performed two of the four tasks assigned to the team. First, Williams visually examined the cars' paint jobs, opening and shutting their doors, hoods, and trunks as they passed through the assembly line. Then, inspecting the car a second time, Williams wiped down each car with a glove. When Toyota's managers decided that members of the inspection team must perform all four tasks, Williams's injury flared up again. Wiping down the cars with a thick type of oil pushed Williams over the edge, triggering her re-injury. Both Williams's and Henry's situations are similar in that their employers knew that they could not perform the essential tasks of the new jobs. What differs is that Williams was a member of a team that had had the rules changed. The additional duties assigned to her, moreover, were similar to her old duties. Williams could wipe down a car with a glove, but when she had to pour a sticky type of oil over the car, this re-inflamed her tendonitis and carpal tunnel syndrome. On what could be described as a diet of motion, it was this last motion that led to Williams's re-injury. The Court ruled that the fact that Williams could not perform this last task was not tantamount to proving that she had a physical impairment that could be considered a disability. She was not given shelter under the ADA.

By contrast, Henry's M.S. would be considered a disability by the federal courts. Unlike Williams, Henry might take medication that could mitigate his disease, but the medication could not mitigate it totally because M.S. is degenerative. Also, Henry's situation differs from Williams's since he was singled out by his employer. Not only was he alone, but Henry's reassignment was unrelated to the work he had done previously for the college. Henry had never managed any sports teams. The president purposefully transferred him to a position that required essential duties that Henry could not complete.

One of the key elements of determining if someone is qualified is to assess the essential functions of a position. Since these involve his mind more than his body, Henry can handle his present position of teaching and advising students. Although the accessibility provisions of the ADA in Titles II and III would require that the college install ramps for people who have impairments that affect their walking, an individualized assessment of Henry's condition under Title I in relation to the position of teaching and advising would conclude that his position has little to do with his ability to walk.

Henry's reassignment would involve a different set of obstacles, however, if he had requested it himself. The federal courts have been divided about whether reassignment constitutes a reasonable accommodation. In *Barnett v. U.S. Airways*, Robert Barnett, a cargo handler who sustained a serious back injury on the job, had been granted a reassignment to work in a mailroom. The Ninth Circuit Court of Appeals held that such a reassignment could be considered a reasonable accommodation as Barnett could no longer carry on at his old position. The ADA, the majority opinion noted, stated that the reassignment could involve a position that the employee either "holds or desires." The Ninth Circuit Court came to this decision after analyzing the text of the law. What would the word "desire" mean, the majority asked, if it did not include reassignment? To read the statute otherwise would make "desire meaningless."[23] As long as a reassignment does not mean that a disabled person receives an unwarranted promotion nor that a job was created specifically for her, an employer must retain this employee. This said, it is up to the employee to decide whether to accept the new job since the move could involve a demotion in terms of pay or status. An employee, for instance, might decide to work only on a part-time basis.

The Ninth Circuit Court of Appeals, which is the most liberal circuit, also examined what is entailed in the interactive process for gaining a reasonable accommodation. This process, which is essentially one of negotiation, is triggered when an employee requests a reasonable accommodation. According to the Senate report, the employer and the employee are to sit down and adopt "a problem-solving approach" to provide reasonable accommodations.[24] Examining the legislative history and the EEOC guidelines, the majority outlined the four steps to the interactive process. First, the employer and the employee are to analyze a "particular job involved and determine its purpose and its essential functions."[25] Second, the employer consults with "the individual with a disability to ascertain the precise job-related limitations imposed by the individual disability and how those limitations could be overcome with a reasonable accommodation."[26] Third, reasonable accommodations are identified. Finally, the employee's preferences should be taken into account.[27] Nothing in this process allows the employee or the employer to unilaterally determine work conditions. The operative word, in other words, is "interactive."[28] The Ninth Circuit majority ruled that Barnett had been given his reassignment to the mailroom as a result of an interactive process in which he engaged with his employers.

The federal courts have ruled that it is up to the employer, not just the employee, to anticipate the employee's needs. While the employer can act only on the basis of information, a company must help accommodate an employee. Federal court judges assume that employers are much more knowledgeable about what kind of accommodations could be made.[29] "Putting the entire burden on the employee to identify a reasonable accommodation," the Ninth Circuit Court ruled, "risks shutting out many workers simply because they do not have the superior knowledge of the worker that the employer has."[30]

In 2002, the Supreme Court overturned the Ninth Circuit Court of Appeals' ruling about Barnett's reassignment, making it difficult for the disabled to pursue one of the primary ways someone could be accommodated—reassignment. (This type of accommodation, moreover, would have been particularly useful to workers who are injured on the job, like Barnett and Williams.) The 5–4 Court majority, however, did not address any of the issues that the Ninth Circuit raised about the interactive process.[31] It stopped short of addressing these issues by ruling in favor of U.S. Airways that an employee cannot be reassigned to a position that violates a seniority system, even if this system was not the result of a collective bargaining agreement. The Court held that while a seniority system does not always "trump" accommodation requests, it will prevail "in the run of cases."[32] Except in "special" circumstances, the Court held, the

ADA gives a worker with a disability no chance of obtaining an accommodation that would violate a seniority system. The Court switched the burden to the plaintiff, who must now go looking for the special circumstances that would make violating a seniority system reasonable. This would jeopardize the "more uniform, impersonal operation of seniority rules."[33]

The majority, however, made no distinction between a seniority system that has been created by the company and one that is a product of a collective bargaining agreement. No one disputes that the seniority system was unilaterally imposed by management. The difference between these two types of systems, Justice Souter explained in a dissenting opinion, is significant since in its personnel handbook, U.S. Airways carefully pointed out that its seniority system should not be misconstrued. It is not a contract. Management can modify any work condition for any employee at will. "With U.S. Airways itself insisting that its seniority system was noncontractual and modifiable at will, there is no reason to think that Barnett's accommodation would have resulted in anything more than minimal disruption to U.S. Airways' operation, at that."[34]

Nonetheless, the *Barnett* Court majority ruled that an employee with a disability cannot request that a work condition be changed if it violates the conditions of the seniority system. U.S. Airways, the Court decided, should make no exception by accommodating Barnett, who wanted to hold onto his position in the mailroom, where he had already been working for two years. It was only when two workers with more seniority put bids in for Barnett's mailroom position that he was bumped. And being bumped back to his cargo position, a position he could not handle given his back problem, meant that Barnett was terminated by U.S. Airways.

In Kuusisto's story, Henry does not ask for reasonable accommodations. Rather, he wants to keep his old job. It is the president who asks him to accept a position that he neither "holds" nor "desires." While in Henry's case the president's request clearly is a ruse, the same situation occurs after a business or corporation has injured someone and then refuses to transfer an employee to a position that she could handle or to modify her job, as was the case with Ella Williams and Robert Barnett. While some companies have reassigned their workers to jobs that they could perform after being injured or getting ill, others have not.

What is more, the Court's ruling about reassignment did not involve a collective bargaining agreement. The Court ruled that any seniority system, whether it is part of a binding collective bargaining agreement or a nonbinding personnel handbook, will be honored. Hence, if a business prefers not to accommodate workers who have become ill and not fully recovered to the point that they could return to their old positions or who have been injured on the job, one unintended consequence of the ruling could be that some businesses might well adopt a seniority system.

Reassignment represents only one type of accommodation, however. The Supreme Court has yet to issue a ruling about other types of accommodation. As it stands in the lower federal courts, for those people who are recognized as disabled, the accommodations have been extensive. Most important, the idea that an accommodation must not cause a company undue hardship, as the federal courts have interpreted it, means that the accommodation to be rejected must put a business or a company in absolute financial peril. The interactive process, therefore, has retained its potential to provide those who qualify for protection under the ADA with comprehensive reasonable accommodations.[35]

[ ] SICK LEAVE AND REASONABLE ACCOMMODATIONS

The situations that Nowak and Felix face help us to examine another form of reasonable accommodation: sick leave. In addition to the question of whether Nowak and Felix each have a disability and thus whether the ADA covers them, these two stories illustrate how they become aware of all of the ramifications associated with telling an employer about a serious illness. As his story unfolds, Nowak explains that he decides whether to reveal the status of his physical condition only after assessing each situation. If a reasonable accommodation is essential, as it was shortly after he was diagnosed and needed to take sick leave for treatment, Nowak will inform his employer. "Revealing my status," he writes, "leaves me more vulnerable than I like to be."

Nowak's story describes how he learns harsh lessons about disclosure. As a result, he only "tell[s] when it suits me, and when it gives me power." What Nowak's story illustrates is that while disclosure might put off creditors, it gives him little power in the workplace. Nowak learns that every time "I announce my medical status, the person that receives my announcement hears something else. I state that I'm HIV-positive, and the person hears I'm dying." This leads to little hope for Nowak's job advancement. Nowak also realizes that the immediate reaction he receives after disclosing he is HIV-positive or has AIDS shows that "there is a fine line between judgment and concern." Nowak never knows where his employer stands. When one employer offers medical advice, he wonders, is she judging him? Or, is she genuinely concerned about his well-being?

If Nowak does needs sick leave, however, he has no choice but to tell his employer that he is HIV-positive. There are several different routes that Nowak could take when he asks for sick leave. First, he could use the sick leave plan that his employer offers. A health plan must provide all employees with the same benefits.[36]

Second, if Nowak's health benefits do not give him enough leave for treatment, he could request up to twelve weeks of unpaid leave under the Family Leave and Medical Act (FLMA) once he has worked the requisite number of hours to qualify for protection under this statute and if his employer has more than fifty employees, which places the company under its jurisdiction.[37] As a result, Nowak's employer would learn of his condition when he submits the medical documents necessary for a leave under the FLMA. Also, Nowak's employer could ask for a second opinion by a physician whom the company would compensate.[38] Once his employer had knowledge of his HIV-positive status, moreover, she could request that Nowak receive medical certification about his "fitness for duty," or his ability to return to work.[39]

Third, Nowak could ask for an extension of sick leave beyond the company's policy or beyond the unpaid policy provided by the FLMA as a reasonable accommodation.[40] For sick leave to be a reasonable accommodation, however, an employer could ask if Nowak expects to return to work.[41] What is more, if Nowak chose to take a few hours or days off here and there, which also surpassed the amount of time allowed by his employer's sick leave policy or violated workplace rules, a different set of issues about reasonable accommodations would be raised.[42] Then, the question is whether regular attendance at the workplace is an essential function of the job. If it is, erratic attendance could provide an employer with grounds for termination. Atkins's character Felix tells a similar story. He also fears disclosure and makes sure that all of the equipment associated with his disease is hidden so that his colleagues will not know that he was once in, and could return to using, a wheelchair.

[ ] THE NEW MEDICAL MODEL OF DISABILITY

Chronic illnesses like the ones that Nowak, Atkins, and Kuusisto describe have been recognized by medical sociologists as different from permanent physical impairments. Indeed, there is a whole body of literature that attempts to strike a balance between the social or societal model of disability and the medical one. On one hand, the social model purports that societal bias, stigma, and prejudice, not the physical or mental impairment, is what debilitates disabled people. Train stations without elevators or ramps, for instance, reflect the able-bodied majority's bias, whether it is intentional or not, toward stairs.

On the other hand, the medical model emphasizes how the person is limited by his physical or mental impairment and largely ignores the obstacles, like stairs, that society places in front of this person. By contrast, the new literature on medical sociology tries to create a happy medium between these two models by "bring[ing] the body back in[to]" the discussion about disability rights and discrimination.[43] Simon Williams, for instance, strikes this balance by adopting what he calls "critical realism." He addresses the body of the person with a chronic illness, and how it affects her outlook, yet he also "critically" analyzes how society views this illness and the person living with it. Williams argues that activists cannot lose sight that "our identities are lodged in our bodies."[44] Similarly, medical sociologist William Bury adopts a "relational" view of disability, which focuses on the interactions between individuals and their social locations.[45] For both of these scholars, societal attitudes cannot account for all of the problems associated with chronic illness.

Echoing just that sentiment, the stories by Nowak, Atkins, and Kuusisto show that their characters cannot simply will away their illnesses. Henry plays with the idea, jokingly referring to Dale Carnegie's power of positive thinking. Yet, when Gibson Meese, the college president, suggests that his poor attitude, not M.S., explains why he does not want to become a sports coach, Henry recoils. Likening Meese to a kidnapper, Henry knows that he would never suffer from the Stockholm Syndrome. He finds Meese's perspective about the will and the attitude of disabled people to be degrading.

Kuusisto's story, along with Nowak's and Atkins's, highlights the balance between the mind and the body. Every day Nowak, Felix, and Henry wake up with the realization that they have severe chronic illnesses. They cannot adjust their disabilities to their daily routines. Rather, their daily routines will be adjusted in accordance with the demands of their illnesses. All three of them may have to take sick leave, for instance. This will not just alter how others perceive them, but in making the decision to stay home or to seek more treatment, they are recognizing that their bodies are too weak or ill to work, and this affects their lives.

[ ] THE PROBLEMS WITH DISCLOSURE

Although, shortly after his diagnosis, Nowak told the Creative Arts Team, Nowak's story shows that he became increasingly reluctant to disclose information about his health condition.[46] When Felix's references informed prospective employers about his illness, he never received any job interviews. After he hid his illness, he was finally called for interviews. Should employees or prospective employees disclose their illnesses?

Felix and Nowak avoid disclosure. Atkins's story, moreover, exposes one irony about the hiring process. It was the people writing the reference letters—his mentors—not prying prospective employers, who tipped off the colleges about Felix's illness, inadvertently warning them against hiring him. When Felix faces his advisors and explains why this information should be kept private, they show little understanding. Atkins's explanation of the advisor's response reveals the limits of the ADA's influence on the hiring process—that employers would not hire Felix despite his illness. Atkins has Felix's advisors echo an age-old theme in disability studies about personal tragedy and triumph. One advisor, for instance, applauds Felix for doing remarkably well given his "circumstances," using the Tiny Tim stereotype to portray him.

While the ADA might not protect prospective employees from being battered by harmful stereotypes, this law and other laws, like the FLMA, have created a set of rules about medical inquiries and examinations for three specific stages of the hiring and employment process.[47] First, during the application process, which is called the pre-offer stage, an employer cannot conduct a medical examination nor make any inquiries about someone's health unless every applicant is required to pass a physical, for instance, to become a police officer.[48] The "don't ask" rule was included in these statutes to ensure that an employer was not discouraged from hiring because of a health condition that has no bearing on the applicant's job performance. Nowak would be covered under the "don't ask" rule if his employer suspected something from his appearance or as a result of an answer to a query.

Second, once the individual has been offered a position, which is referred to as the entering-employees or the post-offer stage, a different set of rules applies.[49] At this stage, some employers may make an offer of employment conditional on the results of a medical examination. This requirement can be made provided that all prospective employees are compelled to take the same medical examination or to submit to the same inquiries about their health. For example, a fire fighter must pass a physical examination as a condition of employment. Once the examination is taken, the information gathered from the physical is treated as a confidential medical record.

What employers can do with this information raises another set of issues. On the one hand, while an entering employee might pass the examination in terms of what the job calls for, it could produce information about a serious health concern, causing the employer to rescind the job offer.[50] If this happened, the employee would have legal protection. On the other hand, if the employer retained the employee, which would have been the case with Nowak and Jaime, supervisors and managers are given information on a "need to know" basis. A supervisor would be informed of Nowak's condition if, for example, he were on a job that had a safety requirement and might need to provide first aid.[51]

Third, employers cannot ask their employees to take a medical examination nor can they inquire about their health without cause. It is at this stage that the ADA and the FLMA give employees the most protection from discrimination.[52] Unlike the post-offer stage, a request for an examination must be "job-related and consistent with business necessity."[53] Offering guidelines, the Equal Employment Opportunity Commission has ruled that medical examinations can be given, which are referred to as fitness-for-duty examinations, if, for example, a serious injury or illness affects the employee's job performance.[54] If a police officer were injured on the job, for instance, she would be required to have a physical examination before returning to work.

Despite these different types of antidiscrimination protection, Nowak's and Atkins's stories reveal the difficulties associated with making decisions about whether to hide the information about their health. As a legal equation, they do not think that statutory protection compensates for the possibility of prejudice by an employer who could not hire, fire, or simply not renew a contract of employment after discovering an employee has an illness, particularly one that is terminal and contagious. Nowak, for instance, explains that he or someone like Jaime might not even know an employer's motivation for the discrimination. It could result from an employer's concern about health insurance premiums. Misinformed ideas about safety issues might also contribute to an employer's decision to fire or lay off an employee. Like all forms of employment discrimination, the reason for termination may not be associated with the employee's illness but with a "witch hunt," as Nowak describes.

Choosing not to release the information, Nowak reveals as he counsels Jaime, is not without cost. Most important, no reasonable accommodations requests can be made. Atkins also arrives at the same realization. Employers have no obligation to provide reasonable accommodations for conditions of which they have no knowledge. Once an employee has revealed his condition, however, one lower federal court has ruled that there is an assumption that the employer has more information about what type of accommodations can be made.[55]

Not asking for accommodations until they become imperative puts Nowak, Atkins's character Felix, and others like them who have invisible impairments in the position of possibly exacerbating their conditions. While Nowak is not explicit, he tells Jaime that he should inform his employers about his condition because of the health problems related to his HIV status. Explaining this, Nowak realizes how vulnerable Jaime is since he faced a similar situation with Olga, the head of human resources. She would have discovered his health condition if she had insisted that he turn in a copy of his short-term disability insurance or explain why he could not obtain it. This insurance policy, however, was not a condition of employment, and Olga decided not to probe any further.

[ ] MISGUIDED PATERNALISM?

While Nowak came to the brink of being discovered with his short-term disability insurance form, the fact that he had HIV would have been revealed had his employer mandated that all employees take a physical. Atkins's character Felix would have been in the same position. Neither the nonprofit work that Nowak performed nor the university teaching that Felix sought required a fitness-for-duty physical. As explained above, an employer cannot demand a physical without cause. Had they taken work that demanded more of their bodies, like being a police officer or an oil refinery worker, they might well have been required to take a physical as part of the job.

In *Chevron v. Echazabal,* a unanimous Supreme Court ruled in 2002 that Mario Echazabal did not have the same opportunity as Nowak and Felix to decide his own fate in the workplace.[56] Performing a fitness-for-duty physical, the physician discovered that Echazabal had hepatitis C. Working in an oil refinery, the doctor concluded, put Echazabal at risk since he worked with toxins that would enlarge his already large liver. As a result, Chevron concluded that Echazabal could not work at the oil refinery. "Moral concerns aside," explained Justice David Souter in the opinion, Chevron "wished to avoid time lost to sickness, excessive turnover from medical retirement or death, litigation under state tort law, and the risk of violating the national Occupational Safety and Health Act of 1970."[57]

The unanimous Court upheld Chevron's decision by adopting the expansive ruling made by the EEOC about endangering the health of a person with a disability. The EEOC had converted the "threat to others" doctrine, which stipulated that an employee with a physical or mental impairment could not endanger the health of others, into a "direct threat" doctrine. Echazabal could not work at Chevron, in other words, since his job endangered his health.

This said, Souter realized that the ADA had been drafted to protect disabled people from misguided paternalism. Defining what this means, he suggested that the ADA should protect disabled people from facing "sham protection."[58] To him, Congress intended to protect persons with disabilities from "refusals to give an even break to classes of disabled people, while claiming to act for their own good in reliance on untested and pretextual stereotypes."[59] Souter did not dispute Echazabal's claim that there had been "no known instance of OSHA enforcement or even threatened enforcement, against an employer who relied on the ADA to hire a worker willing to accept a risk to himself from his disability on the job." Nonetheless, he dismissed it as a red herring, claiming that there is "another side to this." For Souter, "the employer would be asking for trouble: his decision to hire would put Congress's policy in the ADA ... at loggerheads with the competing policy of OSHA."[60] While the courts generally "resolve the tension" when there is this type of "intersection of competing objectives," Souter decided that the EEOC's resolution, which transformed the "direct threat doctrine" into a "threat against one self," had already resolved it.[61]

Perhaps Souter offered this extensive explanation of the EEOC since he realized the irony of the Court's acceptance of its guidelines. In *Sutton*, the Court had categorically spurned this administrative agency's advisory guidelines about what constituted a disability. Now that the EEOC's guidelines gave employers, not this employee, discretion, the Court recognized this administrative agency's authority.

For Nowak and Felix, the *Chevron v. Echazabal* decision might have given them more pause about disclosing their illnesses. If their respective employers brought in medical experts to testify that the stress associated with their high-level positions, for instance, exacerbated their illnesses, could Nowak and Felix be terminated? The Court decision leaves Nowak and Felix with the same dilemma that Echazabal described. Was Echazabal fired for his health? Or was he let go to bolster the health of a company interested in maintaining the lowest insurance premiums possible? Upon taking every new job, and when he advises Jaime, Nowak carefully mulls over these questions.

[ ] A DISJUNCTURE

That the United States has a very strong work ethic is a truism. Americans work longer hours than people in other industrialized societies, surpassing even the Japanese.[62] Disabled people are no different, with over two-thirds wanting to work.[63] So, why are more persons with disabilities not put to work? Disabled people either cannot find work, or when they do work, employers balk at providing reasonable accommodations, which forces them to leave their jobs.[64]

Does part of the answer lie in the fact that employment is private? While the work ethic in the United States is strong, do the Supreme Court decisions under Title I suggest that the belief that employers should have the "right to manage" their workforce is stronger? If so, why do the federal courts believe that employers should retain this right? Should employers, moreover, have the discretion not to hire someone like Echazabal, who knows full well how working will hurt his health? Or should Echazabal be given the autonomy to make this determination himself?

If employers do retain the discretion to hire and fire people given their physical and mental impairments, will this encourage people with invisible physical or mental impairments, like Nowak and Atkins's character Felix, to continue hiding the fact that they have disabilities? How many employees will fear falling into the Catch-22 that makes them not disabled enough to receive statutory protection, but too disabled to perform the essential functions of a position? Will it benefit employers to have their employees keep their disabilities a secret since working might exacerbate their illnesses or conditions?

Finally, should employers who compensate employees for injuries they sustained on the job, such as Williams and Barnett, be compelled to accommodate them? Why does the Supreme Court recognize the intersection between OSHA and the ADA in Echazabal's case, but not the intersection between workers' compensation and the ADA in the suits involving Williams and Barnett? Does the no-fault insurance principle underlying workers' compensation programs work with the notion that persons with disabilities should have the right to work? Or does workers' compensation conflict with the ADA's employment provisions?

LOCAL AND STATE

GOVERNMENTAL SERVICES

(TITLE II)

[8] by Leonard Kriegel

"Speak of me as I am, nothing extenuate," pleads Othello. Moments before he takes his own life, Othello addresses the Venetian ambassadors, hoping to make them privy to his agony. Othello does not seek to excuse the murder of Desdemona. He asks only that, when they speak of the horror they have witnessed, the ambassadors speak also of the rage that led him to kill the woman he passionately loved. That a murderer on the verge of taking his life believes so self-serving a request to be justified is as good an illustration of the Yiddish term *chutzpah* as I know. Yet it is also the sort of behavior that must strike those of us who were born and bred in New York City as neither surprising nor atypical. Acting as if he himself were to the outer boroughs born, Othello seeks what all true New Yorkers seek—not understanding but vindication. He has no interest in justifying the murder of his wife (he believes that the act has guaranteed his eternal damnation) but wants those who will judge him to recognize just what it was that led him to kill that which he most loved in the world.

Whenever I reread that greatest of all death scenes, I am struck by how natural a New Yorker Othello is. We New Yorkers take confession seriously, and had Shakespeare been one of ours, he very well might have made his Moor a product of this city's outer-borough culture. Envision an Othello who has grown up in Queens or in the kind of Bronx neighborhood I grew up in. Like most natives of New York, this outer-borough hero would accept the idea that one must pay the price of desire. And that price, Othello would understand, doesn't change because one chooses to confess one's sins. Our outer-borough spiritual cousin to Shakespeare's Moor (nowhere is that kinship more apparent than in Othello's need to explain himself to the Venetian ambassadors) possesses the New Yorker's peculiar blend of *chutzpah* and self-doubt. It is what stamps him as one of us, a true New Yorker. Those who come of age in this city know that New York is not only the natural center of their imaginations but that the attitudes formed in the street have formed their attitudes toward the world. New York is more than bricks and mortar to those who grow up here; it is a subaltern parent.

Yet even lovers of this city may forget how it exerts its presence most powerfully not in what can be viewed in its streets but in the images that the street imposes upon imagination. Few are more aware of the power of those images than the men and women forced to live in this city with the aftereffects of a serious physical disability. To a man crippled by polio as a child, a man like me, New York is more than its parks and museums and public spaces—not so much city as conduit of love and source of rage. The barriers it chooses to place before me are the barriers it chooses to place before all cripples trying to live as normal a life as the streets will allow. And those barriers feed an anger that is perhaps the most powerful consequence of living as a cripple in a city that cannot allow its cripples to forget how different they are.

What involves the world with New York has always had more to do with the city's image than with its actual physical landscape. It is the city in my mind, more than the physical city I push myself through, at which I am enraged. Even more than the scared streets I push through in my wheelchair, that city lurks in my imagination like a steel and concrete vampire. And that city is the place I am forever trying to come to terms with, as I probe its strengths and weaknesses like an adolescent compulsively returning to the scene of his defeat because he cannot return to the scene of his triumph. I struggle with what New York tells me about myself as much as I do with its crumbling sidewalks and the Coney Island pitch of its broken streets and collapsing avenues. To live as a cripple in New York is to confront a physical world that is one's intimate enemy. However much I love New York, it is my adversary—and I wrestle with it because it insists that I must exist only on its sufferance. Whenever I insist upon my right to live here despite my physical limitations, it insists upon imposing its presence on my body. My response is to try to force my will upon the city. That I choose to live in a place that is indistinguishable from the air I breathe, that I cannot see myself as willingly living elsewhere, doesn't change the role of the city in my life. I hate it. Yet I cherish it as an intimate enemy far more, I suspect, than I could possibly cherish it as a friend—and because it is my enemy, I know not only that I do not trust it today but that I will not trust it in the future.

The structures by which great cities are known—an Eiffel Tower or Empire State Building—focus attention on their representative images. Yet beyond those structures lies the reality of how one lives in that particular city. I doubt that I could ever feel the love, hate, scorn, or anguish New York inspires in me had I not been born and raised here. Even the terrorist attacks of September 11, 2001, reinforced my sense that this city is functionally different from any other city. All New Yorkers struggled with those collapsing towers and fleeing citizens. But as a cripple, I was struck by how little the World Trade Center had to do with images of the city and how much it had to do with actual life here. Those towers were, admittedly, symbols of high finance and global capitalism, but they didn't define the New York I know and love. Forced upon the city's famed skyline, they weren't my image of New York. The towers never embraced for me the inner landscape that lovers of this city carry within themselves. I thought of them, if I thought of them at all, not as "arrogant," as one writer described them after September 11. For me, they marked the boundaries of city quiescence. In spite of all that has been written of the WTC since its destruction, the towers never managed to capture the city's singularity for me—until, at least, they came crashing down to earth. The WTC could never shake free of the hype that seized it the moment it was thrust before the public as a conception. On the other hand, even before it opened in 1931, the Empire State Building embodied the city's soul.

But I loved the World Trade Center, despite those boring towers and despite the hype. I didn't realize how much I loved it until it lay in ruins. I loved its walkways and plazas, loved the sweep of the staircase in the Winter Garden, which invariably brought to my mind, however strange it may sound, the curving sea of steps of the great gothic cathedral in Wells. Most of all, I loved it because my New York is a wheelchair city. And the aspect of walkways and plaza and atrium I loved most was how they offered me access, how open they were, how they led me into the city. Their accessibility was the gist of the identity that made the WTC so important a part of the city. Like most New Yorkers, after September 11, I read everything I could about the city's loss. Yet nothing I read addressed what the WTC had meant to those men and women forced to live in the shadowy confines of the cripple's city. Bland as they were, the towers invited us inside, while the walkways confirmed our sense that we, too, were natural to the chaos of New York. The Winter Garden, for instance, urged my wheelchair across its marble floors unencumbered by the threat of broken sidewalks I usually struggle with as I push myself through the city. I have few illusions about those towers or atrium or walkways. To remind myself of what the WTC lacked in the way of poetry, I need only compare the twin towers to the Empire State Building in the 1933 version of the movie *King Kong*. No one would suggest, even jokingly, that the Empire State Building was built to allow Kong a cinematically poignant death. But the towers not only caricature the great ape's death, they caricature the city where that death takes place. That alone explains why the 1970s version of the film seems so gimmicky, as if the twin towers had been constructed only to afford the great ape a high and dramatic death.

Image demands the kind of empathy that feeds belief. The Eiffel Tower has been the image of Paris in the popular mind ever since it was created for the Exposition of 1889. But ask a Parisian whether he thinks of the tower as a symbol of his city, and he will stare incredulously. Location dominates imagination even more than it dominates the real estate market. Transplant Eiffel's tower to an African savanna and it is just another example of urban kitsch, as laughable as the marble statues lining the entrance to Caesar's Palace in Las Vegas. When he was New York's governor, Nelson Rockefeller tried to remake Albany into a symbol of state power and wealth. He built tall buildings and a sweeping mall—and succeeded only in making a provincial but interesting city more provincial and less interesting. Geography and politics do not make a city memorable by themselves. If they could, then Albany and Sacramento would be among the nation's great cities. No city can simply assume its landscape the way hotels in Vegas or theme parks in Orlando can. Cities are both more and less than the landscapes they fill. Great cities, in particular, must be places where life is lived by people who work, eat, copulate, raise children, and die there. Novelist William Kennedy did more for Albany than those tall buildings and that sweeping mall.

The New York in which I live is not the city made memorable by the dark angles of the *noir* films of the 1940s. My city is a cripple's New York, and despite the images of power it shares with the New York of tourists and beggars, its reality remains singular for those who push through its streets in wheelchairs or walk through those streets on crutches. I know any number of New Yorkers whose passion for this city equals mine, but I don't believe any of them know this city as intimately as I do. My New York has been stripped of sophistication and glamour, and my sense of it has been constructed from the ground up. Cripples who choose to live here are closer than we care to admit to those tourists gaping at the man-made canyons or peering into the restaurant windows in hopes of catching sight of some real-life celebrity. Stuck with our nurtured images and fragile myths, we cannot acknowledge how similar we are to the tourists we claim to despise.

For better or worse, September 11 thrust New York, for perhaps the first time in its history, into the nation's heart. Power and wealth were suddenly humanized by a cataclysm in which the city "took a hit for the nation," as city politicians said. No one expected the generosity with which the nation opened itself up to a city it had scorned as not truly American. That generosity soon ended, as it was bound to end once the initial shock of the attack wore off. Yet prior to that morning in September, a majority of New Yorkers viewed their city as other Americans did. New York was separate and different, in America but not of it. Real New Yorkers didn't ogle "Today" show cameras or allow themselves to be herded behind velvet ropes so that they could wave to some aunt or uncle in Des Moines. Real New Yorkers didn't risk stiff necks to stare up at the city skyline. No, real New Yorkers were a separate species, for whom not looking up was as much a point of honor as not riding the elevator up to the observation deck of the Empire State Building. Real New Yorkers understood that certain journeys were suitable for tourists or oversized Hollywood apes—but that didn't make them suitable for outer-borough Othellos.

The cripple's New York is different from the city to which tourists flock. It is even more different from the city populated by those for whom to live in New York is a mark of distinction in itself. New Yorkers insist on how tough they are because they live in a city that overwhelms the senses. Before September 11, most other Americans felt that the New York toughness was inflated. And most other Americans were correct in that assumption. But a cripple who lives in this city has no choice but to be New York tough. He may try to cast aside the need to be tough; he may scorn it as a philosophy, deny it is the reason behind his being. Yet his survival remains dependent upon how tough he is. Toughness is the guiding principle of life in this city for a cripple, no matter how arbitrary or unreal that may sound. To believe that an ordinary New Yorker is any tougher than a citizen of Chicago or Los Angeles or Des Moines is ludicrous. What sets people in this city apart is not how tough they are but how willingly they live with eyes cast down in a culture that wants us all to look up. The tourist gazes up at the skyline; the New Yorker prefers to stare down at the intricacies of the sidewalk—dog droppings and all. Among the salient lessons this city teaches is, "Don't look up! You may be surprised at what's falling down."

On September 11, the bodies were the first to fall down, and the towers soon followed. To my knowledge, no one reported any wheelchairs or crutches plummeting through the smoke, which is no more than poetic justice, since few, if any, of those who escaped the inferno would recognize the city that cripples confront daily. One man who might have escaped the inferno chose, instead, to remain with his wheelchair-bound friend. Not until his obituary appeared in the *New York Times*'s "Portraits of Grief" months later did I discover that the man had a name. I wish I believed in the kind of afterlife where I might shake the hand of Abe Zelmanowitz's ghost. Yet how ironic that in the millions of words devoted to September 11, no one pointed out that the WTC was one of the few truly accessible areas of the city, almost a wheelchair-rider's dream. It's quite probable that the WTC's accessibility cost Abe Zelmanowitz and his wheelchair-bound friend their lives. For what did those "arrogant" towers and busy walkways offer Abe's friend if not an urban space in which he could not only make a living but where his wheelchair could be as much at home as a car or Abe's legs or a baby carriage. Not until their collapse did those towers assume the kind of New York identity that made them as inhospitable to a person in a wheelchair as the rest of the city is.

I like to think of myself as New York's representative man. Until quite recently, I would fantasize about playing baseball again (as vain and absurd a fantasy as a man in his sixties can have). But fantasy or no fantasy, imagination also insisted that any man who had to stare down at the sidewalk rather than gaze up at the heavens was as representative a New Yorker as could be found. However immodest and self-serving it may be, let me offer myself, one aging cripple, as New York's representative man. That someone forced to confront the city as enemy should see himself as its representative is an image that would tickle Emerson, who invented the idea of the representative man. Yet who knows this city as intimately as a man who must push through its streets in a wheelchair, his eyes glued to the cracks in the sidewalk instead of the stars in the heavens? What choice does such a man have but to seek in those broken sidewalks and hump-backed streets the emblems of his fate? And that is what I must do—in a city that is indifferent to my problems as a cripple. Only a man able to understand what the cracks in sidewalks portend can possibly serve as a city's representative man.

It's a daring hypothesis. But daring hypotheses have always been in vogue in New York. And if this one comes from a self-appointed representative, it yet deserves consideration. To see New York from the ground up is to see how a city shapes its secrets. The first time I pushed through the neighborhood I live in, Manhattan's Chelsea, I realized that I was as representative of New York as any man could possibly be. I was born and raised in the outer-borough Bronx, and New York has been my home for all but the two years I lived in an upstate hospital as a child and the three years I lived abroad as an adult. I am as pure a product of its outer-borough culture as Woody Allen or Pete Hamill. And, as it is for them, my love for this city is so natural that it seems genetically linked to my soul. Yet it wasn't until I was in my fifties and had gone from walking on crutches to pushing through the city in a wheelchair that I recognized how representative a New Yorker I am. I have been formed by the experience of living as a cripple in a city as hostile to cripples as it is indifferent to their needs. New York is my beloved enemy, an enemy that has molded ambition and given anger substance.

New Yorkers view the city's shortcomings as testimony to their own virtue, a virtue built upon the idea that the proof of any individual's humanity is how well he can endure the irritation of living in this city. It is human to suffer, and New Yorkers take great pride in their ability to take whatever indignities the city throws at them. For taking it means that they are tough, and to think that he is tough allows a man to avoid thinking about what the city does to undesirables. It isn't that New Yorkers would deny the difficulties people in wheelchairs face. What they would deny is that the city is in any way responsible for those difficulties. Far from being the radical bastion non–New Yorkers believed it was before September 11, New Yorkers always took great pride in their city's sense of individualism. For citizens of this city, helping someone in a wheelchair confront the problems imposed on him is not really natural. Not that New Yorkers lack generosity. It's simply that it isn't easy for anyone, normal or cripple, to get around here. And so we believe that the city is as difficult for the normal as it is for the cripple—a belief that is absurd, as Manhattan traffic jams and the city subway system testify. My survival may be admirable to New Yorkers. But it is proof not of my endurance but of city toughness. "If you can make it here, you'll make it anywhere," sang Frank Sinatra (a New Yorker from Hoboken), echoing the city's passion for itself. Like the lovers on Keats's urn, the New Yorker's affair with his city is forever young and forever unconsummated.

To be a cripple in New York is to understand how little input one has about one's fate. It isn't by its ability to meet the cripple's needs that this city measures success. Does it matter how tough the cripple must be to survive its battered streets to the normal who calls the city home? It can't matter, for the normal has been conditioned, as I have been, to believe that it isn't through his expectations of the city but through the city's expectations of him by which his worth is to be determined. New York demands that cripples who insist upon living here put up with what is unacceptable even as it demands that they demonstrate their ability to take it. His existence is a test of the cripple's character. And the city, not the cripple, decides whether or not his survival is important. The cripple is asked to serve as supplicant, the very role he has spent a lifetime struggling against. How does he define what his survival means to a city of broken sidewalks and collapsing curbs, which are far more threatening to his existence than snow or ice or rain? Is it just bureaucratic indifference or ineptitude that creates curb cuts with two- or three-inch lips or streets on which a wheelchair pitches and rolls as if it were the Coney Island Cyclone? The question, he realizes, doesn't make sense in a city where both bureaucratic indifference and bureaucratic ineptitude are the norm rather than the exception.

To whom does he complain as his path is blocked by broken plastic boxes emptied of "free" copies of the *Village Voice* or flyers advertising courses that will make the reader a beautician or an ad exec or a novelist in six weeks? Those boxes lean across the curb cuts up which he tries to maneuver. To whom does he send the bill for the broken wheel spokes or casters that plague the man who insists upon his right to push through the capital of the Western world? To what city agency does he protest the rutted streets that would shame Cairo or Calcutta? Does he write his congressman? Or telephone his assemblyman? (I have done both, with results that were equally laughable.) Or does he sue those who sold him that wheelchair with the promise that he would now discover the accessible city? They, too, are New Yorkers—who are less interested in repairing wheelchairs than they are in selling them. In a culture in which they could just as easily sell hot dogs or VCRs, profit and loss alone concern them. What good will it do to remind them that a wheelchair is as necessary to a man like me as legs are to them? That a man will make his dollar any way he can is part of the myth of New York tough. Broken curb cuts and battered streets are no more the responsibility of the normal than they are of the cripple.

Some years ago, I telephoned the city agency in charge of maintaining curb cuts, hoping to demonstrate just what my wheelchair was up against in Chelsea. A fortunate accident put me through to the head of the agency, and I managed to persuade him to accompany me through the neighborhood. Trying to show him what I was up against in my chair, I dutifully pointed out curb cuts with two- or three-inch lips and reminded him that the city had mandated cuts of no higher than an eighth of an inch. He was sympathetic. He understood the difficulties I faced. Only what was it he could do? He could give me sympathy. He could speak to me frankly (like all bureaucrats, he made a great show of how frank he was) and tell me what I knew: that my right of access was a distinctly minor priority to the city. And when that right conflicted with the right of the *Voice* to distribute free newspapers from those graffiti-scarred containers chained to lampposts, he knew that I was smart enough to understand how little power he had. Looked at through his eyes, it didn't matter that those boxes leaned like dead trees across the rutted curb cut. It was obvious which rights were considered paramount. That free *Voice* distribution box chained to the lamppost, along with the delivery bike of the Chinese take-out, which dangled like a huge metal dog from that same lamppost, served urban needs that were more important than my right to access. He was being frank, and I had to be realistic about the priorities of a tough city.

As a representative man, I pride myself on how realistic I am. Eyes on the sidewalk, I continue educating myself. Protest must be limited to what the city considers worth protesting. I know that, as does the cop who guards closed-off 20th Street at 8th Avenue. In fact, he knows nothing better than he knows the limits of his own responsibility—so that when I complain about the empty boxes chained to the lamppost, he nods, frowns, and says, "I'm sorry. There's nothing I can do." It's a tough city. And while in a tough city, cops must show sympathy to crips, his job is to reassure the normal populace. Guarding the Tenth Precinct from Osama's terrorists, he needs no chair-bound crip to tell him what is and isn't important. My right of access is secondary to the right of the people in Chelsea to their free *Voice*. Maybe I should write the editor, ask him why the *Voice* isn't concerned with the problems that crips in this city face. The thought feeds my self-righteousness. Only the *Voice* is no guiltier than the *Times* or the tabloids or the television news when it comes to the problems of crips. Access simply isn't a glamorous media issue. It lacks the immediacy that the news-as-entertainment industry finds attractive, and we crips aren't very fashionable. Even kindly, crotchety Andy Rooney, liberalism's own Dutch uncle, feels no qualms in expressing irritation with us on "Sixty Minutes." What particularly annoys Uncle Andy are those parking permits that allow crips like me to park where even members of the press like him can't. Uncle Andy, like most normal people in New York, expects crips to be supplicants in this tough city. For a tough city can't open its heart to those who lack modesty or gratitude.

To the cop on 20th Street, I am a supplicant, not a citizen. But how do I fault him for that? He, too, struggles with New York mythology. "Go fight city hall!" my immigrant father would cry in disgust in an accent that, forty-six years after his arrival, could still blister tar. He never quite understood America, but he was New Yorker enough to voice futility with an urban bureaucracy whose sole purpose seemed to be ensuring its own continuity. As the cop eyes my purple Quickie 2 wheelchair, he grows flustered. I can see that he knows I have a problem. And he would like to help. Only he doesn't know what a cop can do about accessibility. It isn't what cops are trained for. What he knows is that no one who has the slightest idea of how this city works should pester him about curb cuts. "Try Sanitation," he sighs, "or the Fire Department. If anyone can help, it's the Fire Department." I can hear him thinking, "Just do me a favor. Don't make it a job for the cops."

That my problem disturbs a man guarding me against Osama's legions as they smash the barricades of 20th Street to blow up the precinct house pleases me. I have lived as a cripple in this city since my return from the New York State Reconstruction Home in August 1946. And I am pleased that a guardian of this city is aware of the stupidity that makes a crip's life difficult. But there is nothing this cop, or any cop, can do about the problems of people in wheelchairs. Of course, he has mastered the vocabulary, has learned to speak of "the differently abled." But that isn't of much help as I try to push through this city.

The street he guards is in the neighborhood I have called home ever since I moved from the Bronx to Manhattan in August 1957. I was twenty-four, recently married, and although we did not know it then, my wife and I were to watch Chelsea evolve from a quietly drab neighborhood to one that now hosts overpriced luxury apartment houses, art galleries, restaurants, gyms, and nail salons. For much of that time, Chelsea was represented in the city council by Tom Duane, one of the few city politicians who has actually paid attention to what is now referred to as "the disabled community." (In the Orwellian newspeak of this city, individuals only have problems if they are part of an identifiable community.) Yet many of the new restaurants in trendy Chelsea do not comply with the city access laws, which are stricter, I am told by the young intern in the street-level office of Manfred Ohrenstein, my state assemblyman, than what the Americans with Disabilities Act calls for. Access remains what restaurant owners choose to grant or not to grant. Their whims are my law. Like the constitution of the Soviet Union, laws guaranteeing accessibility are merely "words, words, words." The restaurant owners understand, as I do, that there are few consequences if they choose to ignore those laws. Where right of access is concerned, New York toughness is no more than attitude.

Unable, unwilling, or simply bored, the city bureaucracy is convinced that it lacks power to enforce the law. In defending its inability to act, it reduces civic virtue to numbers. Statistics rule the day, dislodging both the barriers in my path and the incompetence of the bureaucracy. We understand that life is difficult in the tough city. And we expect it to be difficult. That city policies make little sense doesn't force the bureaucracy to pause. Nor is it the city bureaucracy alone to whom the numbers speak. I complain to a friend about how difficult it is to get around in a wheelchair. And he is, of course, sympathetic. But his sympathy is tempered by the numbers. Like those city bureaucrats, he has become a surveyor of emotions. New York, he tells me, has more accessible buses and accessible theaters and accessible landmarks than any city in the nation. I have heard this litany before, and it is as likely to come from a cabby six months off the plane from Pakistan as from my friend or from the cop on 20th Street. In a city that boasts of how it has more of everything worth having, numbers count. They may sound specious, but they are all we know and all we need to know.

The city does have more curb cuts and accessible buses than other cities. That it also has twice the population and at least twice as many streets as any other city in the nation is considered, if considered at all, to be an aspect of the city's singularity. My admittedly informal survey tells me that half the curb cuts in Chelsea are dangerous. Some are completely unusable. That doesn't concern my fellow New Yorkers. Who cares that these rutted and broken sidewalks are today booby-trapped with dog shit and garbage? Who cares that streets in what the *Times*'s real estate section glowingly speaks of as Manhattan's hottest residential neighborhood unfold before me as if they were monuments of devastation? In this city, reality is a number, and numbers don't lie. They may fudge truth, but they don't lie. Statistics are the new urban scripture. Inaccessible buses, broken sidewalks, blocked curb cuts—what do they mean if they can all be canceled out by the numbers? A twelve-year-old boy works out his batting average, and numbers lift the weight of failure from his burdened shoulders. Only the problems of crips have to do not with numbers but with such mundane realities as being able to go where one wants to go.

All politics are local, and all pain is personal. One adapts to the pressure by embracing it. Please don't misunderstand me. I am neither sadist nor masochist, just a man trying to balance the needs of mind and body by facing the reality of his life as a cripple. If I had my druthers, I would ask for the legs that were taken when I was eleven years, two months, and seven days old. Yet fifty-seven years of living as a cripple—most of them in this city—have taught me that I cannot quantify pain. No one can. There is no scale that accurately measures the humiliation a crip must endure in New York. And precisely here, the numbers prove costly. No city in history ever offered average men and women such extraordinary abundance or so powerful a sense of possibility as New York. Yet, in a city itself crippled by September 11, a fixation on the numbers has grown, at least where crips are concerned. City bureaucrats still cite their statistics as willingly as subway drunks cite scripture while working the cars for a handout. New York asks for *more!* because more is what it is familiar with. And more is measurable—more money, more dirt, more roads, more garbage, more tall buildings, more small buildings, more men, more women, more chestnut trees.

Yet more doesn't ease my cripple's heart. Rarely does this city question what it asks of those to whom it offers more. "Live!" is its Jamesean gush of passion. But how does a cripple live with the gnawing humiliations this city insists on? In a curious twist, humiliation proves as singular as the Empire State Building or those smiling tourists waving at the camera outside the "Today" show. Crunching the numbers turns out to be just another way of blocking entrances and exits, of mocking my determination to remain in this city, to *live* here. I am not what New York wants. But I am here and I will remain here, no matter how irritated I grow with the city.

I love living with the enemy, even after I discover that the just-finished, overpriced apartment building on 7th Avenue between 25th and 26th streets lacks the mandated curb cuts. Irritated, I accost the rental agent in the marble lobby. He sizes up my purple Quickie 2 wheelchair, about to say something. He shrugs and then decides to remain silent after he discovers that I have not come to rent an apartment. He seems bored. He sees no reason that he should play cat and mouse with me merely because I am forced to play cat and mouse with the trucks turning west on 25th and 7th whenever I cross the street on my way to the supermarket on 24th Street. Why should he care about curb cuts? This is a tough city—even for rental agents. Maybe the landlord simply forgot to see to it that a proper cut was installed in the rush to finish the building. It's not his problem. He's just a rental agent. The subject doesn't interest him. Perhaps someday, if the landlord's luck doesn't hold, one of those trucks will hit a wheelchair forced to maneuver into the turning traffic. Maybe something will be done after that. Until then, there is nothing he can do.

I parse the numbers, statistician of the soul's anguish. Only the numbers cannot explain why crossing 7th Avenue at 23d Street makes me seasick with its pitch and roll. The numbers cannot explain why there are steps in front of new restaurants in Chelsea or why periodically I am forced to shell out another $100 to fix a caster broken while pushing across these broken streets and avenues. Even a representative man will rage against the city that mocks him. I yet hope to find some bureaucrat in some city agency who will take it upon himself to rid the streets of chained newspaper boxes. I still expect curb cuts to be repaired and restaurants to obey the law. I know what it means to keep my crip's place in a city fixated on the myth of its toughness. If virtue is its own reward, am I really expected to feel gratitude because that cop on 20th Street recognizes that my problems are real?

There was a time when I believed that if I had to be a crip it was best to be a crip in New York. Of course, I never chose to be a cripple, not in New York and not anywhere else. I find the rhetoric of the disability movement as embarrassing as bumper stickers telling the world what great sex plumbers have. When I returned to this city from the hospital ward I lived in for two years as a child, I fell in love with its streets all over again. Thirteen years old, hanging on long-legged braces and crutches, I was unable to take ten consecutive steps. Yet I forced myself through these streets because the very air in this city promised that my coming of age might be difficult but would never be boring. Crippled or whole, New York in the late 1940s was willing to give me a shot at life. And living in the city was crucial to my rehabilitation. I still can't get over how willingly the city allowed me to pursue my life. Because I was physically unable to attend school, it sent teachers to our apartment. Other cities didn't do that back in 1946. I spent my high school years receiving home instruction, and to this day I am grateful for the education the city gave me. I learned to get around by bus and subway in a New York that accepted me—braces and crutches and all. After high school, I went to one of the tuitionless municipal colleges. If one had to be a crip in America during the late 1940s and early 1950s, one was best off in a city where survival was as much a question of attitude as of strength. New York taught me as much about survival and going after what I wanted as Camus or Hemingway or Saul Bellow's splendid cripple, Einhorn. And for that, I remain immensely grateful.

Yet living as a cripple in this city turned out to be not so much a personal as a political problem. It asked me to define what I could legitimately ask of the larger community. Is access a right or a favor granted by the city? Most people, asked to choose between my right to enter a restaurant and the integrity of one or another landmark, would discover that the lame and halt, even if called "differently abled," pose problems they would rather ignore. The now-fashionable Chelsea in which I live wants sculpted and buffed bodies. Cripples are neither sculpted nor buffed, merely broken. Christopher Reeve as Superman was a New York fantasy. Christopher Reeve in an electric wheelchair, speaking with the aid of a computer, makes the city squirm. It's not that the city is indifferent to him but that it wants to keep its distance from his problems. Yet it brags of what it has done, is doing, and will do for cripples like him. It brags that it has more of what we need to live. But the bureaucracy that seeks to define us defines its limitations through us.

That bureaucracy claims it is interested in our welfare. But it is interested only in its own perpetuation. The single most important issue facing cripples in New York is why their lives are still defined by others. "Speak of me as I am," Othello begs, "nothing extenuate." Prepared to relate the Moor's tragic tale, the ambassadors will first praise his courage, laud his soldierly skills, and speak of his service to the state. In death, they will give him the understanding he needs. Only his Venice, like my New York after September 11, is a crippled city. And, like a crippled man, a crippled city, with no choice but to acquiesce to the bureaucracy that runs it, will discover that neither rage nor silence can save it. If that isn't a major recognition, representative New Yorkers like me know that it is the painful price of existence.

PUBLIC TRANSIT

 by John Hockenberry

New York was not like Iran.

It was a shock to return to the United States in 1990, where it routinely took an act of God to hail a taxi. There was nothing religious about New York City, even on Christmas Eve. I had taken a cab from midtown to Riverside Church on the west side of Manhattan only to find that my information about a Christmas Eve service there was mistaken. The church was padlocked, which I only discovered after getting out of the cab into the forty-mile-an-hour wind and the twenty-degree weather. I tried all of the doors of the church and found myself alone at close to midnight, without a taxi, on December 24 at 122d Street and Riverside Drive.

I was wearing a wool sports jacket and a heavy scarf, but no outer jacket. There were no cars on the street. Being wrong about the service and having come all the way uptown was more than a little frustrating. I suspected that I was not in the best psychological condition to watch the usual half-dozen or so New York cabs pass me by and pretend not to see me hailing them. I knew the most important thing was to try and not look like a panhandler. This was always hard. Many times in New York I had hailed a cab only to have the driver hand me a dollar. Once I was so shocked that I looked at the cabbie and said, as though I were correcting his spelling, "No, I give you the money."

"You want a ride?" he said. "Really?"

The worst were the taxis that stopped but had some idea that the wheelchair was going to put itself into the trunk. After you hopped into the back seat, these drivers would look at you as though you were trying to pull a fast one, tricking them into having to get out of their cabs and load something in the trunk that you had been cleverly hiding. Some cabbies would say that I should have brought someone with me to put the chair in, or that it was too heavy for them to lift. My favorite excuse was also the most frequent, "Look, buddy, I can't lift that chair. I have a bad back."

"I never heard of anyone who became paralyzed from lifting wheelchairs," I'd say. My favorite reply never helped. If the drivers would actually load the chair, you could hear them grumbling, throwing it around to get it to fit, and smashing the trunk lid down on it. When we would arrive at our destination, the driver would throw the chair at me like it was a chunk of nuclear waste and hop back behind the wheel. The only thing to do in these situations was to smile, try not to get into a fight, and hope the anger would subside quickly so you could make it wherever you were going without having a meltdown.

There were some drivers who wouldn't load the chair at all. For these people, at one time, I carried a Swiss army knife. The rule was, if I had to get back out of a cab because a driver wouldn't load my chair, then I would give the driver a reason to get out of his cab shortly after I was gone. I would use the small blade of the knife to puncture a rear tire before the cab drove away, then hail another one. A few blocks ahead, when the first driver had discovered his difficulties, he was generally looking in his trunk for the tire jack when I passed by, waving.

The trouble with this idea was that other people often did not have the same righteous attitude that I did about tire puncturing in Manhattan traffic, and using knives to get freelance revenge in New York City under any circumstances. Most of my friends put me in the same league with subway vigilante Bernhard Goetz and concluded that I needed serious help. So I had stopped using the Swiss army knife and was without it that Christmas Eve on 122d and Riverside Drive.

The first cab drove toward me and slowed down; the driver stared, then quickly drove by. A second cab approached. I motioned emphatically. I smiled and tried to look as credible as I could. Out in this December wind, I was just another invisible particle of New York misery. The driver of the second cab shook his head as he passed with the lame, catch-all apologetic look New York cabbies use to say, "No way, Mac. Sorry, no way I can take you."

I had one advantage. At least I was white. Black males in New York City have to watch at least as many cabs go by as someone in a wheelchair does before getting a ride. Black male friends of mine say they consciously have to rely on their ritzy trench coats or conservative "Real Job" suits to counter skin color in catching a cab. If I could look more white than crippled, I might not freeze to death on Christmas Eve. I was a psychotic, twentieth-century hit man named Tiny Tim, imagining all sorts of gory ways to knock off a cabbie named Scrooge. The wind was blowing furiously off the Hudson, right up over Riverside Drive.

A third cab drove by. I wondered if I could force a cab to stop by blocking the road. I wished I had a baseball bat. For a period of a few minutes, there was no traffic. I turned and began to roll down Riverside. After a block, I turned around, and there was one more empty cab in the right lane coming toward me. I raised my hand. I was sitting directly under a streetlight. The cabbie clearly saw me, abruptly veered left into the turn lane, and sat there, signaling at the red light.

I rolled over to his cab and knocked on the window. "Can you take a fare?" The driver was pretending I had just landed there from space, but I was freezing and needed a ride, so I tried not to look disgusted. He nodded with all of the enthusiasm of someone with an abscessed tooth. I opened the door and hopped onto the back seat. I folded the chair and asked him to open the trunk of his cab.

"Why you want me to do that?" he said.

"Put the chair in the trunk, please." I was half-sitting in the cab, my legs still outside. The door was open and the wheelchair was folded next to the cab. "No way, man," he said. "I'm not going to do that. It's too damn cold." I was supposed to understand that I would now simply thank him for his trouble, get back in my wheelchair, and wait for another cab.

"Just put the chair in the trunk right now. It's Christmas Eve, pal. Why don't you just pretend to be Santa for five fucking minutes?" His smile vanished. I had crossed a line by being angry. But he also looked relieved, as though now he could refuse me in good conscience. It was all written clearly on his face. "You're crazy, man. I don't have to do nothing for you." I looked at him once more and said, "If you make me get back into this chair, you are going to be very sorry." It was a moment of visceral anger. There was no turning back now. "Go away, man. It's too cold."

I got back into the chair. I placed my backpack with my wallet in it on the back of my chair for safekeeping. I grabbed his door and, with all of my strength, pushed it back on its hinges until I heard a loud snap. It was now jammed open. I rolled over to his passenger window, and two insane jabs of my right fist shattered it. I rolled around to the front of the cab, and with my fist in my white handball glove took out first one, then the other headlight. The light I was bathed in from the front of the cab vanished. The face of the driver could now be seen clearly, illuminated by the dashboard's glow.

I could hear myself screaming at him in a voice that sounded far away. I knew the voice, but the person it belonged to was an intruder in this place. He had nothing to do with this particular cabbie and his stupid, callous insensitivity; rather, he was the overlord to all such incidents that had come before. Whenever the gauntlet was dropped, it was this interior soul, with that screaming voice and those hands, who felt no pain and who surfed down a wave of hatred to settle the score. This soul had done the arithmetic and chosen the weapons. I would have to live with the consequences.

I rolled over to the driver's seat and grabbed the window next to his face. I could see that he was absolutely terrified. It made me want to torture him. I hungered for his fear; I wanted to feel his presumptions of power and physical superiority in my hands as he sank up to his neck in my rage, my fists closed around his throat. I attacked his half-open window. It cracked, and as I hauled my arm back to finish it, I saw large drops of blood on the driver's face. I looked at him closely. He was paralyzed with fear and spattered with blood. There was blood on his window, as well. A voice inside me screamed, "I didn't touch you, motherfucker. You're not bleeding. Don't say that I made you bleed. You fucking bastard. Don't you dare bleed!"

I rolled back from the cab. It was my own blood shooting from my thumb. It gushed over the white leather of my glove: I had busted an artery at the base of my thumb, but I couldn't see it because it was inside the glove. Whatever had sliced my thumb had gone neatly through the leather first, and as I rolled down the street I could hear the cabbie saying behind me, "You're crazy, man, you're fucking crazy." I rolled underneath a street lamp to get a closer look. It was my left hand, and it had several lacerations in addition to the one at the base of my thumb. It must have been the headlight glass. The blood continued to gush. Wind blew it off my fingers in festive red droplets, which landed stiffly on the frozen pavement under the street lamp. Merry Christmas.

Up the street, a police squad car had stopped next to the cab, which still had its right rear door jammed open. I coasted farther down the street to see if I could roll the rest of the way home. With each push of my hand on the wheel rim of my chair, blood squirted out of my glove. I could feel it filled with blood inside. The cops pulled up behind me. "Would you like us to arrest that cabbie? Did he attack you?" All I could think of was the indignity of being attacked by him. I thought about screaming, "That piece of human garbage attacked me? No way. Maybe it was me who attacked him as a public service. Did you donut eaters ever think of that? I could have killed the bastard. I *was* trying to kill him, in fact. I insist that you arrest me for attempted murder right now, or I will sue the NYPD under the Americans with Disabilities Act." I thought better of this speech. Intense pain had returned my mind to practical matters. Spending the night in jail for assaulting a cabbie after bragging about it while bleeding to death seemed like a poor way to cap off an already less than stellar Christmas Eve.

"Everything's fine, officer. I'll just get another taxi." I continued to roll one-handed and dripping down Riverside Drive. The cops went back to talk to the cabbie, who was screaming now. I began to worry that he was going to have me arrested, but the cops drove back again. Once more, the officer asked if I wanted to file a complaint against the cabbie. As more blood dripped off my formerly white glove, the officers suggested that I go to the hospital. They had figured out what had happened. As I started to explain, they told me to get in the squad car. "Let's just say it was an unfortunate accident," one officer said. "I don't think he'll ever stop for someone in a wheelchair again. If we can get you to the emergency room in time, maybe you won't lose your thumb."

I got in the backseat while the cops put the chair in the trunk. Seven blocks away was the emergency room of St. Luke's Hospital. Christmas Eve services at St. Luke's included treatment of a young woman's mild overdose. An elderly man and his worried-looking wife were in a corner of the treatment room. His scared face looked out from beneath a green plastic oxygen mask. A number of men stood around watching CNN on the waiting-room television. A woman had been brought in with fairly suspicious-looking bruises on her face and arms. One arm was broken and being set in a cast. She sat quietly while two men talked about football in loud voices. The forlorn Christmas decorations added to the hopelessness of this little band of unfortunates in the emergency room.

When I arrived, everything stopped. Police officers are always an object of curiosity, signaling the arrival of a shooting victim or something more spectacular. For a Christmas Eve, the gushing artery at the base of my thumb was spectacular enough. The men sitting around the emergency room shook their heads. The overdose patient with the sunken cocaine eyes staggered over to inspect the evening's best carnage. "Where did you get that wheelchair?" She looked around as though she was familiar with all of the wheelchairs in this emergency room from previous visits. "It's my own," I replied. "That's a good idea," she said. "Why didn't I think of that?"

I got nine stitches from a doctor who suggested politely that whatever my complaint with the taxi driver, I was one person on the planet who could ill afford to lose a thumb. The deep laceration was just a few millimeters from the nerve and was just as close to the tendon. Severing either one would have added my thumb to an already ample chorus of numbness and paralysis. The thought of losing the use of my thumb was one thing, but what was really disturbing was the thought of its isolation on my hand, numb in the wrong zone. Trapped on a functional hand, a numb and paralyzed thumb would have no way of communicating with my numb and paralyzed feet. It would be not only paralyzed, it would be in exile: an invader behind enemy lines, stuck across the checkpoint on my chest.

Today, there is a one-inch scar that traces a half circle just to the left of my knuckle. The gloves were a total loss, but they no doubt saved my thumb. Nothing could save my pride, but pride is not always salvageable in New York City. I have taken thousands of cabs, and in each case the business of loading and unloading delivers some small verdict on human nature. Often it is a verdict I am in no mood to hear, as was the case on that Christmas Eve. At other times, the experience is eerie and sublime. At the very least, there is the possibility that I will make a connection with a person, not just stare at the back of an anonymous head.

In my life, cabbies distinguish themselves by being either very rude and unhelpful or sympathetic and righteous. Mahmoud Abu Holima was one of the latter. It was his freckles I remembered, along with his schoolboy nose and reddish-blond hair, which made his Islamic tirades more memorable. He was not swarthy like other Middle Eastern cabbies. He had a squeaky, raspy voice. He drove like a power tool carving Styrofoam. He used his horn a lot. He made constant references to the idiots he said were all around him.

He was like a lot of other New York cabbies. But out of a sea of midtown yellow, Mahmoud Abu Holima was the one who stopped one afternoon in 1990, and by stopping for me he wanted to make it clear to everyone that he was not stopping for anyone else, especially the people in expensive-looking suits waiting on the same street corner I was. His decision to pick me up was part of some protest Mahmoud delivered to America every day he drove the streets of Manhattan.

His cab seemed to have little to do with transporting people from place to place. It was more like an Islamic institute on wheels. A voice in Arabic blared from his cassette player. His front seat was piled with books in Arabic and more cassettes. Some of the books were dog-eared Korans. There were many uniformly bound blue and green books open, marked, and stacked in cross-referenced chaos, the arcane and passionate academic studies of a Muslim cabbie studying hard to get ahead and lose his day job, interrupting his studies in midsentence to pick up a man in a wheelchair.

I took two rides with him. The first time I was going somewhere uptown on Third Avenue. Four cabs had passed me by. He stopped. He put the chair in the trunk and, to make more space there, brought stacks of Arabic books from the trunk into the front seat. He wore a large, knit, dirty-white skullcap and was in constant motion. He seemed lost in the ideas he had been reading about before I got in. At traffic lights, he would read. As he drove, he continually turned away from the windshield to make eye contact with me. His voice careened from conversation to lecture, like his driving. He ignored what was going on around him on the street. He told me he thought my wheelchair was unusually light. He said he knew many boys with no legs who could use such a chair. There were no good wheelchairs in Afghanistan.

"Afghanistan, you know about the war in Afghanistan?" he asked.

I said I knew about it. He said he wasn't talking about the Soviet invasion of Afghanistan and the American efforts to see that the Soviets were defeated. He said that the war was really a religious war. "It is the war for Islam." On a lark, in my broken, rudimentary Arabic, I asked him where he was from. He turned around abruptly and asked, "Where did you learn Arabic?" I told him that I had learned it from living in the Middle East. I apologized for speaking so poorly. He laughed and said that my accent was good, but that non-Muslims in America don't speak Arabic unless they are spies. "Only the Zionists really know how to speak," he said, his voice spitting with hatred.

I thanked him for picking me up. He removed my chair from his trunk, and as I hopped back into it I explained to him that it was difficult sometimes to get a cab in New York. He said that being in America was like being in a war where there are only weapons, no people. "In Islam," he said, "the people are the weapons."

"Why are you here?" I asked him.

"I have kids, family." He smiled once, and the freckles wrinkled on his nose and face, making him look like Tom Sawyer in a Muslim prayer cap. The scowl returned as he drove away. He turned up the cassette. The Arabic voice was still audible a block away.

The second time I saw him, I remembered him and he remembered me. He had no cassettes this time. There were no books in the car, and there was plenty of room in the trunk for my chair this time. Where were all of the books? He said he had finished studying. I asked him about peace in Afghanistan and the fact that Iran and Iraq were no longer at war. He said something about Saddam Hussein I didn't catch, and then he laughed. He seemed less nervous but still had the good-natured intensity I remembered from before. "Are you from Iran?" I asked him, and this time he answered. He told me he was from Egypt. He asked me if I knew about the war in Egypt, and I told him I didn't.

Before he dropped me off, he said that he wanted me to know when we would lose the war against Islam. He said that we won't know when we have lost. "Americans never say anything that's important." He looked out the window. His face did not express hatred as much as disappointment. He shook his head. "It is quiet now."

He ran a red light and parked squarely in the middle of an intersection, stopping traffic to let me out. Cars honked and people yelled as I got into the wheelchair. He scowled at them and laughed. I laughed too. I think I said to him, "Salaam," the Arabic word for peace and good-bye. He said something that sounded like "Mish Salaam fi Amerika," no peace in America. Then he said, "Sa'at." In Arabic, it means difficult. He got into his cab, smiled, and drove away. On February 26, 1993, cabbie, student of Islam, and family man Mahmoud Abu Holima, along with several others, planted a bomb that blew up in the World Trade Center. Today, he is serving a life sentence in a New York prison.

If you use a wheelchair and you want to avoid cabs in New York City, you can pay $10,000 a year in parking to have your own car, or you can try your luck at public transit. There are para-transit wheelchair vans which are bookable far in advance. Then there is the subway, which has only twenty elevator sites out of hundreds of stations. And there are the buses.

The buses in New York have wheelchair lifts, and if the driver is carrying a key to operate the lift, if the lift has been serviced recently, if the bus is not too crowded, and if the driver notices you at the stop, then you have a chance of getting a ride. Because the fare box is at the front of the bus and the lift is at the back, you can ask the driver to put your bus token into the box, but he will refuse. "I'm not allowed to touch your money" is what they usually say, and so they hand you instead a self-addressed stamped envelope for you to mail a check for $1.25 to the Transit Authority. The bus lifts are better than nothing, except that when the city buys new buses, the new wheelchair lifts don't work properly, so there is a period of months when a bus drives up and the driver shrugs and says that his bus is one of the new ones. Only in New York would the new buses be the ones you can count on not to work.

Attempting to use public transit involves taking the risk of finding no bus lift, no elevator, or that either one will stop working while you are in the middle of using it. The transit system in New York sometimes seems like an elaborate trap for people in wheelchairs, who are lured like mice to cheese with promises of accessible transportation. For years in New York's Herald Square, there were signs indicating an accessible subway station with an elevator. The space for the elevator was a large cube covered with plywood that looked as though it hadn't been disturbed for years. Wheelchair signs had arrived before the elevators, but that didn't keep the Transit Authority from putting the signs up even when there was no way to use the train at this stop. While they waited for the long-delayed elevator, the Transit Authority covered the little wheelchair symbols on the Herald Square subway station to prevent confusion. Today, the elevator works, but the signs for it are still covered. The Transit Authority apparently wants it to be a surprise.

When I returned to New York City from the Middle East in 1990, I lived in Brooklyn, just two blocks from the Carroll Street subway stop on the F train. It was not accessible, and as there appeared to be no plans to make it so, I didn't think much about the station. When I wanted to go into Manhattan, I would take a taxi, or I would roll up Court Street to the walkway entrance to the Brooklyn Bridge and fly into the city on a ribbon of oak planks suspended from the bridge's webs of cable that appeared from my wheelchair to be woven into the sky itself. Looking down, I could see the East River through my wheelchair's spokes. Looking up, I saw the clouds through the spokes of the bridge. It was always an uncommon moment of physical integrity with the city, which ended when I came to rest at the traffic light on Chambers Street, next to city hall.

It was while rolling across the bridge one day that I remembered my promise to Donna, my physical therapist, about how I would one day ride the rapid transit trains in Chicago. Pumping my arms up the incline of the bridge toward Manhattan and then coasting down the other side in 1990, I imagined that I would be able physically to accomplish everything I had theorized about the subway in Chicago in those first days of being a paraplegic back in 1976. In the Middle East, I had climbed many stairways and hauled myself and the chair across many filthy floors on my way to interviews, apartments, and news conferences. I had also lost my fear of humiliation from living and working there. I was even intrigued with the idea of taking the train during the peak of rush hour when the greatest number of people of all kinds would be underground with me.

I would do it just the way I had told Donna back in the rehab hospital. But this time, I would wire myself with a microphone and a miniature cassette machine to record everything that happened along the way. Testing my own theory might make a good commentary for an upcoming National Public Radio program about inaccessibility. Between the Carroll Street station and city hall, there were stairs leading in and out of the stations as well as to transfer from one line to another inside the larger stations. To get to Brooklyn Bridge/City Hall, I had to make two transfers, from the F to the A, then from the A to the 5, a total of nearly 150 stairs.

I rolled up to the Brooklyn Carroll Street stop on the F train carrying a rope and a backpack and wired for sound. Like most of the other people on the train that morning I was on my way to work. Taking the subway was how most people crossed the East River, but it would have been hard to come up with a less practical way, short of swimming, for a paraplegic to cover the same distance. Fortunately, I had the entire morning to kill. I was confident that I had the strength for it, and unless I ended up on the tracks, I felt sure that I could get out of any predicament I found myself in, but I was prepared for things to be more complicated. As usual, trouble would make the story more interesting.

The Carroll Street subway station has two staircases. One leads to the token booth, where the fare is paid by the turnstiles at the track entrance, the other one goes directly down to the tracks. Near the entrance is a newsstand. As I rolled to the top of the stairs, the man behind the counter watched me closely and the people standing around the newsstand stopped talking. I quickly climbed out of my chair and down onto the top step.

I folded my chair and tied the length of rope around it, attaching the end to my wrist. I moved down to the second step and began to lower the folded chair down the steps to the bottom. It took just a moment. Then, one at a time, I descended the first flight of stairs with my backpack and seat cushion in my lap until I reached a foul-smelling landing below street level. I was on my way. I looked up. The people at the newsstand who had been peering sheepishly down at me looked away. All around me, crowds of commuters with briefcases and headphones walked by, stepping around me without breaking stride. If I had worried about anything associated with this venture, it was that I would just be in the way. I was invisible.

I slid across the floor to the next flight of stairs, and the commuters arriving at the station now came upon me suddenly from around a corner. Still, they expressed no surprise and neatly moved over to form an orderly lane on the side of the landing opposite me as I lowered my chair once again to the bottom of the stairs where the token booth was.

With an elastic cord around my legs to keep them together and more easily moved (an innovation I hadn't thought of back in rehab), I continued down the stairs, two steps at a time, and finally reached the chair at the bottom of the steps. I stood it up, unfolded it, and did a two-armed, from-the-floor lift back onto the seat. My head rose out of the sea of commuter legs, and I took my place in the subway token line.

"You know, you get half price," the tinny voice through the bulletproof glass told me, as though this were compensation for the slight inconvenience of having no ramp or elevator. There, next to his piles of tokens, the operator had a stack of official half-price certificates for disabled users. He seemed thrilled to have a chance to use them. "No, thanks, the tokens are fine." I bought two and rolled through the rickety gate next to the turnstiles and to the head of the next set of stairs. I could hear the trains rumbling below.

I got down on the floor again, and began lowering the chair. I realized that getting the chair back up again was not going to be as simple as this lowering maneuver. Most of my old theory about riding the trains in Chicago had pertained to getting up to the tracks, because the Chicago trains are elevated. Down was going well, as I expected, but up might be more difficult.

Around me walked the stream of oblivious commuters. Underneath their feet, the paper cups and straws and various other bits of refuse they dropped were too soiled by black subway filth to be recognizable as having any connection at all to their world above. Down on the subway floor, they seemed evil, straws that could only have hung from diseased lips, plastic spoons that could never have carried anything edible. Horrid puddles of liquid were swirled with chemical colors, sinister black mirrors in which the bottoms of briefcases sailed safely overhead like rectangular airships. I was freshly showered, with clean white gloves and black jeans, but in the reflection of one of these puddles, I too looked as foul and discarded as the soda straws and crack vials. I looked up at the people walking by, stepping around me, or watching me with their peripheral vision. By virtue of the fact that my body and clothes were in contact with places they feared to touch, they saw and feared me much as they might fear sudden assault by a mugger. I was just like the refuse, irretrievable, present only as a creature dwelling on the rusty edge of a dark drain. By stepping around me as I slid, two steps at a time, down toward the tracks, they created a quarantined space, just for me, where even the air seemed depraved.

I rolled to the platform to wait for the train with the other commuters. I could make eye contact again. Some of the faces betrayed that they had seen me on the stairs by showing relief that I had not been stuck there, or worse, living there. The details they were too afraid to glean back there by pausing to investigate, they were happy to take as a happy ending which got them off the hook. They were curious as long as they didn't have to act on what they had learned. As long as they didn't have to act, they could stare.

I had a speech all prepared for the moment anyone asked if I needed help. I felt a twinge of satisfaction over having made it to the tracks without having to give it. My old theory, concocted while on painkillers in an intensive care unit in Pennsylvania, had predicted that I would make it. I was happy to do it all by myself. Yet I hadn't counted on being completely ignored. New York is such a far cry from the streets of Jerusalem, where Israelis would come right up to ask how much you wanted for your wheelchair, and Arabs would insist on carrying you up a flight of stairs whether you wanted to go or not.

I took the F train to the Jay Street/Borough Hall station. The train ride was exhilarating. I had a dumb smile on my face as I realized that the last subway ride I had taken was in February 1976, when I went from Garfield on the Dan Ryan train in Chicago to Irving Park on the north side to visit a friend. The Chicago trains had a green ambient light from the reflection off the industrial paint on all the interior surfaces. The New York trains were full of yellows and oranges. But the motion and sound of the train was familiar. The experience was completely new and just as completely nostalgic.

The Jay Street station was a warren of tunnels and passageways with steps in all of them. To get to the A train track for the ride into Manhattan, I had to descend a flight of stairs to the sub-platform; then, depending on which direction I was going, ascend another stairway to the tracks. Because it is a junction for three subway lines, there was a mix of people rushing through the station in all directions, rather than the clockwork march of white office-garbed commuters from Brooklyn Heights and Carroll Gardens on their way to midtown.

I rolled to the stairs and descended into a corridor crowded with people coming and going. "Are you all right?" A black woman stopped next to my chair. She was pushing a stroller with two seats, one occupied by a little girl, the other empty, presumably for the little boy with her, who was standing next to a larger boy. They all beamed at me, waiting for further orders from Mom.

"I'm going down to the A train," I said. "I think I'll be all right, if I don't get lost."

"You sure you want to go down there?" She sounded as if she was warning me about something. "I know all the elevators from having these kids," she said. "They ain't no elevator on the A train, young man." Her kids looked down at me as if to say, *What can you say to that?* I told her that I knew there was no elevator and that I was just seeing how many stairs there were between Carroll Street and city hall. "I can tell you, they's lots of stairs." As she said good-bye, her oldest boy looked down at me as if he understood exactly what I was doing, and why. "Elevators smell nasty," he said.

Once on the A train, I discovered at the next stop that I had chosen the wrong side of the platform and was going away from Manhattan. If my physical therapist, Donna, could look in on me at this point in my trip, she might be more doubtful about my theory than I was. By taking the wrong train, I had probably doubled the number of stairs I would have to climb.

I wondered if I could find a station not too far out where the platform was between the tracks, so that all I had to do was roll to the other side and catch the inbound train. The subway maps gave no indication of this, and the commuters I attempted to query on the subject simply ignored me or seemed not to understand what I was asking. Another black woman with a large shopping bag and a brown polka-dotted dress was sitting in a seat across the car and volunteered that Franklin Avenue was the station I wanted. "No stairs there," she said.

At this point, every white person I had encountered had ignored me or pretended that I didn't exist, while every black person who had come upon me had offered to help without being asked. I looked at the tape recorder in my jacket to see if it was running. It was awfully noisy in the subway, but if any voices at all were recorded, this radio program was going to be more about race than it was going to be about wheelchair accessibility. It was the first moment that I suspected the two were deeply related in ways I have had many occasions to think about since.

At Franklin Avenue I crossed the tracks and changed direction, feeling for the first time that I was a part of the vast wave of migration in and out of the Manhattan that produced the subway, all the famous bridges, and a major broadcast industry in traffic reporting complete with network rivals and local personalities, who have added words like *rubbernecking* to the language. I rolled across the platform like any other citizen and onto the train with ease. As we pulled away from the station, I thought how much it would truly change my life if there were a way around the stairs, if I could actually board the subway anywhere without having to be Sir Edmund Hillary.

The inbound trains were more crowded in the last minutes of the morning rush, and back at the Jay Street station there was a roar of people rushing to catch that lucky train that might make them not late after all. As I was sliding my folded chair toward the steps down to the platform, a young black man with a backward baseball cap walked right up to me out of the crowds. "I can carry the chair, man," he said. "Just tell me where you want me to set it back up." I looked at him. He was thin and energetic, and his suggestion was completely sensible. I didn't feel like giving him my speech about how I didn't need any help. "Take it to the Manhattan-bound A train," I said. "I'll be right behind you."

One train went by in the time it took to get up the flight of stairs, but going up was still much easier than I had imagined. My legs dragged along cooperatively just as my theory had predicted. At trackside, the young man with my chair had unfolded it and was sitting in it, trying to balance on two wheels. A friend of his, he explained, could do wheelies ever since he had been shot in the back during a gang shooting. "Your chair has those big-ass wheels," he said, commenting on the large-diame-ter bicycle wheels I used, as if to explain why he was having some trouble keeping his balance. "I never seen those kinda wheels," he said, as I hopped back into the chair.

As the train approached, he asked me for some cash. I thought that I must be some kind of idiot to go through all this and end up spending more to get into Manhattan than anyone else on the subway that day. The smallest bill I had was a five. I handed it over to him and boarded the train, laughing to myself at the absolute absurdity of it all. When I looked up, I could see commuters looking up from their newspapers. They cautiously regarded my laughing, as though I had just come from a rubber room at Bellevue Hospital. I let out a loud, demented shriek, opening my eyes as wide as I could. The heads bobbed quickly back behind the newsprint.

On the last flight of stairs leading onto City Hall Plaza at Centre Street and Chambers, the commuters in suits poured into the passageway from six trains. There was not a lot of space, and people began to trip over me. One gray-suited man in headphones carrying a gym bag nearly fell down, but he caught himself and swore as he scrambled up to street level, step-ping on one of my hands in the process. A tall black man in a suit holding his own gym bag picked up my chair and started to carry it up the stairs. In a dignified voice, he said, "I know you're OK, right?" I nodded.

Behind him, a Puerto Rican mother with two daughters identically dressed in fluffy flowered skirts with full slips and holding corsages offered to take my backpack and cushion up to the top so that I could haul myself without worrying about keeping track of the loose things. At the top, as I unfolded the wheelchair, the mother told me that she was on her way to get married at the Manhattan municipal building. Her two daughters were bridesmaids. She said she was going to put on her wedding dress, which she had in her gym bag, in the ladies' room before the ceremony. I wished her good luck and hopped back up into the chair as the commuters streamed by. It was a familiar place, the same spot I always rolled to so effortlessly off the Brooklyn Bridge.

I turned to roll away and noticed that the two little girls had come back. In unison, they said, "We will pray for Jesus to bring back your legs, mister." "Thank you," I said. As though I had just given them each a shiny new quarter, they ran back to their mother, who was waiting for them with her hands outstretched to take them across busy Centre Street. It was not the sort of thing I ever cared to hear people say, but after the ordeal of the subway, and the icy silence of virtually every white person I had met, I didn't mind at all. For once, I looked forward to riding home in a cab.

Since 1976, I had imagined a trip on the subway. I knew it was possible, while my physical therapist had known it would be utterly impractical as a form of transportation. We were both right, but neither of us could have imagined the America I found down there. The New York subway required only a token to ride, but on each person's face was the ticket to where they were all really going, the places they thought they never had to leave, the people they thought they never had to notice, or stop and apologize to for stepping on them. Without knowing it, I had left that America behind long ago. I discovered it alive and well on the F train.

TAXIS, TRAINS, AND SIDEWALKS Navigating

the ADA's Mass Transit Provisions

[10]

The stories by Hockenberry and Kriegel reveal the tremendous frustrations felt by persons with disabilities using public transportation. For Kriegel, navigating his chair along New York City sidewalks is perilous, though not as tough as facing the bureaucrats who explain why so little is done to remedy the poor conditions that face persons with disabilities. Meanwhile, John Hockenberry not only conveys his immense aggravation with taxi drivers who routinely pass him by because of the effort they would have to expend putting his chair in the trunk, but he also describes a venture into the subway with the aid of no ramps or elevators. Hockenberry takes on both the drivers and mass transit, proving that despite the odds and the architectural obstacles, he can do it, if only once.

Hockenberry's experiences using a taxi and a subway underscore a vital point about the problems people face in enforcing civil rights laws. While a taxi should be the easiest form of public transportation he could use in an urban area like New York, it is not necessarily available to him.

Nor can he use litigation as a means of making it more available. This stems from the fact that it is the cab driver's attitude that prevents Hockenberry from relying on this form of transportation. The cause of the driver's attitude—whether it is laziness and apathy or bias and malice against people who use wheelchairs—makes no difference. Hockenberry has little opportunity to sue any one driver who refuses to make his services available. By contrast, the physical barriers that both Hockenberry and Kriegel face in the subway and on the sidewalk are easier to remedy. Litigation or the threat of litigation under the ADA could help remove physical obstacles like nonworking elevators or dangerous curb cuts.

Hockenberry and Kriegel also touch upon a prominent theme in disability studies by juxtaposing the individual and the societal models of disability. The field of disability studies emerged, in large part, because of the frustration that persons with disabilities felt about how doctors and other professionals involved in rehabilitation turned the individual—the person with an impairment—into the problem. This idea, as Simi Linton, a disability studies expert, explains, is embedded in the rhetoric of "personal triumph over a personal condition."[1] Or, as Kriegel commented in another of his essays, the common perception of a person with a disability is a variation of the Tiny Tim story.[2] Persons with disabilities must take responsibility for their impairments and figure out ways of circumventing the obstructions before them. The consequence of this disability model means that the individual should accommodate society, rather than having society accommodate those with disabilities. Should Hockenberry have given up on taking a taxi or the subway? Or should he fight the existing public transit system, forcing it to take him into account either out of good will or, if that isn't effective, at least shaming public officials into doing it?

Disability studies protests the individual explanation, arguing that it is "ablism," or discrimination in favor of the able-bodied.[3] As a result, one of the dominant models within disability studies argues for a social conception of disability, which emphasizes society's failure to adapt to persons with disabilities by alleviating environmental obstacles, like stairs.[4] As disability rights theorist Jenny Morris explains, "Disabled people are those people with impairments who are disabled by society."[5] The social model rejects the personal-tragedy theory and argues that disabled people are held back not by their impairments, but by the obstructions that society places before them.[6] Stairs rather than ramps, curbs instead of sloping curb cuts, the inconvenience of putting a chair in a trunk—all impede persons with disabilities more than their actual impairments. Indeed, disability studies is not the first field to criticize architecture for poorly serving certain groups in society. Criticism has been leveled against architects for perpetuating gendered, racial, and other divisions in metropolitan areas.[7]

[ ] GETTING THERE

Nowhere is the societal form of discrimination more apparent than with architectural obstacles. One of the biggest impediments a disabled person faces is the lack of good public transportation. Overall, 24 million disabled people depend on public transit, including more than 4 million people who are legally blind or so severely impaired that they cannot drive.[8] What good is a ramp to an office building if someone cannot move from her home to the office?

As early as the 1970s, the federal government recognized this dilemma and began passing legislation to give persons with disabilities more access to mass transit. Even before the passage of the Rehabilitation Act of 1973, the first antidiscrimination legislation—the urban mass transit and highway legislation—had stipulated that persons with disabilities should have the same rights as those without them.[9] To effect this change, the Department of Transportation issued regulations that required transit systems to make "special efforts in planning public mass transportation facilities and services."[10] The Department of Health, Education, and Welfare also issued its own guidelines when the Rehabilitation Act passed, which mandated that any public transportation system that received federal funds had to make its system "readily accessible to and usable by handicapped persons."[11] Then, in 1979, the Department of Transportation drafted comprehensive guidelines that made alterations across the board. Every bus purchased, for example, had a wheelchair lift installed by the end of 1989. As a result, approximately half of all buses in the United States became accessible to those in wheelchairs.

The 1979 regulations did not stand, however. In one critical case, a federal court ruled that they were too stringent, holding that only "modest, affirmative steps to accommodate disability" were necessary.[12] To lighten the burden, this court ruled that persons with disabilities could be accommodated by making regular service accessible, or it also allowed a transit system to create a paratransit system, which is a separate transit system for people with special needs, which runs parallel to the mass transit system that serves the public at large. The court also recognized a "safe harbor provision," which relieved public transit of the obligation to serve persons with disabilities as long as the system spent 3.5 percent of its funds on such services. Then, in 1982, Congress and President Ronald Reagan passed the Surface Transportation Act, which codified the federal court's ruling.

Following the federal court's ruling, the Department of Transportation's new regulations mandated that only 3 percent of a transit system's overall budget needed to be used for accommodations.[13] The Supreme Court, however, struck down the spending limit as arbitrary and capricious, noting that in cities of less than one million, disabled people might well have no access to public transportation at all. As a result of this decision, many systems started buying buses with lifts. By 1990, when the ADA passed Congress, 35 percent of all buses and 50 percent of newly purchased buses were accessible.[14]

Given the checkered history of transit accommodations, when the ADA passed in 1990, specific sections of Title II outlined what was required of a public transit system. One section provides that when a public entity buys or leases a new bus or rapid or light-rail vehicles, it must make them "readily accessible to and usable by individuals with disabilities, including individuals who use wheelchairs."[15] This is not to say that these systems must buy or lease anything new. Another section maintains that all fixed-route bus systems must provide paratransit as a safety net.[16] These provisions do not ensure public transportation, rather they make what does exist comparable for people with and without disabilities.

The Department of Transportation immediately issued regulations enacting the ADA. These regulations mandated that the vehicles already accessible remain that way. The department also went so far as to outline what was involved in maintaining the lifts and mandated that paratransit systems be created. Fares on paratransit, moreover, could not exceed twice the fixed-route fare. The regulations forbade the systems providing paratransit from prioritizing who was served first on the basis of the trip's purpose. Taking those with visual impairments into account, the regulations required bus drivers to announce major bus stops and to find means of helping visually impaired people to identify the bus. The regulations mandated that public transportation systems make all of the changes known to disabled people.[17]

[ ] TRANSPORTATION UNDER LAW

Although the Supreme Court has not heard any ADA cases about mass transit, a body of law has been established in the lower federal courts about this subject.[18] To begin with, the courts have asked how a reduction in services affects persons with disabilities. In one case, a person with a disability sued for a preliminary injunction to stop a transit system from closing the nearest station to his house.[19] The closing meant that the nearest station would have been four miles from this person's home, a distance that he could not easily walk. Nor could he afford the taxi fare.[20] The judge, however, refused to stop the transit system from closing the station, arguing that the ADA did not require it to keep all stations open.[21] The system had the discretion to open or close stations as long as its policy harmed people with and without disabilities in equal measure. This ruling concerned disability activists not because they thought all stations should stay open, but because they hoped that the federal judge would reaffirm the distinction in the legislation about key and nonkey stations and not allow key ones to be closed.

Public transportation cases also revolve around what Kriegel faced as he ushered the bureaucrats around his neighborhood: service slip-ups. Here, the federal courts have ruled that these slip-ups only constitute discrimination if they are perceived as "egregious."[22] Giving some indication of what this means, one federal court ruled that seventy-six incidents in little more than one year was egregious.[23] In another case, where the rider found a bus to be unreliable nineteen times, the court did not rule in favor of the plaintiff. Rather than making a determination about the egregiousness of the service, however, the court noted that the evidence submitted had been about the drivers' failure to check lifts, not maintain them. While these two cases had different outcomes, both were consistent with the leading case in transportation and disability, which holds that a transit agreement violates the ADA through consistently inadequate service.

The question that Kriegel kept raising about curb cuts or ramps has been addressed by one federal court. At issue was whether the city of Philadelphia had an obligation to provide curb cuts when it resurfaced a street. Did resurfacing constitute an "alteration" within the scope of the regulation? The district court held that it does and ordered the city to install curb ramps on the portions of city streets that it was resurfacing.[24] The court recognized what Kriegel described as a very perilous choice of either traveling on the streets or getting stuck on the sidewalks.

Some federal courts have ruled on whether a person with a disability can compel a city to provide a paratransit system that is almost as effective as the mass transit system. People have sued because paratransit systems do not offer on-time service and because they miss trips.[25] Some suits have also been filed to make drivers more sensitive and responsive to the needs of persons with disabilities.[26]

Finally, the federal courts have ruled about damages. If public transit systems fall short of the ADA, the federal courts have concluded that no damages can be awarded unless discriminatory intent has been found. A mass transit system must have planned on keeping disabled people out before it is held accountable. This emphasis on intent effectively undermines the provisions. The legislators who drafted the ADA had explicitly stipulated that no plaintiff need prove intent for the transit system to be held liable. Creating an inaccessible transit system, whether the officials had purposefully designed it this way or not, is discriminatory. Understanding the intent behind the design, in other words, should be irrelevant.

[ ] PUBLIC TRANSIT IN PERIL

While new suits and the suits described above will continue to shape the ADA's scope, the biggest problem facing persons with disabilities is that public transit itself is in peril, and the mass transit sections of the statute provide only that disabled people be treated like everyone else. As the pub-

lic transit system becomes weaker, it affects disabled people disproportionately since they rely on it more than those without disabilities.

In 1900, most people in urban areas could get somewhere by streetcar,
whereas now mass transit is available to little more than half of the people
in the nation.[27] In 1921, the federal government began to support highway
building by enacting the Federal Road Act. By the 1960s, it also started sub-
sidizing public transit. The car, however, had already won the battle. By the
1990s, the public transit system had shrunk 37 percent in terms of mileage.
It is not that state and local governments have made up the difference.
Mass transit only accounts for 2 percent of public spending.[28]

Rather than citing a shift in priorities away from public transit, some
mass transit officials have actually blamed the disability rights movement
by suggesting that the ADA's mandates account for their financial woes. A
survey by the American Public Transit Association revealed that 31 percent
of transit systems reduced service, increased fares, or laid off employees to
meet the costs of ADA compliance, and 29 percent considered doing so.
This survey was conducted during the 1990s, when Michael Lewyn, a law
professor, shows that "federal support was cut nearly in half." As he
explains it, the ADA has "essentially pitted disabled riders against other
passengers."[29] Yet, with studies showing that in all but a few cities it is
cheaper to make transportation systems accessible than to operate paratransit systems, the American Public Transit Association figures seem
grossly inflated.[30] As Jo Davis, the cofounder of the Access Now Coalition
in Boston describes, "Persons with disabilities [are] being used as scape-
goats. Some writers, for instance, blame the ADA for rising subway fares,
neglecting to mention the role of draconian cuts in federal aid to mass
transit."[31]

Just as Kriegel's essay points out the frustration of the bureaucrats
themselves, the problems of mass transit reflect the larger problems of
society in general. And again, the resolution of the larger problem
redounds on the persons with disabilities themselves. Should they go private or continue to battle the public? Mass transit officials would say it is
these few individuals who spoil the system, and Hockenberry and Kriegel
would retort that the burden should not be placed solely upon them. No
matter whom should receive the blame, without mass transit, persons
with disabilities cannot fully participate in society. Although there is little

more basic than being able to leave your home, should the burden fall on the state and society or on individuals like Hockenberry and Kriegel? Even if the state used the full vigor of the ADA to enforce disability rights, would this assure that all or even most taxi drivers would stop and pick up either Hockenberry or Kriegel? Is it the attitudinal or the environmental barriers that are the most difficult to remove in American society?

THE PERILS OF GETTING A DRIVER'S LICENSE

[11] by Joan Tollifson

I've been putting off going to the DMV to exchange my California license for an Illinois one. I grew up in Illinois, and when I got my first license here, they slapped all kinds of restrictions on me because I'm missing one hand. I had to have a spinner knob on the steering wheel and could only drive a car that had an automatic transmission and power steering. I hated that spinner knob, which got in my way. Together with my parents, we finally succeeded in getting the DMV in Illinois to drop that restriction, but the others they kept.

When I was twenty-two, I moved to California, where they eliminated all the restrictions on my license without my even asking. Before long, I was driving a stick shift without power steering. I drove a truck. I've been driving now for almost four decades, and I consider myself an excellent and safe driver. I've never had an accident.

When I was in my forties, I lived and worked for five years at a retreat center in rural New York state. The retreat center required everyone on the staff to take a driving lesson with a local driving teacher because, as part of our job, we had to ferry retreat participants back and forth from the airport in the center's van, and for liability purposes, the center had decided it would be good to require a driving lesson. I dreaded going, because after my experience in Illinois, I was leery of what might happen. I had avoided getting a New York driver's license, fearing that the state might put restrictions on me, and this was going to bring the whole issue to a head.

Reluctantly, I went.

I parked the van on the street where the driving teacher lived, got out, and walked toward his house, where he met me on the sidewalk. He was an older man who took one look at me and said, "Oh! You have one arm. Do you have a spinner knob on the steering wheel?" I said no. I explained that I had one back in Illinois when I first learned to drive, and I found that it was not useful and actually got in my way. I even felt it was a safety hazard. I told him that Illinois had dropped the restriction, and that California never put any restrictions on me. I told him that I had been driving safely for thirty years.

"Well," said he, "you need a spinner knob. I used to teach the handicapped to drive, and I know what you need. You'd drive better with that knob." This was before we even got into the van.

Before I could turn on the ignition, he had written out his report, recommending a spinner knob. This "expert on the handicapped" with two hands was going to tell me how I should drive, discounting my thirty years of actual experience, without even bothering to check it out by seeing how I drive!

I felt powerless in the face of the injustice. I felt humiliated, stripped of the image of myself as a competent and skillful driver. I felt discounted, not heard, not understood, not respected, not taken seriously. I imagined what it would be like if the center where I worked was forced to attach a spinner knob to the wheel of the van because of me. I imagined myself picking up passengers and having to hear their comments about what a wonderful device the knob was and how amazing it is what the handicapped can do. I'd be endlessly tempted to offer bitter sarcastic retorts, while feeling inwardly enraged and humiliated. And surely the other staff drivers would resent the steering wheel being messed up by my "special equipment."

My own car at that time was a Toyota Corolla—with a stick shift and no power steering. What if the state of New York told me I couldn't drive my own car?

The situation triggered some of my deepest, oldest, most volatile feelings. I was afraid, I was angry, and if it hadn't been for the wonders and insights of meditation, I would have been in a tailspin of anxiety, rage, and depression, feeling hopeless and defeated by life.

None of that happened, but there was still an underlying worry and upset.

Fortunately, a call to the DMV the next day established that such a knob would not by any means be automatically or usually required in my situation. The department said that I would most likely be given an unrestricted license, the same as I had from California. Furthermore, I figured out that I could reasonably claim that I was in a training program and thus avoid having to even apply for a New York license. I was spared. I was able to operate the center's van without restrictions and to continue driving my own car.

But I was aware that it could have gone differently. If the driving teacher, or someone with his mentality, had been working at the DMV, it could have been a whole other story. I went through weeks of low-level anxiety, worry, and stress that no one else on the staff had to go through, one of the side effects of living with a disability in a world where nondisabled individuals and bureaucracies often have the power to determine our fate. The thought of applying for a new driver's license has appeared a number of times in my mind as a reason not to move to another state.

This year, I moved back to Illinois to be closer to my mother, who is now in her nineties, and the law says I am supposed to exchange my California license for an Illinois one. For most people, this is a simple, routine procedure. You fill out a form, take the written test, turn in your old license, pay the fee, and they give you a new license. But for me, depending on the person who happens to be at the window when I get there, I might be subjected to a road test and possibly to a whole new set of restrictions on my license.

I put it off for months. Once again, I felt dread and anxiety. I felt powerless in the face of bureaucracy, like someone trapped in a Kafka novel with no way out. This time, I had no excuse, no choice. I had to do it. Finally, I bit the bullet.

I stood in line for five hours at the DMV. As the line inched slowly toward the counter, hour by hour, we all observed that there was one particular civil servant who was giving almost everyone a hard time and doing it loudly enough so that the whole line could hear. We all prayed that we wouldn't get him.

At the exact moment that I reached the front of the line, the man who was giving everyone a hard time went on his lunch break. Another man with a sweet smile waved me forward. I was filled with relief, although I couldn't totally relax yet. This was the critical moment, the moment I had dreaded and avoided and postponed for so long.

We began the paperwork, the routine questions. He definitely saw my arm (the one without a hand), because I had it on the counter several times, holding down papers I signed while he watched. Finally, he asked: Do I have diabetes? No. Am I epileptic? No. Do I have any disability that might impair my ability to safely operate a motor vehicle? No. It was a perfectly honest answer. I don't. And, it's what the officer in California who road tested me told me to say. So I said it. The man behind the counter smiled sweetly. I was sent on to the cashier.

I paid my fee, I passed the written test, I was photographed. And finally, they handed it to me: an unrestricted Illinois driver's license. Happy and relieved, I headed home.

What if I had gotten the guy who hassled people? Would he have hassled me? What if I had gotten someone like that small-town driving teacher in New York? What if I had naively answered "yes" to the question about having a disability that might interfere with safe driving, and that "yes" had been punched into the computer and the official bureaucracies of the state had stepped in to decide my fate? It seems upon reflection that my good outcome was a somewhat fragile and lucky affair. It could have gone differently, and if it had, I'd likely be in a protracted battle with the machinery of the state. Anyone who has done such battle knows how time-consuming and how wearing it can be.

I don't want people who can't safely drive a car to be out there on the road driving. If I felt it was unsafe for me to drive, I wouldn't want to drive. My mother voluntarily turned in her driver's license when she turned eighty. Of course, I realize that some people don't operate that way. Some people, for a variety of reasons, will continue to drive even if it isn't safe. Hence the need for regulations. I understand and support that.

But the place where it can go astray is when people without disabilities are deciding what people who have disabilities can and cannot do. When we imagine what it would be like not to have a right hand, or when we try to function for a day without using our right hand, this does not tell us at all what it is like to actually be without a right hand for many years and to have the full use of a right arm. No one can accurately imagine this without experiencing it. What we imagine is usually much worse and much more limited than the actuality. Quadriplegics can and do drive, although that might come as a surprise to many.

So, this story has a happy ending. But as I answered the questions at the counter, I thought of my friends who have epilepsy (and who drive). I thought of my friends who are diabetic (and who drive). I thought of those folks with disabilities who are not white, articulate, college-educated Americans (as I am), who face double or triple jeopardy at the counter. I thought of those people with disabilities who are going through this stress without the benefits of meditation and familiarity with disability rights and supportive friends, and perhaps with the added stresses of poverty and having children to care for. I thought of those folks with disabilities who live in small towns and rural areas, where things are perhaps not as advanced as they are in bigger cities, where they are maybe more likely to find that driving teacher of mine behind the counter.

For many years, I've lived with the fear that changing my residence to another state might mean a restricted driver's license. Today, that fear has lessened considerably. But it is not completely gone. After having an unrestricted license now from two states and after forty years of safe driving experience, my chances of being hassled are ever-declining. But it is always a possibility that next time around I will meet someone like that driving teacher behind the counter and that the machinery of the state will grind out some less favorable outcome.

PROBING ACCOMMODATIONS

Testing, Testing, and Retesting the (Dis)abled

Tollifson's story about her trip to the Department of Motor Vehicles (DMV) in Illinois leaves the reader with questions about testing. These questions do not involve disputing the DMV's role in testing, however. The federal, state, and local governments must set standards for people safely to operate all types of equipment and to conduct a myriad of services without endangering anyone relying on these services. Rather, the issue underlying the debate about testing in disability studies and in Tollifson's story centers on *whom* should conduct the test? Should it be an expert? If so, what type of expert? Does distinguishing between experts mean, moreover, that no conflict of interest will result? Should the person undergoing the test—the person with a disability—have any role in the process?

[ ] DIAGNOSING DISABILITY OR DISABLING DIAGNOSES

From World War I until the 1970s, the medical model of a disability reigned in the United States and other industrialized nations.[1] This model gave physicians the discretion to diagnosis a chronic illness or a permanent injury.[2] A medical model locates the source of disability in the individual's deficiency.[3]

The medical model evaluated by students of disability studies was not restricted to doctors, however. Initially, it involved physicians who made breakthroughs in treating chronic illnesses and injuries, which in the words of one historian later developed into a whole rehabilitation empire in the United States.[4] "When care calls itself therapy," Henri-Jacques Stiker wrote, "the doctor is already more than a doctor."[5] To him, the "medical view of the disabled evolved as more paternalistic than clinical."[6]

In the United States, the role of physicians expanded as did those of the professions that worked closely with medicine, such as physical therapy, occupational therapy, vocational rehabilitation counseling, psychology, and social work. Persons with disabilities came under more and more scrutiny by the different "caring" professions. As Abberley explicates, "The problem comes when they determine not only the form of treatment (if treatment is appropriate), but also the form of life for the person who happens to be disabled."[7]

Beginning in the mid-1960s, disability rights activists insisted that they no longer be seen as "non-people with non-abilities."[8] The first struggle the disability rights movement undertook was with the rehabilitation experts. In the mid-1970s, the movement successfully confronted the cult of experts in public education when the Education for All Handicapped Children Act passed.[9] This legislation gave students individualized educational programs, which the parents, sometimes the students themselves, and teachers devised together.[10] Educational experts no longer dictated what students needed. The parents of the students and sometimes the students themselves had a role in the process.

One of the disability rights movement's legacies then was the functional definition of disability, which takes into account the individuality of the person in question. The federal regulations under section 504 of the Rehabilitation Act and the Americans with Disabilities Act do not recognize someone as disabled on the basis of a medical diagnosis. People are defined by what they can and cannot do, not by what impairment or disease they have.[11]

The problem that Tollifson faces with the functional model, which is based on what she can and cannot do, is that testing is essential. When it is unclear whether or not her disability rises to the level of being an impairment that substantially limits the major activities in her life, an individualized assessment of Tollifson's functionality is necessary. For her, testing evokes all sorts of fears. Having taken the driving test before, Tollifson realizes that she faces an official who wields tremendous power over her daily life. The official DMV tester could deprive her of a driver's license even though she has no record of violating public safety.

Alternatively, this tester could impose some restrictions that she believes would not enhance her ability to drive. Judging for herself, Tollifson realizes that she drives better without a spinner knob on the steering wheel. This knob, moreover, potentially stigmatizes her, as she feared when she shared the driving at a retreat. It underscores what makes her "different" from the others and might well impede those who share driving duties with her. While no one expresses this concern, Tollifson feels compromised by just having this piece of equipment on the steering wheel.

Tollifson's fear also stems from her realization that the official tester making the decision might let his own bias or personal prejudice against persons with disabilities interfere with his judgment. Will the DMV official follow his instructions about how to apply the ADA, she wonders? What type of instruction did he receive about the ADA? Were his supervisors conscientious about educating their staff about whether to and how to conduct tests under the ADA? Or, will the official rely on a visceral reaction to her impairment? Years earlier, a thoughtful official gave Tollifson some invaluable advice about what to say to the tester at the counter, which gave her a better understanding of the logic underlying the process.

Finally, Tollifson knows that whenever a bureaucrat gives some person with a disability a hard time, all those watching realize that it would be easiest if they just hid their impairments, rather than disclose them. While Tollifson cannot hide the fact that she is missing a hand, she knows that other people with invisible impairments might hide them as a means of avoiding what could turn into a demeaning process.

[ ] TESTING TEST CASES

To date, no Supreme Court case has tested the local and state government-service provisions that address testing. A number of cases, however, have been brought before the lower federal courts about the driving test, establishing a small body of law. The primary question in these cases involves whether the DMV can make the driving test mandatory for persons with disabilities. The lead case included a plaintiff, Theriault, with cerebral palsy, who had been awarded a license eight years earlier and had to take the driving test again. Theriault protested, arguing that his visible impairment was what made the DMV officials single him out for the test, whereas people with invisible ones were not compelled to take the test. It was "demeaning," he explained, "to be asked repeatedly to prove his ability to drive."[12]

Under Title II of the ADA, the DMV is forbidden from "administering a license or certification program in a manner that subjects qualified individuals with disabilities to discriminate on the basis of disability."[13] This is not to say that federal, state, and local governments lack the authority to determine "essential eligibility requirements" or if someone with a disability poses a threat to the health and safety of others.[14] The federal courts have had no difficulty accepting that the ability to safely control a car is an essential eligibility requirement.[15]

In *Theriault*, the federal court argued that the plaintiff had not been denied meaningful access to a governmental benefit or program since the New Hampshire DMV did not foreclose people with cerebral palsy from driving. There was no evidence, in other words, that Theriault had been singled out because he had this condition. Rather, the DMV officials expressed concern about the symptoms of the condition—that he had limited use of his hands. Then, the federal court suggested that it was relying on Supreme Court precedents on individualized assessment.[16] This is "not only permissible but also the state's obligation in balancing the rights of people with disabilities with the responsibility to ensure safety on the roads." The standard for the court was about what is "objectively appropriate."[17]

Challenging the court's ruling that this did not constitute discrimination, one concurring judge stated that it did, but that this discrimination was permissible. This distinction, the concurring judge argued, was vital because it meant that instead of imposing the burden on Theriault, it would be placed on the government. The New Hampshire DMV had to prove that the discrimination was necessary for another reason, which in this case was public safety. The burden would fall on all local, state, and federal governments, rather than on Theriault, to justify all discriminatory actions.

[ ] WHO ARE THE EXPERTS?

Tests are a vital aspect of assessing someone's (dis)ability. This does not resolve the question of whom should conduct the tests. Tollifson herself expressed her concerns about whom is qualified to give a test. The disability rights community, however, has been divided over the larger issue of testing and legal experts. On the one hand, the movement came into its own disputing the role that both testers and legal experts played in the rehabilitation process. On the other hand, it has relied on experts in and out of the courtroom to lessen concerns about public health and safety issues.

What role legal experts should play in helping determine disability rights first occurred in the *Davis* decision, when the Supreme Court upheld a community college's rejection of a student who had a congenital hearing impairment. Already a nurse, Davis sought more education so that she could become a state-certified nurse.[18] Writing for the majority, Justice Lewis F. Powell deferred to experts and the institution to determine public safety.[19] He ruled that they should take into account not only experts the college had hired from Duke University Medical Center, but also its own nursing staff. Powell expressed no concerns about a potential conflict of interest. It was the college that would have to pay for Davis's accommodations. Meanwhile, no experts had been appointed by, or for, Davis herself to contest their opinion.[20] Unable to present her own defense, Davis considered herself trapped within the medical model.

While the *Davis* decision disappointed most disability rights activists, they used legal experts themselves to demonstrate that a risk is not a *real* risk in two other Supreme Court decisions that involved people with contagious diseases.[21] Dropping their critique of professionalism, these activists suggested that the disability rights law should rely on scientific data and analysis as a means of curbing the bias, prejudice, and negative stereotyping that persons with disabilities encounter.[22] As Samuel Bagenstos, a Harvard law professor, described the rationale behind this position, "Disability rights law does nothing more than replace irrationality with rationality, prejudice with science. Who could be against that?" But as Bagenstos elaborates, this position conflicts with the disability rights activists' earlier position, which contested the legitimacy of science and medicine.[23]

To Bagenstos, the best means of reconciling this conflict involves examining what *type* of expert should be used. Generally, experts are associated with technocratic approaches that uphold a conservative public policy agenda. Conservative Republicans and many members of the business community, for instance, rely on the idea of risk aversion. That is, they use mathematical equations like the "risk per averted death" to scale back many business regulations, especially those involving environmental and worker-safety concerns. The proponents of this approach then maintain that the equation, not a value judgment, determines whether the federal government should adopt a regulation.

Adopting a technocratic approach to disability rights, Bagenstos argues, may have helped in the decisions about contagious illness, but it will not always serve the interests of disabled people. What he suggests is that the disability rights activists reject the technocratic approach and adopt a "democratic" approach to experts. This approach would not dismiss the utility of expert opinions altogether. Instead, it would give deference to public health officials, who differ greatly from technocratic experts.

Public health officials, having received training in epidemiology, serve the public at large rather than one specific industry. Concerned with the probabilistic nature of risks and harms, public health experts collect a vast amount of information from a huge array of sources. They weigh the society-wide costs of proposed courses of action against the society-wide benefits.[24]

By contrast, experts found within industry-specific regulatory agencies, like the Federal Communications Commission (FCC), are less likely to advance the public good. Indeed, a large body of literature on "capture theory" has long shown that the industry-specific regulatory agencies respond more to the concerns of their specific constituencies, whether they are businesses or organized labor, than the public interest. A high-level public official noted that the Occupational Safety and Health Agency (OSHA), for instance, did more harm than good to persons with disabilities by allowing employers to prevent people with tuberculosis from working. The employers created more stringent standards than the federal courts would have in a disability rights decision.[25]

The fundamental difference between public health and industry-specific experts, Bagenstos argues, stems from the fact that the former recognize the moral and political nature of their decisions, whereas the latter do not. Public health officials place the evidence they collect in a political context.[26] Citing the work of two well-known progressive law professors, Cass Sunstein and Richard Pildes, he suggests that the process about qualifications must be examined.[27] The "direct threat doctrine" used under the ADA, for instance, differs greatly from the "bona fide occupational qualification" test conducted by OSHA. While the direct threat doctrine prohibits employers from making categorical judgments about safety issues, the bona fide occupational qualification doctrine gives experts that right.

Bagenstos examined the Supreme Court's position on the role that testers played in weighing regulations and public safety in the 1999 *Albertson's* decision.[28] Truck driver Hallie Kirkingburg had been terminated once the grocery store Albertson's discovered that he had monocular vision. A unanimous Supreme Court had declared that this truck driver was not qualified for the position since he had failed to pass the vision test given by the Department of Transportation. When Kirkingburg found out that a waiver existed that would have exempted him from this test, he had asked Albertson's if he could return to work. Albertson's, however, refused to rehire him, and the question before the Court was whether Albertson's should rehire Kirkingburg.[29] Was Albertson's obliged to accept the waiver?

Justice David Souter and his eight colleagues decided that Albertson's was not so obliged. The federal government could not require employers to follow every change in standards, particularly since the Department of Transportation had granted this waiver as part of an "experiment to provide data."[30] The Court's decision showed that corporations could hide behind those industry-specific or subject-specific agencies, which do not weigh the public interest as a whole.[31]

[ ] PARTIAL OR IMPARTIAL TESTERS AND EXPERTS

With the functional definition of a disability, testing has become a great part of practicing disability rights law.[32] On the one hand, testing reflects the nonmedical model. On the other hand, judges interpreting these suits have put persons with disabilities in the same type of Catch-22 position that those interpreting the employment provisions face. If you have no disability, then you cannot be accommodated. Yet, without an accommodation, you may fail a qualifying exam. It is the process—not the medical versus the functional model—that should now be examined. It should also be noted that the federal government does not have a consistent view of legal experts or testers. Who instructs someone about how to conduct a test and who conducts a test or renders a legal opinion helps shape public policy. How physicians work under the workers' compensation programs represents one example.

Under this program, physicians take on the role of legal experts and are treated like lawyers in an adversarial system rather than as impartial testers or experts. Each side—the worker and the employer—receives a doctor. Since this leads to corrupt doctors, who do not even bother to create a facade of professionalism, workers' compensation recognizes the discrepancy in expert determination. It gives both the injured worker and the employer the chance to have input into who will offer an expert opinion. This scheme recognizes that employers and injured workers are entangled in an antagonistic relationship, and it attempts to provide an impartial expert by allowing each side to help choose one.

It is unclear what would work best for persons with disabilities. If Tollifson's official tester had not given her a license, should she have gone straight to court with legal experts who would fight for her, as is the case with workers' compensation? Or should she have questioned how the DMV instructed its staff about the ADA? Should a new system of judging the testers and the legal experts be put in place were the ADA to be amended? Or should persons with disabilities have confidence that the state officials do a thorough job of training their staffs about how to test them?

SOVEREIGNTY

[13] by Jean Stewart

First off, I should tell you that Zoe's heart is fine. There's a bunch of other things that are *not* fine, not one bit fine, but Zoe's heart is not on that list. She sailed through both surgeries, the long-ago one and now this recent one, and it seems like now her heart is stronger than ever.

I tell you this up front so you won't pester me—"Forget about all that, what about *her heart*?"—while I'm trying to tell you about this other stuff. I mean, I'm the president of her fan club, so don't go thinking I played my violin while Rome was in flames.

The point is, so many things can go wrong if your daughter has heart trouble and is deaf. For one thing, you'll probably spend some time in ERs, hearts being the incorrigible organs they are, refusing to time their acting-out episodes to coincide with regularly scheduled doctors' appointments. Which means you'll spend some time interpreting, until a certified interpreter arrives.

And things get messy real fast when you're interpreting for your daughter. Like the minute they ask, "How long has your daughter been having chest pain?"

That's always their first question. You'd think these doctors would direct their questions to the owner of said chest—she's forty-eight years old and smarter than me by far; wouldn't you think that would count for something?—but no, they always ask me: your daughter this, your daughter that. Doctors and nurses seem to assume that since I'm the one who's talking, the heart must therefore somehow be *mine.*

You might think this benign, like a mechanic asking you, "So how long has your gas tank been leaking?" instead of asking the car. But it irks Zoe, who feels like an eavesdropper (she calls it "eyedropper") on someone else's conversation. It's not an issue when I'm her interpreter, since I tend to edit and interpret the question as if it were asked directly, so she's unaware of the insult. Professional interpreters—the really meticulous ones—interpret the question exactly as it's asked, but I'm no pro and don't have time for niceties like the code of ethics; it's all I can do to keep up with the speaker.

Zoe being Zoe, she rarely responds with a specific number of months, weeks, or hours, which would constitute one correct answer. On October 4, 2000, her answer is, "Well, it's been creeping up on me; it didn't just happen overnight. It's been incremental."

Maybe it's "incremental" that throws this doctor. Maybe he assumes a gold-plated word like that can't possibly issue from Zoe's brain. I can see him looking her over. My daughter's not gold-plated, mind you, her bones stick out, she slumps her shoulders, her socks smell. Used tinfoil, more likely, though her dark eyes, like her hands, crackle with life. You can see the doctor thinking: Yeah, right. Women like that, *who can't even talk,* don't use words like *incremental.*

Actually I'm pleased to report that it's exactly the right word for the particular combination of signs she used: *over-the-course-of-time slow pop-up-intermittently worse-worse-worse.* Anyway, as I relay the query to Zoe and then wait for her reply, my eyes already have annoyance in them.

It's not a great idea to have annoyance in your eyes when you're interpreting, unless the person whose message you're conveying is annoyed.

People think it's just a matter of flailing hands, as if facial expression were an interesting but ultimately distracting optional extra. Let *them* try interpreting for Zoe in an ER. Luckily for both of us, she accommodates me as she struggles to make sense of what I sign, knowing that in ERs I'm usually upset and worried, especially before the interpreter arrives.

Probably she accommodates me too much. She sees the stress and misery in my face and feels bad, feels herself to be the cause of it, wants it to go away, and so pretends, sometimes, to understand when in fact—owing to my inadequate skills—she doesn't. She of course remembers what I went through with her dad, especially toward the end. Hearts that fail are not new to me. It pains Zoe to subject me to the same wringer that Hank's heart put me through. So, sometimes, she lets comprehension slide, which is perhaps OK when the subject under discussion is the weather and the speaker is Zoe's friend at the greenhouse. It's not OK when the subject is Zoe's heart and the speaker is a doctor who's charged with figuring out what's wrong with her heart and fixing it before it kills her.

The doctor briefly ponders *incremental* and then tries a different tack: "When did your daughter first start experiencing shortness of breath?"

Zoe shakes her head. "I don't have shortness of breath."

The doctor, whose name badge says "Dr. Atwood" but who did not introduce himself when he entered the curtain area, barely pauses. He's in a hurry, has other patients to see. "OK, let's start over. Why doesn't she describe her symptoms to me and tell me when they started."

Zoe, whose symptoms have subsided now, slips into storytelling mode. "It felt like"—her hands gently wring an invisible sponge in the area of her heart—"like squeezing. I noticed it this morning when I reached down to lift something. I was transplanting my mother's potted fig tree, and I got hold of it by the trunk and started to lift, and it was kinda heavy, and all of a sudden, I felt this squeezing. Ever transplant a fig tree?"

"So, when did it start, this squeezing sensation?"

Zoe concentrates. "I think it was about 9:30 this morning." She pauses, glancing into his face, and adds: "Real figs!"

"Excuse me?"

"It produces real figs. It's not the ornamental Ficus, it's got real edible figs! Ever eat a fig fresh off the tree?"

Nonplused, Dr. Atwood is briefly silent, his little mouth bending into a pucker of acknowledgment. "Can she tell me when was the first time she felt this sensation?"

It occurs to me to wonder: how come Zoe has the grace to address him directly in the second-person pronoun, but the guy—who has a whole lot more education—can't accord her the same courtesy? I feel like the kid who's forced to play shuttle diplomat between warring parents: "Tell your mother if she wants the car repaired, she's going to have to take it to the shop herself. I'm not doing it." "Remind your father that it's *his* car and he can go to hell." Except that in this case only one of the parents is at war; the other responds sweetly: "OK, I'll take your car in, no problem." There's no reciprocity, no balance.

Stifling an urge to supply the reciprocity myself, to fill in the disrespect that's missing from Zoe's half of the dialogue, I try to convince myself that at least this time, the parent who's exhibiting warlike behavior doesn't know he's doing it; isn't that a mitigating circumstance? Wouldn't it be worse if his rudeness were intentional?

"Um, look," I say, stepping out of the role I've been assigned, trying to flatten the edge in my voice. "Her symptoms have subsided. Why don't we just wait for the professional interpreter to arrive before we go any further?"

"Professional interpreter?" Dr. Atwood snips his words. Zoe's eyes are fixed on me.

"The admitting nurse said she'd call an interpreter." I check my watch. "That was half an hour ago. I don't think we'd have very long to wait. You could go tend to other patients 'til —"

"*You're* the interpreter," Dr. Atwood crows. "Why do we need anyone else? You're doing great," he adds, apparently thinking I'm in the grip of a confidence crisis.

"Thank you, but I'm not."

"You're not—"

"I'm not an interpreter, and I'm not doing great. Anyway, how would *you* know?" I hiss.

"I know because she's answering my questions appropriately." Dr. Atwood looks smug, a man who's just played his trump card. He's impeccably groomed, middle-aged, receding hairline. Nondescript, except for his eyes, which I study briefly. I have this habit of holding up a sheet of mental cardboard in front of people's faces, blocking out the nose, mouth, and cheeks, so that whatever is contained in the eyes will swim into the foreground. Or sometimes I hold my imaginary cardboard vertically, bisecting the face along the length of the nose, looking first at one side of the face and then the other, to see what contradictory messages might be contained in the two halves of eyes and lips. But Dr. Atwood doesn't hold still long enough for me to wield my cardboard, though I do glimpse something in his eyes and scribble in my mental notebook, *feral*, thinking to ponder it later.

"Dr. Atwood, interpreting for a family member in an ER is a very bad idea. What if her symptoms were to get worse? It's happened to us, more than once."

"If her symptoms were to get worse, I'd feel safer with you as her interpreter than with a *professional*," he declares, his lip curling at the word, as if he himself were a hobbyist. "After all, she's your daughter. You know what she *means*. Even if her sign language got a little shaky because of pain or stress, you'd know what she was *trying* to say."

"Not necessarily!"

The vacancy in Dr. Atwood's stare is inauspicious. "Look," I say, feeling suddenly sorry for him, a man alone in a foreign country. "You can't rely on me. I'm *family*. I might make an assumption about what I think she's signing, based on my *vast knowledge* of Zoe"—I can't help returning his sneer—"and I might be *wrong*. I might be *seriously wrong*."

I'm gathering steam. "Besides, aren't you forgetting something?" Dr. Atwood glares and waits. Offense sits in his dark little eyes; he looks appalled to find himself thus challenged. "Aren't you forgetting the other half of the equation? I mean, yes, of course it's important for you to understand what she's saying. But Zoe's gotta understand you too!"

At this Zoe explodes: "Right! Right!"

"I mean, maybe that doesn't matter to some patients, maybe they just want you to cut to the chase, fix what's wrong, so they can get out of here. . . . But that's not Zoe. She wants to know what you think is wrong, and she wants to know WHY. And I'm no good at that. Interpreters go through lots of advanced training to prepare for these situations—"

"She's not an interpreter!" Zoe bursts in, to my relief. "She's never been trained! She doesn't know medical terminology." She signs *medical big-words*. "She gets upset! She's worried and scared about my heart.... It's not fair that she should have to interpret when she's so worried and scared."

Thank you, Zoe, thank you. "The point is, worry and fear affect my judgment. When I'm scared and upset, I can't trust my perceptions. My clarity is shot to hell. What if I make a mistake? Hearts are—" I grope for words. "Hearts are hearts! I mean, there isn't a whole lot of room for error, is there?"

"Anybody can make a mistake," Dr. Atwood fires back. "Doctors make them!" I suppress a giggle at his delivery of these words. *We're really no different from you, we're just flawed human beings!* "I'm sure *professional* interpreters make them too!"

Zoe speaks up again. "I have a right to an American Sign Language interpreter." Her signs are quiet and formal. "The ADA says so."

"Fine!" Atwood snaps. "I've got other people to attend to. Let me know when you're ready to continue. This is a waste of my time." He rises from his chair, facing me. "Be glad her symptoms have subsided, otherwise she might be dead by now, while you quibble about *linguistics!*"

He strides out of the examining area, pausing at the nurses' station to order an EKG for Zoe. Lucky thing the curtain's not a door, I think; the whole building would have shuddered when he slammed it.

Zoe remains seated on the end of the examining table. I've done my best to interpret the entire exchange, though the more my bile rises, the more my ASL falls apart. "Cheap bastard," Zoe says, shaking her head. "It's all about money!"

I shift in the uncomfortable chair. The exam area feels suddenly confining; I pull back the curtain, as if flinging a window wide. "I don't know," I say. "Yeah, he wants to save a lousy buck, but even if interpreters were free, he just doesn't get it. He sees us talking together, and my sign looks fluent to him."

Zoe frowns. "Same old thing," she says, rolling her eyes. (Her sign is *same same same*, a circular motion perfectly suited to its meaning.) "Next time we go to an ER or a doctor's office, we should both just sit on our hands until the interpreter arrives." She peers down at the appendages in question.

I love Zoe's hands. They're never still. When she fingerspells, they have snap, authority; and when she signs, they have all the qualities I associate with music: phrasing, intonation, rhythm, melody, harmony, improvisation. Clearly, they love language; they are not shy.

"Asshole," Zoe signs.

We smile, shaking our heads. Zoe looks around at the curtain, the medical equipment, the nurses and technicians and doctors bustling past. I look at Zoe. "How do you feel?"

"Fine," she laughs. "Normal. Wanna go home?"

"We can't!" I wail, and then, echoing Zoe's sign: "Asshole!"

Reader, maybe all this sounds like a caper to you. I mean, we're laughing, we won the argument with Dr. Atwood. What's the big deal?

Since we're sitting here in the exam area with not much to do, waiting for the interpreter to arrive, let me take a moment to tell you about the Big Deal. I might have to stop abruptly, depending, as they say, on developments.

There was another time, another emergency room. Eleven years ago, Zoe's heart gave out for the first time. In case you're thinking she was grieving for her dad, this was sixteen years after his death. Zoe's husband had just left her (she wasn't grieving for him either), so Zoe decided to sell her house and move back home with me, which we both considered a brilliant idea. She'd just been promoted to manager of the greenhouse where she worked, so for once we were flush, though she didn't really want the new job. She said that desk jobs freeze the brain; she much preferred burying her hands in warm soil, which she said smells much better than computers. But the paychecks were bigger, which helped with her daughter's college tuition. Anyway, I rushed her to the local ER, and they in turn rushed her to a hospital upstate, where she was pronounced to have a 90–95 percent occlusion of the coronary artery. The doctors recommended immediate angioplasty. "OK," said Zoe, "go ahead and do it. But don't forget that I need an interpreter."

We'd started asking for interpreters the moment we'd arrived in the first ER. None was forthcoming, but since Zoe was being transferred to a different hospital, we held our tongues, so to speak, and prayed that St. Joseph's would accommodate her. When we arrived in Albany, she again requested an interpreter. "We'll try," they said with elaborate tolerance, as if she'd just demanded a mocha latte, or whatever the equivalent would have been in 1989.

Unfortunately, Zoe's heart chose a bad historical epoch in which to give out. The Americans with Disabilities Act did not yet exist, and its predecessor, a gutsy piece of legislation with good intentions and an inferiority complex, was routinely ignored by nearly everyone. Disability agencies would periodically issue earnest pamphlets with titles like "Know Your Rights: Deaf People and Section 504 of the Rehabilitation Act of 1973," explaining that deaf people had the right to an interpreter if the situation involved a hospital or institution which received federal funds. But since no one seemed to know about 504, its mandates weren't taken very seriously. Interpreters were scarce, and calls for them scarcer still.

"*We'll try*," said the good nurses of St. Joe's, but when the hour arrived and a terrified Zoe was being wheeled down the corridors toward the OR, no interpreter was at her side. Only her mom was there, along with a gaggle of technicians, orderlies, and nurses, one of whom observed that since said mom seemed to know sign language perfectly well, what was the problem?

And so I was pressed into service, interpreting for my daughter's heart surgery. If Hank had been there, he could have done a nimble job of it, being a native signer, the child of deaf parents. But Hank had died of premature heart disease when he was forty-two. His death crackled all around me now like an electric storm.

Did I protest? you ask. I knew our rights, knew the situation was preposterous, fraught with risk, and I knew they'd had ample time to find someone. I'd even given them names and phone numbers. "But she needs the surgery now," the nurses and doctors declared. "The OR is booked. If she cancels this slot, there's no telling when we'll be able to fit her back into the OR schedule. She needs to go now, she can't wait."

"But I told you before!" Zoe exploded. "She's *my mother*. She's not an interpreter! You don't get it, do—"

Oops, storytime's over. A young woman dressed in gray sweatpants and a black windbreaker has just shown up and is standing in front of us in the exam area. She points at Zoe and fingerspells, "Z-O-E T-E-N-B-R-O-K-E?"

"T-E-N-B-R-O-E-C-K," Zoe corrects, extending her hand. "This is my mother. You must be the interpreter!" She beams; her puppylike relief makes the muscle of my heart contract.

A plump hand replies, fingerspelling the name: "I'm M-A-R-G-I-E. I got here as soon as I could. I was out running. . . . Have you been waiting long?"

Zoe and I exchange glances. Shall we give her the short answer or the long one? "A while," I sign. "The doctor wanted to proceed without an interpreter, but we insisted."

"He's an asshole," Zoe supplies, but her eager cheer at Margie's arrival has replaced all anger and frustration.

Margie takes off her windbreaker and drapes it on the back of a chair. "Yeah, they're not uncommon in the medical profession," she smiles. "What's his name? Maybe my agency has dealt with him before."

"A-T-W-O-O-D," Zoe and I chorus. Zoe's fingerspelling has her trademark snappy flair; mine is wearier and charged with contempt.

"A-T-W-O-O-D," Margie repeats. "I'll check with my boss and see if he has a history. So," she gestures, open-handed. "Where is he now?"

Off I go in search of Atwood who, according to a nurse, is seeing another patient. "I'll let him know the interpreter is here," she says. "I'm sure he'll be with you shortly." I glance at my watch (1 p.m.), which prompts her to glance at hers. We smile; I return to curtain area 3, where Zoe and Margie are animatedly conversing about bats.

"Fruit bats!" Zoe is exclaiming. "They were huge." The sign for *huge* is a sort of fish-story gesture; Margie is suitably impressed.

I interrupt to relay the nurse's reassurances, then head toward the waiting room vending machines, leaving Zoe and Margie to their bats. The curtain circumscribing area 2 has been incompletely drawn; as I pass, I glimpse a broad-beamed woman with a long black braid seated beside an examining table on which lies someone very small. . . . The woman's voice trails me down the hall, speaking urgent rapid Spanish. *Hijo*, I pick out of the tumble of words. *Le duele. No se, no se que paso*, followed by a child's voice saying, "She don't know what happened."

Snickers, Hersheys, Fritos. My brain seems stuck elsewhere, snagged on something just out of reach. Distractedly, I rummage in my pockets for coins, push various buttons, pile little packages of peanuts and pretzels in my handbag. Hurrying back down the corridor, a bottle of juice in each hand, I find that Zoe and Margie have moved on from bats to caves.

"Salt, white flour, chemicals. All the major food groups," I announce. Zoe tucks into her peanuts and juice with enthusiasm, her long-fingered hands stopping their conversation to tear open the bag and unscrew the bottle cap. Our curtain is still pulled back, so when a doctor, recognizable as the one I'd just seen with the braided woman and the boy, approaches the nurses' station and says, "Can you page Mercedes? I need her to interpret in 2," we see and hear him clearly.

And now the memory that was stuck when I was studying the contents of the vending machine comes unstuck, shaking itself free: Zoe, lying before me on a table in an OR, fully conscious. The doctors are explaining that they need her to be alert during the "procedure" in order to ask her questions and monitor her responses.

Procedure! I want to snarl. "It's surgery, let's be frank. You're about to operate on my daughter's heart without general anesthesia, and you want me to interpret for her. . . ." But I don't snarl. I grip Zoe's hand, then release it to sign to her: "They can't knock you out because you need to be aware. They're going to ask you some questions—."

"I know," Zoe says, her sign a bit less crisp than usual from the med they've given her to dull anxiety. "You already told me." She's addressing the doctors, but now she turns to me. "Don't worry, I'll be OK."

Now this memory conflates with another, a different room. Zoe is in bed; she hasn't yet been wheeled into the OR. A doctor stands beside her and reads from a form while I, seated on the edge of the bed, am expected to convey to her its content. When the paper is proffered for her signature, we see that it has four paragraphs, which the doctor has just read, very fast. Only long Latinate words seem to be on the form, though two monosyllabic exceptions leap at my eyes: *stroke* and *death*. Zoe, ghastly pale, bony, gapes at the paper, then asks what is meant by *myocardial infarction*. My hands are choking; I can't get the signs out. I try not to read the expression that sits in her eyes.

"Should I do this?" she signs to me. "Maybe I should cancel, maybe the problem will go away on its own. This sounds bad. . . ."

"It's just a routine consent form, honey. . . . The doctors all say this is a very safe procedure. Very high success rate. . . ."

Zoe—fatherless Zoe—of course knows better. Knows terror when she sees it. "If it's so safe, why would they come up with this form? I need more time to think this through. . . ."

"Zoe, your heart is in bad shape" is what I attempt to sign to her. "You may not live without this operation. I don't think we have much choice."

I try to interpret the four paragraphs, but though I do my best, the *medical big-words* are beyond me; what comes out is mostly mush-sign. I see her struggling to comprehend, and then something shifts, something that was in her eyes is no longer there. She's trusting me, I think, panic squirming like a worm inside my brain. Since she can't understand enough to make an informed decision, my middle-aged daughter is leaving it to me. The weight of her trust presses down on my shoulders. It occurs to me that I might vomit in the OR. What then?

Zoe's signature on the release—a precarious wobble—doesn't much resemble the jaunty flourish in which she takes such pride. The doctor leaves the room, and we stare at each other, our hands silent, gripping one another.

Margie pulls me back to the present. "Maybe I should go see what's taking him so long," she suggests. "This is costing them money. . . . I'll be right back." She vanishes, and I find Zoe's eyes. Caught as I've been in webs of memory, expecting to see naked horror, I find instead only the cheerful beneficence for which my daughter is justly famous. "She's cool," she says, her sign for *cool* a little twist of hooked finger on cheek. "She explores caves. She says it's called S-P-L . . . ." She tries to recall the finger-spelling.

"S-P-E-L-U-N-K-I-N-G," I supply.

"Right!" Zoe beams, then examines my face more closely. "Are you OK? You look tired—"

"I'm fine. I was just remembering when you had your surgery before. I sure hope we don't have to go through that again."

"Yeah." Zoe tears open a bag of pretzels. "At least this time, we'd have an interpreter." She chews thoughtfully, signing with her mouth full: "You think I might have to have it done again?" Her sign for angioplasty is a balloon inflating in front of the heart.

"I don't know. The doctors warned us, remember? They said it probably would have to be repeated. That was eleven years ago. Maybe your number's up."

Zoe ponders— "You think they'll want to do it today?" Then she brightens: "Maybe Margie can interpret," referring to her by her sign name—the letter *M* at the chin—which she used to introduce herself.

Head-shake, eyebrow-raise, shoulder-shrug: Who knows?

It occurs to me that, when it comes to the subject of hearts and the medical care delivery system, we seem to spend an awful lot of time head-shaking, eyebrow-raising, shoulder-shrugging. I'm reflecting on this thought when Margie reappears, *sans* Atwood. "He's got an emergency," she says. "He'll come when he can."

Zoe takes this in, puzzled. "I thought *we* were an emergency!" It doesn't make a lot of sense; the man who was too cheap to support the idea of an interpreter is now racking up her bill while he tends to other patients who could presumably be seen by another doctor. Maybe he doesn't know the meter is running.

Margie decides again to find Atwood, to clarify the situation. Of course, if he really is tending to a life-threatening emergency, it seems tacky, perhaps even dangerous, to interrupt with something as banal as a billing matter. She opts to leave word with a nurse, who can convey the information to Atwood at the right moment. The nurse promises to let him know at the first opportunity. "He's not interruptible right now," she explains.

Margie returns to our little encampment, which is by now strewn with backpacks, jackets, handbags, newspapers, peanuts, and pretzels. An hour passes, during which we hear about Margie's brother's house in El Paso, her degree in sociology, her daily exercise routine. A convivial older woman shows up and takes an EKG; when she leaves, I take the opportunity to tell Margie a little about Zoe's heart.

"You interpreted for your daughter's heart surgery??!" She uses one of Zoe's favorites, the *you-can't-be-serious-my-eyeballs-are-popping-out-of-my-head* sign. If she were speaking, her shriek would cause heads at the nurses' station to turn.

"Yeah, well. . . ." Feeling rather stupid, I watch my hands trail into silence. Margie and Zoe wait. "This was pre-ADA, don't forget. Maybe you're too young to remember those bad ol' days."

And so I tell her the story: how they strapped Zoe down in the OR . . . It's crucial that she not move while we're doing the procedure, they explained. . . . Zoe screamed, and I protested: "But you said you wanted to ask her questions, how do you expect her to answer if you strap down her hands?" "Can she speak?" *They want to know if you can speak,* I signed to Zoe. *I speak with my hands,* Zoe mouthed, tears flooding her cheeks. "That was good," they trumpeted. "Her speech is clear enough. We'll be fine," and they began to look for a vein. . . . But Zoe's veins did not cooperate; the more they gouged and probed and prodded her, the more elusive were her veins. She was bleeding copiously and weeping in pain, and I was weeping too, Zoe couldn't quite make out what I was signing because my facial expression was so distorted, nor could she see my signs clearly through her tears, which no one was bothering to wipe away—

"Don't let me interrupt you," a male voice intrudes. It's Atwood, standing a few feet from Margie, arms folded across his chest, his expression unreadable. Engrossed in conversation, none of us noticed him reenter the curtained area.

At last, the examination commences in earnest. He starts from the beginning, taking Zoe's medical history, examining her carefully, his former truculence gone. Is he impressed by how elastic communication with a deaf person can be in the presence of a skilled interpreter? At any rate, he seems willing to let bygones be bygones.

Soon, we're trooping up to the third floor for a stress test, which Zoe declares she will most certainly ace. But after a few minutes on the treadmill, she starts to feel light-headed. The test is stopped; Zoe, out of breath, steps down. Dr. Atwood is summoned; he in turn calls in a colleague; they consult. An angiogram, they decide, would be "helpful." Accordingly, they schedule one for the next day, and Zoe is admitted overnight "so we can keep an eye on her."

Reader, if you detect a speeding-up of the narrative here, you're right. I have no intention of boring you with the details of Zoe's second angioplasty, except to say that, as I said in the beginning, it seems to have been successful. Margie, who cleared her schedule to interpret the procedure, has since become what Zoe calls a *heart-friend*, intending the pun. She's taken Zoe spelunking, and Zoe has in turn given her a tour of the greenhouses.

The friendship was fast and deep and from the outset encompassed me as well, which was a blessing, especially when that first bill arrived from the hospital. I called Margie, who assured me it was a simple bookkeeping error and advised me to call the hospital billing office. The woman who answered seemed confounded when I explained that my daughter had mistakenly been sent a bill for interpreting services rendered on two successive days, totaling $350. What should the correct amount be, the young woman, who said her name was Tammy, wanted to know, and I explained that it was not the amount that was in error—

"So, you're saying your daughter should not have received that bill."

"Exactly."

"So who should the bill be sent to?"

"No one. I mean, the hospital is required to pay for interpreting services, not the deaf client."

"No, ma'am, we don't pay for that. We just provide medical care."

"No, you're mistaken," said I, but obdurate Tammy stuck to her guns. So I asked to speak to her superior, Mrs. Terhune, who listened politely as I explained that the ADA requires hospitals to make their facilities and services accessible for people with disabilities. She said she'd "look into the matter" and promised to get back to me.

When no one called, I assumed the interpreting bill had been paid by the hospital, but a month later, another bill arrived. This time when I called Margie, her agency called the billing office and, as Margie put it, "duked it out with them."

Months passed. The interpreter agency continued to dispatch monthly bills to the hospital, each more emphatically worded than the previous bill; each was ignored, to Margie's consternation. Eventually, the hospital's counsel sent Margie's boss a legal opinion, which laid out the hospital's position: under the Eleventh Amendment to the Constitution, the hospital was not obligated to pay for interpreter services for a deaf patient. This was because, the document explained, it is a public hospital funded by state monies, and—I'm not making this up—the state has a "sovereign immunity" from federal law.

Well, I'm all for sovereignty, but this was wrong. Zoe, whose heart was ticking along nicely now, called a special meeting of the local deaf club to discuss the situation and prepare an organized response to what she saw as a crisis of major proportions for deaf people. I, of course, attended, as did Margie and several other interpreters, but in truth I was only half listening, besotted with pride in my daughter who, having "dressed up" for the meeting (meaning, her jeans were clean, her shirt tucked in, her copious salt-and-pepper curls brushed), sat in a straight-backed chair in front of the group and told her story, emphasizing that it could have happened—and sooner or later probably *would* happen—to every deaf person in the room. She said that the only reason Margie's agency had not yet submitted the bill to *her* was that a decision had been made to challenge the hospital's position. If the agency lost in court, deaf people would henceforth be expected to pay for their interpreters when they undergo treatment at public hospitals that receive state funds.

I tried to follow what everyone said after Zoe spoke her piece, though let me tell you, when deaf people get together in a room, sign language bounces like popcorn from hand to hand. People wanted clarification on this *sovereign immunity* thing. How can a state be exempt from the law? S-O-V, uh, would you fingerspell that for me one more time? A plot was hatched: the deaf club would call a press conference and organize a demonstration outside the hospital gates. Many pairs of hands participated in the discussion, which was punctuated by a few mantras: *What about the ADA? We're already paying through the nose for medical care! Are they nuts? Where do they think we're going to get enough money to pay for interpreters? They can't thumb their noses at the ADA! Sovereign immunity, that's a good one! Shame on them! They think they can fuck us over because they've got all the power and we're just a few dumb deafies! What about the ADA?! They'll be sorry!*

Zoe the catalyst, having struck the match that ignited this fire, sat back and watched it roar, periodically casting her sly grin across the room at me. I don't mean to say she wasn't pissed, not engaged, but part of her rejoiced.

That night after the meeting, we sat at the kitchen table. Still non-plussed, I murmured some cliché about hoping to see justice served. . . . Zoe was silent for a moment, gazing at the floor. "People think justice is a concept," she said then. "That's why it's so easy to disregard"—her hand flicked justice away—"because you can't eat it or drink it or fuck it. But it's a living thing, like a tree" (hands planting a seed, patting down the soil). "It starts out wobbly and weak, but given a little encouragement it grows into —" She paused, chewing her lip. "I felt its presence in the room with us tonight. It spread out its branches" (arms cast wide, as if in benediction) "and breathed on us. I felt it."

You're wondering, of course, about the outcome. Bad news: we lost. Not five months after our encounter with Dr. Atwood, the Supreme Court ruled on this Eleventh Amendment business in relation to an ADA violation of some sort in some other state, and the ruling went against us. But we decided to go ahead and raise a ruckus anyway; as one TV pundit covering the story observed, we turned our judicial loss into a public relations gain.

"Just because the Supreme Court says it, doesn't make it right or just!" Zoe declared at the press conference, her eyes locked onto her interpreter, none other than Margie, who sat facing her in the front row, her voice as impassioned as Zoe's sign. "Who sits on the Supreme Court? They're not deaf, that's for sure. . . . They're mostly rich, white, hearing men! What do *they* know? Do they represent *me*? Do they comprehend the day-to-day experience of discrimination we deaf people face?" Zoe was briefly still; I imagined I could see her nostrils flare. Then the sign for "pigs" waggled at her chin, followed by the verb "fly," hands flapping together, dipping and soaring around her upper body like butterflies. She finished with a question mark aimed at the reporters. From where I stood on the side, I watched every pair of eyes in the crowd follow the arc of her finger through its rhetorical curve and poke.

It was a hearing expression, one she'd picked up from me. As Margie delivered it into English—*Do pigs fly?*—with just the right mix of humor and disgust, I glanced nervously around at other deaf people, who were exchanging looks of puzzlement (pigs? flying pigs?) and knew, with a mother's certainty, that my daughter was making a mental note to explain this locution to her comrades as soon as the reporters had left. Probably, she would apologize.

The press conference led to newspaper and talk show interviews. We've pioneered deaf radio, Zoe gloated. The demonstration was likewise a hit: a small but spirited band of deaf people and their families and friends circled in front of the hospital gates carrying signs that read: Hands Off the ADA! and Sovereign Immunity, My Ass! and No One Is Immune from the Law! and Deaf Sovereignty! The media loved us, and another demonstration was called, this time at the office of the state attorney general, who had publicly commiserated with the beleaguered hospital. By the time that demo was over, Zoe's group—our group—was calling itself a *movement*. We even coined a name: DSN, Deaf Sovereignty Now! Our dozens became hundreds as people with other disabilities climbed aboard, along with a couple of immigrant rights groups, which reasoned, correctly, that an interpreter is an interpreter.

As I write this, evening has turned to night. Zoe's just home from another meeting (I begged out of this one, too tired); from my bedroom, I hear her car pull up in front of the house. Car door, front door, refrigerator door, open, shut. Plate on kitchen table, kitchen chair scraping floor. Bread being lowered into toaster, bread popping up. Cupboard opening, closing, glass on kitchen table. The sounds of Zoe living her life. If I listen very closely, I can almost hear her heart beating.

I know exactly what she's eating and drinking: sliced banana on toast, grapefruit juice. I know she's sitting at the kitchen table, chewing her toast, reviewing the meeting in her mind, planning the next move. I can see her long strong fingers gripping the glass.

CHEATERS AND COPYCATS

[14] by Ruth O'Brien

I walked up to the metal detectors, my pupils adjusting from the glare of the June sun to the cool mosaic of marble in the dim foyer. I was headed for the Manuscript Division of the Library of Congress. Pulling back one of the doors to the reading room with some difficulty given the flesh-colored casts wrapped around both my forearms, I admired the way the brass outlined the thick panes of glass with a clean, modern design.

I went toward the guard, registered, and received a key for a locker. Looking past him, I saw an airy room filled with desks, which was not too full yet. As I tried to open the locker, the hook from my right cast that wrapped around my thumb kept hitting the lock. Working at it, I remembered that the last time I'd used these lockers I was a graduate student. Then, suppressing this hint of vanity, I stashed my purse, keys, and a comb in the locker and approached a desk. I carried my new tool in hand, a slim metal arm with a rubber thumb, which helped me turn pages.

Looking around to see if any heads had turned, I put the arm down on the desk and went off to the alcove reserved for finding aids. I strode toward the alcove, trying to appear as if I knew what I was looking for. Opening the binder, I started reading the subheadings and immediately got lost in their promise—George W. Norris's early years, the Trade Disputes Act, the National Labor Relations Act. The numbers next to the boxes made my blood rush faster. I adjusted the brace that held my pencil and started scribbling, filling in the forms necessary to get the papers.

Waiting the few minutes while an archivist pulled the boxes from the closed stacks, I scanned the room again. The people at the desks were flipping through papers, taking notes on the large index cards supplied by the reading room, or tapping on their laptop computers. Before long, an archivist wheeled out the boxes on one of the overburdened walnut-colored trolleys.

With the top shelf of the trolley just above the desk I was using, it was not hard to pull down a box, slide it toward me, and flip open the top with my thin metal arm. The folders inside were packed in tightly. It was only the first folder that presented a problem. I lifted the other folders out of each box without much effort.

After sifting through a dozen or so boxes, the muscle around my thumb started to twitch. My fingers were getting tired. I decided to slow down. I didn't want to pay tomorrow for this excess of movement today. My mind was calculating how the newfound material would fit in and advance my book's thesis, just the way I had hoped. It seemed as if I had a mound of valuable documents before me but such a short amount of time to go through them. I panicked at the chance of missing one key letter or memorandum that would give my book the counterintuitive twist I wanted.

Trying to stay calm, I comforted myself with the thought that this metal arm, with its raised rubber nibs at the end, gave me more speed than my own thumb would have. The rustle of the pages I'd sped through was satisfying. Maybe I could run through the material again without opening any new boxes?

Looking back over at the trolley, with the lid of every box open, revealing all the flags for photocopying, I sighed. I made my way up to the reference desk. Standing behind a circular counter on a dais more than a half a foot off the ground, the archivists peered down at those who were asking about sources that were dear to them. Always earnest, the archivists gave each one an explanation, dotted with references that showed their knowledge about other useful sources.

Waiting my turn, I, like the rest of the researchers in line, was eavesdropping. Listening to each person, I felt both petrified that someone might be exploring *my* set of papers and lonely, knowing that this competitive impulse could keep me from talking to people with similar interests. I momentarily forgot why I was there. Then, I steadied myself. How should I start the explanation about my health?

Before I'd mapped it out, one of the archivists turned to me. I drew close to him as I didn't want people behind me listening in as I had.

"I have this hand problem," I said. His eyes narrowed, almost squinting, and I felt less hopeful. I let out a tumble of words.

Had I said too much or too little? In speaking before a class, I never lacked this sense of proportion. With practice, I'd learned how to give my lectures the force (spiced with some self-deprecating humor for relief) necessary to perk up students.

Feeling the ears open behind me, I grew warm. I started getting agitated about having to share this information. I plowed on anyway.

"I can't write because of this problem, and I have to photocopy everything. Could I just take all the papers to one of the machines and copy with the lid up? You see"—I held my hand in front of him and pinched my thumb and forefinger together—"I can't do this."

The archivist stepped back, ignoring my visual demonstration. "You're going to have to speak to the head archivist," he said coldly.

"No one," he added, "can copy with the lid up."

Pointing, he directed me toward a glass cubicle where a woman sat, in the middle of a row of cubicles that lined the front wall. In her early forties, she looked like someone I might sit with on a committee at my university. She had midlength hair, vaguely shaped in a bob, a plain silk blouse, and a slim-fitting skirt.

With a quick, muffled hello, I walked into the small room. Standing to the side of her desk, I ran through the explanation again. She stared at me; I could feel her resolve against me.

"We can't have you photocopying with the lid up. You see, it costs the library a lot of money in terms of ink."

Aha, I thought, this was a problem that could be solved.

"Well," I asked, "what if I tape paper over the part of the machine that gets exposed, or maybe use some cardboard, if you have it in the back?"

This time, she just shook her head.

"Everybody will start asking to do this," she said. "No, you have to go to the photocopying department in the old annex. They can do it for you. Someone will take your trolley over and copy it there. But instead of ten cents, it will be fifty cents a copy." She paused and then added, "Because of their labor."

"Fifty cents," I spat out too loudly. "It only costs ten cents if I do it."

"You'll have to talk with them. There's nothing I can do," she retorted. She stood up, asking me to leave with her body language.

"Well, where is this office located?" I asked, refusing to let her chase me out. I felt my throat closing. Tears were close, so I got up anyhow. I wasn't going to let her see me any more exposed than I already was.

Leaving the brisk air-conditioned environment, I felt comforted by the hot sun as I headed over to the annex. Still, this didn't stop the tears, and in childlike anger, I walked on the grass, ignoring the walkways. It was humiliating to ask for help.

Before my injury, I had enjoyed figuring out little ways of making my scholarship progress faster. The more my time-saving strategies took into account my good and bad habits, I'd discovered, the better they worked. I also knew that if I hadn't trained myself to sit at a computer for such long stretches of time, with all the books I needed for a morning's work around me, I might not be wearing casts now.

Having to ask several guards before I found B-342, I finally went into an office with an entryway shortened by a countertop. The counter swung up, giving people in the office access to their metal desks. The neon lights above and the teal green walls, more military than Maybelline, dispirited me. A person in a glass cubicle probably had more discretion than someone with a metal desk.

My spirits were somewhat buoyed when the front clerk, whom I had hoped to bypass, directed me to her supervisor, who sat at a desk tucked in a windowless office. The man inside had gray hair that needed cutting, casual navy pants, and a crisp, well-washed shirt of baby blue broadcloth. Guessing that he'd started working sometime in the 1970s, I thought he looked sympathetic.

Prepared for my inquiries by the head archivist, he explained how the copying process worked and how long it would take. Neither his explanation nor demeanor inferred that I was exaggerating claims about my health. Nor did he suggest that I was looking for any unfair advantage others might demand as well.

"What about the price?" I asked.

At that, he shook his head slightly and said he would see what he could do, but yes, each page would cost fifty cents.

Going back across the street, I tried to walk with the same amount of purpose that I had that morning. When I took my seat, no one looked up, and I busied myself with the stack of papers still on my desk. Fifty cents times a thousand was $500, and two thousand pages would be $1,000. Wow.

I started looking at the papers with a sharper eye than before. Was a document with four lines of material really necessary? Who could I get to take notes for me? I thought of my husband, who was sitting in the main reading room doing his own work. He needed his time too. Still uncertain, I thought, what's $500 or even $1,000? We had the money. I could do it. *Don't get upset*, I chanted in silence.

After a few more days in the reading room, I discovered that the National Archives had a set of papers I should look at. I walked down to this building, which was located at the other end of the mall, close to the White House. With its grand, gray sculptures and dark paneling, it had a different ambiance than the Manuscript Division.

A train station's worth of people scurried around the reading room with its high domed ceiling. Here, the archivists at the reference desk leaned over a counter that was almost level with the public. They lacked both the officiousness and the pride of their colleagues. Reaching the head of the line, I quickly went through my situation. Again pointing, the archivist referred me to her supervisor. This time, I was directed to a small, white-haired man who was standing off to the side of the counter. I waited as he finished talking with another librarian. Then he signaled me with his eyebrows.

"Can I help you?" he asked.

Again, I hurried through my explanation, trying to find the right balance. Embarrassed that I looked so healthy otherwise, I showed him my fingers and forearms tucked inside their casts.

Struck by how he lit up as I rattled off my explanation, I didn't hear his exact response. He told me about an aunt who, having lived with a disability for thirty years, had needed help and how uncomprehending "some people" could be.

Returning to my specific request, he said, "I can just have one of the staff copy the material when you're done."

Then, he signaled an African-American woman in a khaki skirt to come over. Still stunned, I didn't come up with any small talk. I just followed her to the desk she indicated and started working.

Two afternoons later, I was finished. The woman who had copied papers for me had done it as I went along. We had found some subjects in common and chatted, though she tactfully never asked about my problem. With her help, my stay in the reading room was shorter than I anticipated.

Collecting all my photocopies, I went to thank the archivist. I found him in a back room, behind a heavy bronze door to the side of the main reading room. Embarrassed by my gratitude, he listened but gave me little room to elaborate. Not wanting to make him uneasy, I felt unsatisfied but didn't say more. We both realized that my effusive response said as much about the other people I had approached as it did about him.

Back on Constitution Avenue, I saw that it was only 2 p.m. I still had time to go back to the Manuscript Division.

After I had gone through several more trolleys of documents over the next few days, the research trip was finished. I leafed through the last of the material I wanted copied and went back to the annex for the bill.

When I got there, a clerk at the front desk rang up the charges, $135 for 1,350 pages. What? This wasn't fifty cents a page.

Knowing that I shouldn't push it, I asked the clerk for an explanation. "Yes," she said, they had charged me ten cents a page. "Though," she added, "there was no reason behind this." Their generosity had not established any precedent.

A year later, my pleasure at receiving another travel grant was balanced by the prospect of going to Washington again. To lessen my anxiety, I thought, *why not give them a quick call?* I'd see if the photocopying office would do the same thing this summer. After finishing my explanation about my health, the person on the phone told me there was no policy of charging people who could not copy for themselves the same price as those who could.

Feeling comfortable and safe in my home office, I started welling up with rage. I sat down and wrote a letter to Senator Frank Leuchtenberg. Responding in less than two weeks, a member of Leuchtenberg's office told me they would forward my complaint to the EEOC. Less than ninety days later, a fact that was noted in the margin for bureaucratic purposes, I received an official reply from the EEOC. Agencies like the Library of Congress, it said, were not covered by the public accommodations provisions of the Americans with Disabilities Act. Federal agencies do not necessarily follow federal law.

Stewart's character Zoe and O'Brien faced similar difficulties when they asked that semipublic or public places provide them with reasonable accommodations. Officials told them that they could not receive these accommodations because they fall outside the reach of the Americans with Disabilities Act (ADA). The hospital did not believe that it needed to give Zoe a sign language interpreter. As a semipublic state agency, the hospital might well have immunity from a federal law. Similarly, while O'Brien receives help from the Manuscript Division of the Library of Congress, the officials serving her insist that this help should not be misconstrued as a reasonable accommodation. Federal institutions need not follow federal law. The Library of Congress has no legal obligation to make the Manuscript Division accessible. This chapter explores the paradox that federalism—especially in its newest form, which emphasizes state immunity—poses for the enactment of the ADA.

While examining issues about reasonable accommodations, both of these stories also examine the reactions that Zoe, her mother, and O'Brien encountered when they asked for them. Zoe and her mother, having dealt with some variant of the issue since Zoe could sign, have gained a strong sense of who will be helpful. By contrast, O'Brien, having sustained a workplace injury in adulthood, is struck by the wide range of reactions that she encounters.

[ ] SQUARE PEGS, ROUND HOLES, AND POWDER KEGS

By nature, jurisdictional questions are primarily procedural rather than substantive. Federalism, for example, raises jurisdictional questions since it involves delineating what are state and federal powers. While procedural issues are so vital to the rule of law, they also help people understand its limitations. As Martha Fineman explains, law is problematic in that it is based on categories and classifications; law is a system of rules and regulations.[1] Some people and objects fit well into certain categories and classifications, whereas others do not.

Whatever stretches and strains these categories and classifications, moreover, sometimes calls into question law as a vehicle for social change. Whether there is a good fit, in other words, matters. If a court ruled that an accommodation imposes too heavy a financial burden on an institution, for instance, some people would support the ruling, whereas others would not, though everyone still would be embroiled in a substantive battle. By contrast, if the court decides that someone cannot have an accommodation because of a jurisdictional issue, a different political reaction most likely would be generated.

On one level, jurisdictional issues are seen as technicalities—they highlight the artificial nature of categories and classifications. Often, opposition about the appropriateness of such a category turns into a fight over rules and regulations. No one need express her opposition or support for an accommodation since this person can recite the rule. It is the rule, not the underlying issue, that defeats the person making the request. On another level, the discrepancy between the jurisdictional rule and the outcome could ignite public outrage. At the end of Stewart's story, Zoe's outrage transforms her into a political activist.

Activism often stems from fear, dependency, and humiliation, which are transformed into outrage. Having to sign for her daughter during a tense time in the emergency room places Zoe's mother in a perilous position, making her an activist as she battles with Dr. Atwood about his reluctance to wait for an interpreter. Fearing for her life, Zoe's confused. Coming to the brink of this fear and confusion, Zoe's mother sees that her own daughter realizes that she must rely on her mother. This makes Zoe feel protective about her mother. Zoe can see her mother's anxiety. While O'Brien's situation places her in no harm, she shares Zoe's feelings about dependency. O'Brien relays how humiliating it is to ask for help repeatedly.

While the ADA might not resolve the attitude of the patronizing doctor and the archivists, it was drafted with the idea of providing services like sign language interpreters and photocopying. Zoe and O'Brien fail to receive these services not because of what they asked for, but because of where they were. Zoe had surgery in a hospital that received *state* funds, and O'Brien was conducting research in a *federal* archive. If the Supreme Court had an expansive concept of federalism, Zoe and, possibly, O'Brien would have been in the right place at the right time. They would have received the requested services.

[ ] NEW FEDERALISM

Since the specific procedural question that these two stories raise involves U.S. federalism, which is a vital issue, it merits some elaboration. Federalism is a dual system of governance, which divides power between central (national) and local (state) authorities. To ensure that legislation follows this division of power, the Tenth Amendment of the Constitution stipulates that Congress may pass laws that deal only with its enumerated powers of foreign relations and interstate commerce. All laws pertaining to intrastate commerce and state police power or the power to promote the health, safety, morality, and general welfare were reserved for the states.

Since most industrialized countries have unitary sovereignty, the U.S. government's notion of dual sovereignty is unique.[2] What dual sovereignty means, however, is constantly evolving. In the Supreme Court's first important decision, in 1793, *Georgia v. Chisholm*, a citizen from South Carolina sued Georgia for not paying him for goods he had delivered. The Court upheld his right to sue, undermining Georgia's sovereignty.[3] As Bernard Schwartz reports, the decision "fell upon the country with a profound shock" and led to the passage of the Eleventh Amendment, which restored state sovereignty.[4]

Then, in 1800, Chief Justice John Marshall gave the federal judiciary a much larger role in defining federalism via the power of judicial review. Using the newly established power of judicial review, which meant the Supreme Court could declare laws null and void if they violated the Constitution, Marshall, an ardent nationalist, essentially transformed dual sovereignty into national power by rendering a weak interpretation of the Tenth Amendment.[5] "Not until after the Civil War," constitutional law expert Edward Corwin explains, "was the idea [created] that the reserved powers of the [s]tates comprise an independent qualification of otherwise constitutional acts of the [f]ederal [g]overnment."[6] It took a tax case in 1871 to hold that a national income tax could not be levied against the official salaries of state officers.[7] Further, in 1918, the Supreme Court rendered a more expansive interpretation of state powers with its interpretation that the Tenth Amendment had "expressly delegated" the "reserved powers of the states."[8]

The relationship between the states and the national government changed most dramatically during the New Deal, when the Charles Evans Hughes Court gave a broad rendering of the Commerce Clause. It went "full circle," as Corwin explains, and "restated Marshall's thesis" on national supremacy.[9] While Congress has gained power to legislate from a number of constitutional clauses, most federal legislation is based on the Commerce Clause.[10] Beginning with the second New Deal, Congress and the president passed many pieces of regulatory legislation that were based on it, giving the federal government the power to legislate issues that affected health, welfare, and morality.

Both the Earl Warren and the Warren Burger Courts further broadened the scope of the Commerce Clause in the 1950s, 1960s, and 1970s, recognizing congressional authority over non-economic regulatory issues like the Civil Rights Act of 1964. While this legislation also derived some congressional authority from the Fourteenth Amendment, the Commerce

Clause makes it operative. The Supreme Court upheld the statute by holding that Congress had the authority to regulate motels that housed interstate travelers.[11]

The expansive reading of the Commerce Clause in particular and the perception of national sovereignty as opposed to dual sovereignty was so firmly entrenched that before 1995 most legal scholars and political scientists assumed that this expansion would change little.[12] One of the standard texts on constitutional law states that "with the exception of one decision . . . , the Supreme Court since 1937 has invalidated no act of Congress because of conflicting state prerogatives."[13] Put differently, the same text said, "By 1937, the Court had largely resolved that conflict in favor of national power."[14]

The idea of national power extended not just to public law, but also spawned a whole body of literature in political science and sociology on the creation of the American social welfare state, which depended on it.[15] Quite simply, Congress and the president built the American social welfare state on the Commerce Clause. In the 1970s and 1980s, Presidents Richard M. Nixon and Ronald Reagan began giving some power back to the states under a policy of devolution, but the reach of the Commerce Clause remained unchallenged despite these new public policies.[16]

Then, beginning in 1996, a five-person majority narrowed the scope of both the Commerce Clause and the Fourteenth Amendment. The William H. Rehnquist Court created a "set of federalism doctrines," which forbade Congress from regulating what he called "non-economic activities."[17] That is, Congress could no longer use the Commerce Clause to gain authority to pass legislation that affects the states.[18] For the first time, the Court ruled that the Eleventh Amendment impeded the operation of the Supremacy Clause when private parties had been explicitly authorized by Congress to enforce their federal rights against the states.

Creating a boundary between what is national and local, the Rehnquist Court has ruled that Congress must keep its hands off "traditional" local subjects, like crime and the family.[19] Federal laws controlling guns and prohibiting violence against women by allowing them to sue their attackers cannot be applied to the states. Also, antidiscrimination laws protecting people from age discrimination cannot be outlawed by the federal government. The new states' rights doctrines have undermined the hate crime legislation sought by liberal Democrats. These doctrines will also hinder the conservative Republicans' present attempts to regulate human cloning.[20]

Another way of characterizing the debate over federalism is that those favoring states' rights maintain that these rights ensure political accountability, whereas the proponents of stronger national power argue that their position supports the rule of law.[21] "If a state violates your federal rights," writes law professor Cass Sunstein, "are you allowed to sue it in court? In a society proudly committed to the rule of law, you might think that the answer would be yes. But the Rehnquist [C]ourt has often said no."[22]

The argument underlying state sovereignty is that the judiciary should not compel a state with national legislation because the state should be accountable to the people. The elected branches, Justice Antonin Scalia argues, cannot slough off responsibility for their political choices onto the judiciary.[23] By contrast, critics of state immunity argue that while the state may be accountable to the people, the concept violates the rule of law.[24] They cite Chief Justice Marshall's famous dicta that the United States should be ruled by laws, not human beings.[25]

Given the substantive goals that have driven the battle over states' rights, such as the defense of slavery or opposition to child labor laws, there is a link between the rule of law and the highest law, constitutional law. Critics like Jack Balkin, a Yale law professor, maintain that the "real issue is what sort of liberty we are trying to protect." "Is liberty to lynch people worth preserving?" he asks. Or "is the liberty to clone people worth preserving?"[26] Responding to Stewart's story, this interpretation of federalism would mean that the state legislature would decide if Zoe will get a translator. The California state legislature, which is in charge of the budget, should decide if she receives this help, not the courts.

[ ] NO CONSTITUTIONAL GUARANTEES

The Commerce Clause does not represent the only means of bestowing congressional authority, particularly for antidiscrimination legislation. The Fourteenth Amendment offers another means of gaining congressional authority. This amendment passed after the Civil War to eliminate the nullification doctrine, or the notion that states need not follow federal legislation. It reestablished a conception of state sovereignty as subordinate to congressional action.[27] One of the Fourteenth Amendment's principal sections—section 5—gives Congress enforcement powers. Congress can pass any "appropriate" laws to ensure that the states do not deprive any person of life, liberty, or property without due process. Also, state legislation cannot deny someone equal protection under the law.

Given its new position on state sovereignty, the Supreme Court has circumscribed Congress's enforcement powers under the Fourteenth Amendment. First, it held that although Congress can create legislative remedies for violations of rights, these remedies cannot alter substantive rights.[28] Second, the Court ruled that Congress must delineate precisely what rights are being violated before it enacts remedial legislation.[29] As one law professor described, "Absent extraordinary circumstances, such as the national government bringing suit on an individual's behalf, states may violate federal statutes and remain immune from civil action."[30]

While section 5 bestows upon Congress the power to remedy violations by passing legislation, judicial review constitutes the other means of protecting people from discrimination. That is, the Supreme Court can scrutinize the constitutionality of a statute that targets a group of people. There are three types of judicial scrutiny, which offer different, descending levels of protection when a federal court evaluates a statute: strict scrutiny, scrutiny on a rational basis, and heightened scrutiny. To determine which level of scrutiny is applicable, if any, a court will conduct a "test." This test would reveal whether a law was discriminatory—if it singled out a protected class of people—unfairly.

In the 1970s, the disability rights movement hoped that disabled people could become one of the protected classes. Activists proposed that the laws affecting disabled people should come under heightened scrutiny. The least-stringent standard of judicial scrutiny, the heightened scrutiny test already had been applied to criminals and the poor under the Burger Court.[31]

Disability rights activists realized that laws that had an impact on disabled people would never receive strict scrutiny. The Court reserved this level of scrutiny for groups like African Americans, who have endured a long history of discrimination, have an immutable characteristic like race, and have had both the state and society render them powerless.[32] Persons with disabilities do not fulfill these three criteria.

The rational basis test constitutes the second strongest test for determining whether a law provides a class or category of people with equal protection. The Court had applied this test to laws concerning women.[33] Although nothing substantive distinguished people of different races from one another, a woman's capacity for reproduction made her different from a man. This difference justified some laws on the basis of gender.[34]

Once the Supreme Court recognized that laws targeting the poor, criminal suspects, illegitimate children, and the disenfranchised should be held to a higher constitutional standard under the heightened scrutiny test, disabled people thought this test should be made available to them too.[35] This test delineates that while a statute need not rest on a rational basis, it requires a substantial governmental objective. For instance, although a child's right to support from his parents, for instance, is not fundamental, the Supreme Court invalidated statutory classifications that eroded this right. A standard of reasonableness had to be established that had a fair and substantial relation to the object that a piece of legislation sought to achieve.[36]

The Supreme Court dashed the disability rights activists' hopes in several cases.[37] The coup de grace fell in 1985, when the Court took up the question of the constitutionally guaranteed rights of disabled people when Cleburne, a city in Texas, denied Jan Hannah, who had plans to build a residential group home for the mentally retarded, a building permit.[38] Justice Byron White drafted the opinion, which held that neither strict, rational bases nor heightened forms of scrutiny should be applied to laws targeted at persons with disabilities.[39] While persons with disabilities had a long history of discrimination, the state and society had been empathic to their plight by passing pieces of legislation that created programs designed to help them, like special education and vocational rehabilitation. The legislation proved that persons with disabilities were not powerless. Hence, the disabled did not become one of the protected classes, and legislation that affected them was not given any level of scrutiny. Disabled people, in other words, could be singled out as a class without having the federal courts determine whether such a statute was discriminatory.

[ ] FEDERALISM, PROTECTED CLASSES, AND DISABILITY

In 2001, the Supreme Court's new position on state sovereignty directly affected the Americans with Disabilities Act when a 5–4 majority prohibited two people from collecting monetary damages from the state of Alabama under the ADA's employment provisions in *Board of Trustees of the University of Alabama v. Garrett*.[40] The suit involved Titles I *and* II since the people, Patricia Garrett and Milton Ash, worked for a state agent—a public university. Because this university was a state agent, the Supreme Court majority decided, it had immunity from suits involving monetary damages under the Eleventh Amendment.

Although well aware that the majority's new federalism doctrine might affect its interpretation of the ADA, disability activists were still dismayed by the ruling. In part, this stemmed from the Court's first decision about state and local governmental services under Title II. In 1999, the Court handed down a ruling that gave mental health patients the right to leave mental health institutions and move to small community homes whenever they and their physicians think they are ready to do so.[41] Some members of the disability rights community heralded this decision as a "milestone."[42] While Justice Scalia wrote a dissenting opinion that deferred to state sovereignty, the majority did not defer.

Just two years later, Scalia's minority position became the majority in the *Garrett* decision. While the Court concluded that the rational basis test was the appropriate equal protection standard for scrutinizing laws that discriminate on the basis of disability, it also ruled that the two private parties involved—Garrett and Ash—could sue for monetary damages because Congress had not validly abrogated the Fifth Amendment. The gap between the amount of state action that the employment provisions required and the requirements that the Constitution imposed on states, the Court held, was too large.[43]

Drafting the dissenting opinion, Justice Stephen Breyer argued that Congress could break the states' immunity given the legislative powers under Article I of the Constitution.[44] Breyer did not question the logic underlying state sovereignty, however. Nor did he argue that disabled people should become a protected class under the Constitution. Rejecting the idea that state and local statutes should be scrutinized to determine if they violated the rights of disabled people, Breyer suggested that section 5 of the Fourteenth Amendment confers broad powers upon Congress to legislate remedies that uphold the Equal Protection Clause. These remedies need only be "appropriate." Underscoring his point, Breyer added, "And that is all the Constitution requires."[45]

To the minority, the Rehnquist majority conflates judicial scrutiny—in which the judiciary invalidates a law—with Congress's authority to draft a legislative remedy that enforces the Equal Protection Clause. "Unlike courts, Congress directly reflects public attitudes and beliefs," which is why it has this power to fashion and refashion legislative remedies.[46] And to Breyer, Congress had collected powerful evidence of "discriminatory treatment" against persons with disabilities. "To apply a rule designed to restrict courts as if it restricted Congress's legislative powers is to stand the underlying principle—a principle of judicial restraint—on its head."[47]

To arrive at this decision, the Court had to distinguish its decision from another ADA case that involved the Fifth Amendment. In 1999, the Supreme Court ruled in *Olmstead v. L.C. by Zimring* that it would be discriminatory for a state not to release two women, who had cognitive disabilities, from their institutional settings into community-based treatment programs.[48] According to law professor James Leonard, the difference between *Olmstead* and *Garrett* revolves around the fact that "segregating rules or results are suspicious in ways that general rules are not." The Court perceived institutionalization as segregation, which had long been condemned by the courts as discriminatory, whereas reasonably accommodating the plaintiffs in the *Garrett* decision was not discriminatory since the nurse and the security guard were asking for "the waiver of a generally applicable work rule."[49]

The *Garrett* decision caused the disability rights movement great distress. As Leonard elaborates, "There is great uncertainty about the effects of the Court's renewed federalism on the power of Congress to impose the ADA's non-discrimination mandate on state and local governments."[50] Neither the majority nor the minority opinions left much room for legal redress or recourse. First, the majority's state immunity doctrine meant that the ADA could not reach the states. While this was only about monetary damages, did this mean that section 504 of the Rehabilitation Act could also be repudiated? The impact this decision has had on section 504 remains unknown.[51] Second, the minority indicated that disabled people should not be considered a protected class. If Congress amended the ADA, specifying that it was such a class, the Court would probably strike it down.[52]

[ ] CONGRESSIONAL CIRCUMVENTION

Many members of the legal community have been critical of the Court's new position on state sovereignty, or what has been called the Tenth Amendment renewal. As Mark Tushnet, a well-known legal historian, describes it, this new position on federalism opens three paths. First, the Court could restore the meaning of federalism first articulated in 1789 and reinstate "proper relations" between the federal and state governments.[53] To do so, it would be overturning Chief Justice Marshall's interpretation of federalism in the landmark decision *Gibbons v. Ogden*, which made congressional authority over commerce complete.[54] Second, the new federalist doctrines could follow a revolutionary path that would essentially undo the New Deal and the Great Society policy programs, which are all based on an expansive reading of the Commerce Clause. Finally, the Court could follow a constrained interpretation of state sovereignty that would not involve invalidating any major laws. Instead, this path would undermine what Tushnet describes as the "new feel good" statutes, which have little public or legislative support, though they claim credit for tackling tough issues like violence against women.

To Tushnet, the constrained view probably will define the Rehnquist Court. This perspective, however, does not allay the concerns of the disability rights community since it characterizes the ADA as anything but a "feel good" statute. Like the federal Age Discrimination in Employment Act, the ADA represents an extension of civil rights. Members of the movement are more apt to concur with what Balkin argued. "The Supreme Court," he said, "should scrap its ill-considered doctrines and recognize that the national government has the power to make all laws that it considers to be in the national interest."[55]

Recognizing the dilemma that the ADA faces, other law professors have suggested that this statute would profit from a new enforcement mechanism. For instance, Marc Falkoff submits that the Supreme Court could not undermine the ADA if Congress created an administrative tribunal to uphold the law. In fact, as Breyer noted, the *Garrett* majority was penalizing Congress for drafting the most "decentralized remedy" of using private damage actions to enforce the ADA. If Congress had originally created a more uniform remedy, like issuing federal standards or creating an administrative tribunal, the ADA would not have been affected by the Court's new federalism doctrines. Congress could also regulate adjudicative administrative agencies in what are called legislative courts.[56] Being politically accountable bodies, these courts, which are located in the executive branches and are not regular courts of law, allow individuals to sue the states. A legislative court neither violates sovereign immunity nor functionally undermines political accountability concerns.[57]

Should Congress change the ADA's enforcement mechanism to circumvent the federal courts' interpretation of it? In *Garrett*, Breyer noted the irony of this possibility, if Congress changed the ADA's enforcement mechanism. He explained that all the other remedies, like an independent regulatory agency, "are sometimes draconian and typically more intrusive" than having people file private suits to enforce the ADA.[58] Hence, will a conservative Supreme Court's new federalism doctrine push Congress into building a stronger administrative state?[59] Or will this federal statute not apply to the states? How does the fact that the ADA was passed by a large bipartisan majority affect the chances that it might be amended?

[ ] EXEMPTING FEDERAL AGENCIES FROM FEDERAL LAW

While state immunity stops Zoe from having a translator paid for by the hospital, O'Brien faces a battle in a different jurisdiction: the federal rather than state government. For O'Brien, the federal government has taken a self-interested position in not regulating itself. The official immunity doctrine stipulates that the federal government cannot be sued by private citizens. As Corwin explains, there is a "universally accepted maxim of public law that the sovereign may not be sued except on his own consent."[60] Indeed, it was during the ratification debate over the Eleventh Amendment that John Jay argued that not just the states, but the U.S. government itself must be sovereign. The only time any branch of the federal government can be sued is when it has given its consent. Congress must agree that it can be sued.

Congress first rendered its consent under the Tucker Act of 1877, when the United States agreed to be sued in the Court of Claims at Washington on all claims founded upon any express or implied contract. It also gave this consent for suability under the federal Tort Claims Act of 1946. Here, Congress agreed that it could be sued for injuries "caused by the negligent or wrongful act or omission of any employee . . . acting within the scope of his office or employment."[61] Congress, however, did not consent to litigation under the ADA. Hence, the head librarian at the Manuscript Division of the Library of Congress is fully entitled to reject O'Brien's requests for reasonable accommodations. Title II provides accessibility for a state or local governmental service, not a federal one. Of course, this makes the situation no less ironic. The very library that houses the papers of many of the critical lawmakers—presidents, members of Congress, and Supreme Court justices—is inaccessible.

O'Brien's story underscores another difference, albeit not a legal one, between her and Zoe. While Zoe has an easier time anticipating the reaction of those she asks for help, O'Brien does not. Is this because O'Brien has not had enough experience making requests for accommodations? Is it born out of the fact that she does not have a visible impairment? Or does it depend on the person she encounters? Are different people's reactions explained by their political positions? Is someone who identifies with other liberal causes, like civil rights or gender rights, more likely to be empathic? Or does the reaction of the people whom O'Brien encounters come from their experience with other disabled people? Is someone's position on disability rights personal or political? Further, can a law—the ADA—affect someone's attitude? Or does the bias that both Zoe and O'Brien encounter reveal how limited is the ADA's reach?

PUBLIC ACCOMMODATIONS OF PRIVATELY

OWNED BUSINESSES

(TITLE III)

WHACK!

[16] by Shawn Casey O'Brien

I thought I was being a good neighbor, picking up my friend and neighbor Sal for the long ride down the 405 freeway to Long Beach and the Coastal Commission, where, for next to nothing, I'd do a little legal research on some beachfront property he was hot on last night, over drinks. "We have to move fast," Sal had said with slurred urgency. "Seven in the morning, pick me up. We'll get in before they open up." Not quite possible, but I knew what he meant. Next morning, having given him the benefit of doubt, I was there at 8 A.M., and he still wasn't ready. Apparently, last night's urgency had given way to this morning's hangover. As he showered, I decided to have a little breakfast at a small café across the alley.

Again, I thought I was being a good neighbor as I attempted to move my obtrusive Ford Granada out of the narrow alley. My intention was to park it in the café's lot, which included a regulation handicapped-parking blue zone. "Lucky me," I said aloud. Then, peering over the steering wheel, I looked closer. Seems my intention would remain just that, for there, before me, was a chain, which with brute effectiveness obstructed the entrance to the blue zone and thwarted any effort I made to pull into it.

"That's kinda weird," I said to myself. But I figured it was an oversight. So, with the grunting Granada askew next to the oddity—a chained-off handicapped parking stall—I got out of the car, grabbed my sticks, and approached the walk-up window with a simple request.

"My friend, coffee, please," I said to the counterman, wanting to make sure he understood that I was a paying customer, before I made my more pressing request.

Automatically, he put a cup in front of me and filled it. He is your down-to-earth, hard-working Hispanic man. One pleasant peasant giving another a cup of coffee, almost before I could finish the thought. From my fatigues, I pulled out a dollar, and tossed it on the countertop. "Thanks," I said, as he grabbed the buck with a smile. "And could you please unlock the handicapped parking spot?" I pointed at it with my crutch, to empha-size that I am one of the anointed.

His smile became sad, and he rolled his eyes the way people do when-ever they have to do something they don't particularly want to do. When he told me, "No, no, señor," I could see he was not proud of it.

Again it was weird, and I thought that perhaps there was a communi-cation problem. With the mighty wide wonder percolating in the alley, this was no time for misunderstandings.

"Manager, por favor," I said, hoping to speed things up.

Off he went, as I poured cream into my coffee and wondered if my attempt at Spanish was in bad taste.

As I stood there stirring my coffee, I slowly surveyed my surround-ings. Venice Beach. Venice of America, as it's better known to the rest of the world. A most agreeable, if offbeat, neighborhood. I took a deep breath of the ocean air and watched some scantily clad Asian women roller-blade down the boardwalk with the same rhythmic grace as the deep blue Pacific behind them.

I exhaled thoroughly and contemplated how I was going to get my steaming cup of joe over to one of those plastic white table-and-chair sets that one too many Home Depots have foisted on us. My lower back hurt just by eyeing them, but I figured I could endure them long enough to have breakfast. Once again, hunger pains beat out physical pain. It was after all, a stunning day, with a breeze that would keep both the acrobats on the boardwalk, as well as the ones on crutches, cool, calm, and dry. "Count your blessings," I reminded myself, "you live here."

I blew on my coffee with some contentment. I treasure my waterfront neighborhood, having lived nowhere else as an adult, and was happy to see one more blue zone in it. It would make this café a cool little place to breakfast with friends and family. Now, if I could just get the heaving Granada parked, my contentment would be complete.

I was about to sip a little off the top of the cup in preparation for a landing at a nearby table, when John, the manager, came around the corner.

Blond greasy hair. Bad teeth. From the skeletal remains of John, one could tell that he worked at a hamburger stand, and probably did a little too much speed. He was agitated from the start.

"What's the problem?" he asked roughly, wiping his hands on a dirty dishrag.

"No problem," I answered, setting the coffee back down. "I just wanted to use your handicapped parking spot and have a little breakfast."

"Can't do that," he said.

"No, I'm a patron," I explained, pointing to my cup of coffee.

"This is private property. No one's allowed to use the parking lot," he said, putting an even nastier edge on his voice.

I dropped my head in disbelief, keeping one eye squarely on him as the BS detector in the back of my brain went off. I felt the frustrated boxer in me gearing up to dispute this clown.

"This is a public accommodation," I said with all the necessary emphasis. "I am the public, and that is a handicapped parking spot." I pointed to it again. "I'm handicapped," I continued indignantly, stepping back so that the whiz kid could get a full view of my magic sticks. "And that spot was put in place to facilitate the handicapped citizen's patronage of this public accommodation. To give us an equal opportunity to eat in your fine establishment."

OK, I was perturbed, maybe even sarcastic, but under the circumstances, I didn't see that as such a sin. Speedy here didn't know it, but he was messing with my civil rights, and I thought about giving him a deeper appreciation of the ADA, explaining how *that* law, via *that* blue zone, guaranteed me "equality of opportunity" and all. But, considering the chemi-

Whack!

cally altered and addled masses of his brain, I knew this would be lost on him. So, I opted for the much more emphatic "And that's the law!"

He was somewhat startled. So was I—it had come out so smoothly—but I didn't let on. "We know how to deal with people like you," he snarled.

What'd he say? I asked myself. People like me? People like me!

The nausea began to kick in. The discomfort of it made me realize, as always, that I was dealing with another punk. Yet again, I faced a bully. And worse, previous experience told me that if I wanted relief in both my gut and my conscience, I'd have to deal with him head-on.

I couldn't just walk away. I had learned that early.

My mind flashed back to my first bullies. Those petty thugs, Big Mike and Victor, my hearty childhood tormentors, who not only beat up on me regularly but would, when the opportunity presented itself, throw me into a garbage can and kick it down the nearest hill. The dizzying ride and my already screwy equilibrium brought on the worst nausea—that feeling I hate above others—and of course, on my way down the hill, I would throw up in a whirl. My tormentors would then run off scared when they saw my garbage-encrusted, vomit-covered carcass crawl out of the can and fade into the grass.

It wasn't just the vertigo and sickness either. Ultimately, I would have to crawl back up the hill and (hopefully) find my crutches. Yeah, I knew something about bullies. You have to stand up to them, and just as the top of the hill was always better than the bottom, sooner was always better than later.

Quite amazingly, when I did finally hit Big Mike squarely over his head with a crutch—taking a blow or two myself in the process—he *and* Victor left me alone. Yep, they could still kick my crippled butt, but now, if they did, there was a price to pay. I wasn't afraid to fight. Whack!

The remembered whack brought me back to the bully at hand.

"People like me. No, John, you don't know how to deal with people like me," I assured him sternly.

He got all offended, as bullies do whenever you stand up to them, turning themselves into the victim.

"Are you threatening me?" he demanded, flinging the dishrag to the counter.

"Threatening you," I snorted. This guy was a real prize. "No, John, I don't make threats. I make promises, and I promise—that chain is coming down!"

I fought off the urge to knock over my untouched coffee and create a mess, knowing that the guy who would have to clean it up was my sad-eyed friend. No justice there, either. I stormed off, back to my car. As I drove around looking for a parking space, I became even more enraged at how unnecessary it all was. The pettiness of it.

All they had to do was unlock the chain. A simple act of no more than a few seconds, and they wouldn't do it. What cretins. How many other hungry cripples did they chain out of the blue zone?

Beautiful blue zone, too. Perfectly up to code. They'd never have gotten their license to open the café if it wasn't. There was something incoherent about a chained-off handicapped parking zone. A handicapped parking zone is supposed to be a blue beacon of accessibility, something that brings people in, and here they were chaining it off. In my own neighborhood, too. Damn. I knew I couldn't live with that.

And I was a paying customer, too. "Hey, wait a minute," I wondered, "did I get my change back?!" Salting the wound, I realized that I never did. Nor had I gotten even a sip of coffee. I'd left it steaming on the counter.

Now I was steaming as I parked in front of the nonfunctioning gas station on Windward Circle, that now-paved-over "grand canal" of early Venice with the weird green swoosh of sculpture haphazardly plopped down in the middle of it, serving (just as haphazardly) as the center of town.

I made my way back over to Sal's apartment, which overlooked the café, and commandeered his phone.

I called everyone, and not by choice, either. The mayor's office referred me to Disabled Access, which said it handled only "on-street" parking spots, and told me I really should be talking to Building and Safety, which, when I did, wasn't sure if handicapped parking was within the purview of their authority, and thus told me to call the mayor's office. Circle completed.

I tried to be wryly amused at the way no one accepted responsibility for enforcement of such an obvious violation of the law. Being an optimist, I preferred to believe I'd started a blizzard of faxes within the bureaucracy, and someone would go out and let John know that chaining off the handicapped parking wasn't only in bad taste, but it was illegal.

Over the months that followed, I began to wonder if the gods were with me, or just egging me on. For nothing happened. I would sit up in Sal's apartment, stare out his big picture window, and alternate between feeling like a second-class citizen and summoning up the boxer in me.

I had met Sal during my days as a rock 'n' roll singer and all the hard partying that entailed. A bit slippery in his business dealings, he rationalized it all away with a dog-eat-dog mentality, as well as some drugs and booze to deal with the crueler aspects of that perspective. An Italian boy to the core, this made him sentimental, tyrannical, and generous.

Sal liked to carry himself like a tough guy, but he wanted to be loved much more than feared. He just relied on the latter, when he was hurt in the former. In between, he liked to party and do real estate deals as fast and loose as possible.

Truth is, he could be a lot of fun. Even when his definition of fun included going down to the Coastal Commission to look up conditional use permits—which, as mentioned, was what we were going to do the day I went to have breakfast at the café. Had he been on time, I would have never tried to park in the blue zone, and none of this would have come to pass.

Talk about dumb luck.

It confirms my belief that the fates do strange things—give you weird enemies like the kooks at the café and even weirder friends like Sal. And now it was Sal, standing at his big window, who spotted Mr. Daar, the owner of the café, down on the boardwalk. "There he is," he said, taking a drag off his cigarette. "There's your boy, the owner."

It was funny how Sal, so instrumental in helping me, couldn't have cared less about the chain. Most people would have gotten a kick out of helping bring it down. Not him. Nothing that high-minded for him. He liked to *see* a good fight, as opposed to fighting one, and that, I'm sure, is why he pointed Daar out to me.

I walked over to the window and looked down on Mr. Daar. He was a rumpled little man from that vantage point. I needed a closer look. I bolted out the door and down the stairs, my crutches slung over-arm rhythmically clanging like busted bells as they hit the concrete stairs behind me.

Here was my chance to reason with Mr. Daar, I figured. Neighbor to neighbor. As I made my clangorous way down the stairs, I decided to appeal to his better nature and, much to Sal's chagrin, avoid a fight.

Daar was walking between his café and Sal's place. Hearing the noise, he looked over as I turned at the bottom of the stairs, and we stared at each other for just a second. Me sizing him up, him wondering what all the racket was about.

"Mr. Daar," I called to him.

"Yeess," he said, his speech slightly accented.

"I am your neighbor, sir," I said respectfully, "and as a disabled citizen, I would very much like to use your handicapped parking spot, so that I may patronize your restaurant."

"What is this?" he asked, surprised.

"It's a request, sir."

"This is private property," he said.

"And it's the law, sir," I said firmly.

"So, now you're going to tell me the law?" he asked, perturbed.

"No, sir." I sighed. "I just hope you'll do the right thing and let disabled citizens who wish to eat at your restaurant use the parking. That's all," I said evenly. I thought I was getting through to him. Putting a face on it for him.

He looked me over for a moment rather disapprovingly and asked, "What do you want from me? Hot dogs? Forget about all that." He waved off the zone with a flick of his hand. "I will give you hot dogs," he said gruffly.

I took a step back. I needed a second to think. *Did this guy just try to bribe me?* I asked myself. And worse, did he just try to bribe me with *hot dogs?*

I took another step back, fighting my initial impulse to punch him upside his head with my crutch. *Hot dogs!* I thought to myself. All my diplomatic skills melted as it became apparent to me just how Mr. Daar operated.

"No, Mr. Daar," I said, containing myself. "I don't want your silly hot dogs. I want that damn chain to come down. Do I make myself clear?" I had to fight real hostility.

"This is private property. Screw you!" he shouted.

"No, smart guy. This is a public accommodation," I shouted back. "And I'm going to do everything legally within my power to bring down that chain. Got that, hot shot?"

"Are you threatening me?" he asked.

These guys must practice together, I thought to myself. That being the case, I figured I might as well practice my Clint Eastwood persona one more time and give what was fast becoming my stock reply to all victimized bullies.

"I don't make threats, sir, I make promises. And I promise you that that chain is coming down." As before, I used this as my exit line.

All the way down to Long Beach, Sal laughed about it—being bribed with hot dogs. Admittedly, it was embarrassing. Sal loved it. "I'll try that the next time I'm arguing with a city inspector," he said. I sat there and said nothing.

After a time, Sal asked in his most sincere voice, "A hot dog for your thoughts . . ."

"Very funny, Sal, very funny."

Down at the Coastal Commission, after we pulled the permits Sal wanted, I pulled Daar's. It turned out that my neighbor was in violation of *all* of his permits that concerned parking. The chain around the handicapped spot was just the beginning. Daar was supposed to provide parking for his patrons in his larger lot, but he had chained that off too. He was messing with everybody.

Weird business philosophy, if you ask me.

All the way back, I could hear Daar's imaginary mouthpiece: "We discriminate against everybody, so we aren't discriminating against anybody. You're being treated just like everyone else."

But I knew that when Daar locked everyone out of his parking lot and tried to palm that off as "equality," he was still violating my rights.

I realized that it was time to go to court.

The next day, I went to the law library, got out the pleadings and practice book for civil rights litigation, and did what most lawyers do. I copied the standard complaint out of the book and (with yellow legal pad in hand) began to fill in the blanks with my particulars. And again, the question rang out in my head. How many others? How many, indeed. As I scribbled away, I couldn't shake the feeling that in fighting this fight, I really was being a good neighbor.

[17]

The parking space, with the wheelchair insignia embossed in blue on the tarmac, constitutes arguably the most recognizable sign of a public accommodation in the United States. That blue spaces are ubiquitous, however, does not eliminate or even reduce the controversies involved with gaining this accommodation. O'Brien's story offers a good illustration of this point. The parking problem that he faces revolves around enforcement.

O'Brien perceives controversies about enforcement as a battle, and he fights the good fight for himself and his neighbors. O'Brien is very aware of his rights, buying coffee to show that he's a paying customer and entitled to parking, yet he knows that not all persons with disabilities are the same. Some disabled people are not conscious of their rights. Others might get discouraged by the bureaucratic run-around following the initial confrontation with a recalcitrant owner like Mr. Daar.

This said, not all those who seek the ADA's enforcement have encountered people like Mr. Daar. Many lawsuits have been settled against public and private places of public accommodation, like schools, offices, and stores, making them accessible to persons with disabilities.[1] Precisely how successful the ADA has been at this stage is difficult to assess. There are no records of settlements that are comparable to suits that go to trial. More often than not, one of the conditions of settlement is that the details remain private. Nonetheless, when someone like O'Brien faces an owner of a place of public accommodation who refuses to pull down the chain across the parking lot and settle, enforcing Title III of the ADA becomes much more difficult.

One of the primary difficulties associated with taking a case to trial stems from the problem of authority—who has the power to tell whom. For O'Brien, who has obvious mobility issues, the trouble is that he sought parking on private property. O'Brien discovers that one of the ADA's most distinctive features—how far it reaches—presents enforcement difficulties. No city official will come and pull down the chain blocking the parking space. O'Brien notes the irony in this situation when the local building inspector, who gave Mr. Daar the necessary permits for operating his restaurant, has more of an impact enforcing the ADA than do the provisions for enforcement listed in this federal law. To enforce the law, O'Brien must go before a federal judge, initially at his own expense, and request an injunction or otherwise file a lawsuit. Alternately, the attorney general of the United States could take O'Brien's case before the federal court. But given how few resources the Department of Justice devotes to litigation, this scenario is remote. O'Brien's greatest chance for success stems from the threat of a lawsuit, not from actually pursuing it in court.

[ ] WHO IS COVERED

What types of establishments are required by the ADA to provide accommodations for persons with disabilities? Title III offers a long list of private entities, which includes private transportation systems, hotels, restaurants, theaters, auditoriums, retail stores, service establishments, like a physician's office or insurance company, parks, museums, zoos, social service centers, like daycares, and places of exercise, like gyms or private golf clubs.[2] Compared to other civil rights legislation, this list is extensive, which makes the ADA more far-reaching than the Civil Rights Act of 1964. Robert Burgdorf, a disability rights law professor, describes the public accommodations provisions as "unprecedented [in] scope."[3] These provisions ban discrimination against disabled people not only in hotels and restaurants, but in every "mom and pop" store, which civil rights legislation failed to reach.[4] Another law professor observed that the public accommodations provisions cover more than 5 million establishments.[5]

Initially, most people envisioned concrete accommodations, like building modifications. To be sure, the public accommodations provisions offer two standards for buildings. Architectural obstacles in existing buildings must be removed. If getting rid of a barrier in an existing establishment is not readily achievable, alternative methods can be utilized. According to the *Americans with Disabilities Act Handbook*, "achievable" means "easily accomplishable and able to be carried out without much difficulty or expense."[6] For example, if the bar area of a restaurant is inaccessible to someone in a wheelchair, the restaurant may seat this person in the adjoining restaurant. Determining what is readily achievable involves examining ten factors, including the nature and the cost of action, the overall financial resources of the facility involved, and the effect on expenses and resources.[7] If O'Brien went to court, his request to have the chain removed undoubtedly would be described as readily achievable.

Newly constructed buildings also must be made accessible to persons with disabilities. If disabled people have "reasonable grounds" to suspect that they are "about to be subjected to discrimination" before a building is completed, a judge may grant them an injunction ensuring that it is made accessible. Architects are supposed to make new facilities accessible. Yet, this is not to say that architects are liable for noncompliance. Issuing its own guidelines, the Department of Justice has interpreted the provision about new facilities so narrowly that only those who both "design and construct" them are accountable. In other words, liability is limited to owners, lessees, lessors, or operators, but architects are not liable.[8]

Freeing architects from liability is unusual in comparison with other forms of civil law and civil rights law. Architects have long been held liable for inadequate design. If someone falls because of a faulty handrail or if a whole building collapses, the architect would be liable under other kinds of civil law.[9] Further, civil rights law holds a secondary professional, like a licensed real estate agent, accountable if, for instance, she abided by an owner's request not to show a house to African Americans.[10] The Department of Justice's guidelines about being the designer and the builder of a new facility are therefore different from other types of civil laws.

Most important, the idea that someone must design *and* construct a building creates a huge loophole not just for architects, but also for contractors and owners. This stems from the fact that the Department of Justice advises owners that as long as a new facility was initially designed in compliance with the ADA, they are not liable for any alterations made when it was built.[11] Although only one federal court has accepted the Department of Justice's interpretation, its guidelines constitute one of the rare instances where the executive branch's interpretation of this statute is more restrictive than that of the federal courts.[12]

Some persons with disabilities also have pursued cases that were not about concrete physical changes like ramps or elevators. Although the ADA is unclear on this point, there has been some question about the services that different establishments provide. Most notably, disabled people have challenged insurance benefits, arguing that some policies have not been accessible (read: available). While the matter is not entirely settled, these cases have been ruled largely in favor of the insurance carriers. The federal courts have held that the facility, not the service itself, be made available to persons with disabilities.[13]

By contrast, the greatest success for plaintiffs under the public accommodations provisions that did involve a service was *Bragdon v. Abbott*, the Supreme Court's first decision interpreting the ADA.[14] As explained in chapter 3, this decision was extremely important in determining how the federal judiciary would define who had a disability. Yet, it also represented a victory for disability activists fighting for public accommodations provisions since the Court ruled that Randon Bragdon, the dentist who insisted that he treat Abbott in a hospital two hours away from his practice after the latter had informed him that she had the HIV virus, had discriminated against her by making this request. Bragdon, the Court concluded, must treat Abbott in his office like all his other patients. He should follow the "universal precautions" approach advocated by the American Dental

Association, which stipulates that all dentists and hygienists adopt precautions against all contagious diseases that might, or might not, be disclosed to them.[15]

Finally, suits about entertainment in arenas and large auditoriums have raised questions about ticket pricing, which go beyond architectural obstacles. Members of the disability rights community have pressed not just for access into a theater, for example, but also for equal seating in the different price ranges offered.[16] Yet, the public accommodations title does not require that accommodations place disabled people in the same situation as people without them. For instance, as stated earlier, a restaurant need not provide a menu written in Braille as long as a waitperson will read it aloud to a person with vision problems.

[ ] LITTLE REMEDY FOR THIS RIGHT

While the disability rights movement hailed *Bragdon* as a great victory, the public accommodations provisions taken as a whole have not provided many disabled people with relief. Ruth Colker, a disability rights law professor, goes so far as to argue that "the lack of success under ADA Title III has been hidden by the seeming success of the plaintiff in *Bragdon v. Abbott*."[17] To her, Title III has not achieved its civil rights goal of making public accommodations accessible because of "underenforcement."[18] Instead, people like O'Brien have been forced into the awkward position of suing to help himself and others. Tracing the legislative history that accounted for this weak enforcement mechanism, Colker explains how it gives plaintiffs little incentive to bring lawsuits.[19] O'Brien, for instance, must either obtain an injunction or sue the owner of the parking lot. Such a suit would come at great personal expense and, since there are no possible punitive damages to be won, no attorney would take the case on a contingent-fee basis.

Colker has demonstrated that between June 1992, when the legislation first went into effect for larger places of public accommodation, and July 1998, only twenty-five cases had been heard before the courts of appeals. Juxtaposed against the number of cases brought under the employment provisions during roughly the same time period—475 in the courts of

appeals—the limited number of lawsuits under the public accommodations provisions looks even smaller.[20] While the twenty-five cases that
Colker cites is too small a sample to provide a good overview of how the
federal courts will interpret the public accommodations provision, it
should still be noted that 72 percent of the cases were decided in favor of
the defendant or the establishment contesting the accessibility issue.[21]
This figure is only marginally different from the employment provisions.
Coming to a similar conclusion, another law professor noted that most
places of public accommodation, like restaurants, were still not in compliance nearly four years after the ADA became federal law.[22] As she explains
it, "To a great extent, compliance must be voluntary."[23]

What is more, all but one of the cases taken before the federal courts
of appeals involved more than discrimination under the public accommodations provisions.[24] These cases combined a serious personal-injury
claim caused by the poor accessibility standards along with the discrimination claim. This combination gave the plaintiffs more of an incentive to
litigate since they were also eligible for damages under negligence per se
theory for a violation of a substantive standard that led to an injury. Most
of the plaintiffs were awarded around $10,000.[25]

The other possible outlet for O'Brien and all those who encounter an
inaccessible place of public accommodation is to file a complaint with the
Department of Justice. This complaint-driven enforcement agency, however, has been particularly slow in obtaining settlements.[26] As of September 1998, Colker reports that the Department of Justice had settled forty-
six cases. While this number is larger than the cases brought before the
federal courts, it nonetheless amounts to less than one per month. From
1998 until 2002, this figure approximately doubled. Most of the settlements, however, have been exceedingly small with the Department of Justice receiving $50,000 for the plaintiff in only one case. The settlement
amounts in other suits ranged from $250 to $10,000.

Placing the attorney general's settlements in perspective, Colker compared it with Maine's antidiscrimination statute. This state law gave places
of public accommodation more of an incentive to become accessible since
a $10,000 fee is levied against first-time offenders; second-time offenders
must pay a $25,000 fee; and third-time offenders have the fee doubled
again to $50,000.[27] Perhaps, Mr. Daar would have honored O'Brien's

request for accessible parking if it had been followed up with an official levying one of these fines against his restaurant.

Overall, Title III's emphasis is on injunctive relief with no possibility for punitive damages. Someone can ask a federal judge to issue an injunction against a company which is erecting a building that will be inaccessible, for instance, because the entrance has stairs but no ramp. Rather than waiting until the building is complete and then taking its owner to court for violating the ADA, injunctive relief stops this owner from making the building inaccessible in the first place. While an injunction is a powerful legal remedy, Colker concludes that without punitive damages, Title III provides limited relief. It also means that a judge rather than a jury makes the decisions about its enforcement. What concerns her is that without a strong legal remedy, disabled people will not find relief. Places of public accommodation, in other words, will have no incentive to become accessible. It may be less expensive not to abide by the law.

[ ] ANGLING FOR ACCESS

Accessibility involves much more than removing architectural obstacles. It also raises issues about authority. How much can the state impose on a private business? How much can the state interfere?

The question of authority manifested itself in the Supreme Court's second case about private accommodations: *PGA Tour v. Casey Martin.* This decision involved someone like O'Brien, who also had a mobility problem. Casey Martin, however, was not seeking a parking spot but the right to use a golf cart during a minor-league tournament in Florida.

Martin, who has a rare circulatory disease that makes it difficult for him to walk and puts him in what his doctor describes as extreme pain, had asked the Professional Golfers Association (PGA) for permission to use a golf cart.[28] When the PGA officials refused, Martin sought a temporary injunction from a federal court under the public accommodations provisions of the ADA. Injunction in hand, Martin used a cart during the tournament.

Covered by nearly every sports reporter in the country (in addition to some legal analysts), Martin's request for a reasonable accommodation received more attention than any other legal action involving the ADA. For the first time, the legislation underwent great public scrutiny. Martin's situation, however, was not unique. O'Brien's resembled it. Both men challenged the authority of those in charge of the public accommodation: the tournament and the parking lot, respectively.

To prove that a reasonable accommodation must be rendered under the pubic accommodations provisions, Martin's attorney had to prove that his client had a disability. The attorney also had to demonstrate that the tournament was inaccessible to people who had disabilities. However, the issue of accessibility was lost to many members of the press. They characterized Martin's request for a reasonable accommodation less as a plea for the ADA's enforcement and more as a contest of wills between him and the PGA officials. Many articles portrayed the PGA as the rightful authorities who were fighting to preserve the integrity of the no-cart rule, which protected the fair and equal treatment of all professional golfers.

For both Martin and O'Brien, it took a great deal of courage to challenge the authorities, whether they were PGA officials or the owner of a small fast food restaurant. Further, they must have known that not only their requests, but their lives, would be up for public scrutiny. *Martin* received more press than any other suit under the ADA thus far, and Sal, O'Brien's friend, laughed at him, given what he sees as the fun in the fight. Not all of the disabled—just as not all the able-bodied—have the time, the strength, or the stamina to fight such battles.

[ ] "THE RULES ARE THE RULES"

Despite Martin's distinctions between walking and playing golf, many journalists gave air to the view that using a golf cart meant Martin was getting something for nothing—a break from the rules by which everyone else had to abide—which prompted other golfers to express their resentment of Martin's "privileged position."[29] As the PGA tour commissioner, Tim Finchem, elaborated, "To afford one player a competitive advantage over the rest of the field is neither fair nor wise, and it is inconsistent with the fundamental aspect of the sport—that the playing field be level for all competitors."[30]

Insisting that a disabled person could be an athlete, Martin advanced the argument that he had no problem playing golf, despite his inability to walk from tee to tee." The cart aids my leg," explained Martin. "It doesn't aid my golf game at all."[31] Or as Eric Johnson, a former PGA tour player, put it, "Just because he's got a cart doesn't mean he's got a free ride to the PGA Tour. It doesn't matter how you get to the ball, you still have to hit it."[32] The Supreme Court ultimately ruled that walking was not essential to the game. Most important, it rejected the PGA's lawyers' argument that the small private club hosting the tournament should be exempt from governmental interference.

Whether the cases involve employment discrimination, receiving governmental services, or accessibility, the greatest conflict over the ADA revolves around the disabled person's request that someone change the rules.[33] But who is in a position to decide when the rules should change? Again, the issue shifts to whether the state has the authority to impose change.

Justice Antonin Scalia addressed this issue head-on in his *PGA Tour v. Martin* dissent. To him, the federal courts are not in the position to determine the fundamental attributes of the game of golf. Just as he argued that the Virginia Military Institute alone should decide whether to accept women, so he concluded that the PGA should decide what its tournament rules are.[34]

O'Brien's story shows him facing a discriminatory issue with parking, not riding in a golf cart. Nonetheless, it involves the same elements of authority and control: a fight by persons with disabilities over accessibility. The owner turned the issue into one about control over his business by locking O'Brien out of his parking lot. Why is it that control issues, not the actual accommodation, represent the biggest hurdle for disabled people?

Given that one of the central issues involves challenging the rules, what happens to the disabled who face inaccessible buildings but are uncomfortable with standing up to the authorities who made the rules that lock them out? Do they go home? Should the disabled or their families fight to enforce the ADA? Or should the law be given more teeth for enforcement?

AFTERWORD

[18]

The eloquent contributions in this volume give readers a look into the lives of persons with disabilities. By letting each contributor use his or her own voice, the volume opens doors of imagination in many diverse locations. It restores some balance to the overall narrative about disability by having people with impairments speak for themselves. In the past, it has been able-bodied authors like William Shakespeare and Victor Hugo, just to name a few, whose stories have shaped our views of disability.[1] "Non-disabled people have had, and largely continue to have, 'absolute power' over narratives," explains social policy specialist Jenny Morris, "when it comes to the representation of impairment in literature, film, television, [and] art."[2]

This volume also advances legal narration as a genre by moving its application from the lives of people of color to the lives of persons with disabilities. In the words of political theorist Larry Preston, "the imaginative reach of personal narrative" gives "us important access into the lives of particular people in particular places."[3] Or, as Toni Morrison succinctly explains it, "Narrative remains the best way to learn anything."[4]

What readers may have learned, however, is not uplifting. The stories in this volume are not tales of personal triumph like those of Charles Dickens's Tiny Tim or Horatio Alger's boys who inevitably beat the odds. Nor is there one suitable for the *Reader's Digest* series called "Drama in Real Life," the modern-day versions of the Horatio Alger story. The contributions in this volume depart from the traditional disability genre, which contains stories that disability rights advocate Mary Johnson criticizes for having "inspirational features about disabled people who [have] overcome personal affliction with a smile and a bundle of courage."[5] By contrast, the narratives in this book illustrate how the protagonists have been pushed up against the limits of the ADA. They show how difficult it is to change views—whether born from ignorance or malice—about persons with disabilities. Unfortunately, societal attitudes change slowly.

Reading the stories alongside the commentary, or their legal shadow, moreover, demonstrates how narrowly the federal courts have construed some of the ADA's titles. Title I, or the employment provisions, has had the least success protecting persons with disabilities since it overwhelmingly favors employers. By contrast, parts of Title II, or the governmental services provisions, have had more success. As shown in chapter 12, however, this title has been affected by the Supreme Court's new federalist doctrine. And the problem with Title III, or the public accommodations provisions that cover privately owned offices and businesses, is not so much the provisions themselves as the difficulties involved in enforcing them.

So where does this leave us? Is the ADA a monumental piece of civil rights legislation—or not? In the Bay Area, some members of the disability rights movement celebrate the day of its passage every year. Yet, what are they heralding? Are they confident that the law will be more broadly construed over time? Or do they think the ADA takes a vital step in the right direction, but it still needs modification?

If the ADA did undergo a legislative overhaul, what could happen? Would amending the employment provisions, for instance, endanger the governmental services provisions? Can the ADA be modified, in other words, without jeopardizing the provisions in it that have been successful? Will redrafting the ADA make it vulnerable to amendments that might make the law weaker rather than stronger? Could the law be strengthened by developing a more precise definition of what constitutes a disability? Should a different enforcement mechanism be built to further bolster the law? Can anything be done about the Supreme Court majority's position on federalism? Could amendments help rectify the ambiguities in the law that Justice Sandra Day O'Connor has underscored in her opinions and before business groups without making it less effective?

To work through some of these questions, readers should first analyze why the federal courts have interpreted Title I differently than Titles II and III. What are the differences among employment, governmental services, and accommodations in privately owned businesses? Why are persons with disabilities more likely to find public services and buildings more accessible than workplaces?

Readers should also ask: is there is a backlash against the ADA, as some authors in disability studies have maintained?[6] If so, does this backlash come from the public, the federal courts, or any other group or institution in the political arena at large? Is this backlash against the entire piece of legislation or just parts of it? Finally, how has the federal courts' interpretation of the ADA helped or hindered public support for this legislation? This volume raises these questions with the hope that its contents will help people find some answers.

APPENDIX

ABRIDGED AMERICANS WITH DISABILITIES ACT

Passed July 26, 1990. 104 Stat. 327

(42 U.S.C. 12101) Sec. 2—Findings and Purpose

(a) Findings

The Congress finds that—

(1) some 43,000,000 Americans have one or more physical or mental disabilities, and this number is increasing as the population as a whole is growing older;

(2) historically, society has tended to isolate and segregate individuals with disabilities, and, despite some improvements, such forms of discrimination against individuals with disabilities continue to be a serious and pervasive social problem;

(3) discrimination against individuals with disabilities persists in such critical areas as employment, housing, public accommodations, education, transportation, communication, recreation, institutionalization, health services, voting, and access to public services;

(4) unlike individuals who have experienced discrimination on the basis of race, color, sex, national origin, religion, or age, individuals who have experienced discrimination on the basis of disability have often had no legal recourse to redress such discrimination;

(5) individuals with disabilities continually encounter various forms of discrimination, including outright intentional exclusion, the discriminatory effects of architectural, transportation, and communication barriers, overprotective rules and policies, failure to make modifications to existing facilities and practices, exclusionary qualification standards and criteria, segregation, and relegation to lesser services, programs, activities, benefits, jobs, or other opportunities;

(6) census data, national polls, and other studies have documented that people with disabilities, as a group, occupy an inferior status in our society, and are severely disadvantaged socially, vocationally, economically, and educationally;

(7) individuals with disabilities are a discrete and insular minority who have been faced with restrictions and limitations, subjected to a history of purposeful unequal treatment, and relegated to a position of political powerlessness in our society, based on characteristics that are beyond the control of such individuals and resulting from stereotypic assumptions not truly indicative of the individual ability of such individuals to participate in, and contribute to, society;

(8) the Nation's proper goals regarding individuals with disabilities are to assure equality of opportunity, full participation, independent living, and economic self- sufficiency for such individuals; and

(9) the continuing existence of unfair and unnecessary discrimination and prejudice denies people with disabilities the opportunity to compete on an equal basis and to pursue those opportunities for which our free society is justifiably famous, and costs the United States billions of dollars in unnecessary expenses resulting from dependency and nonproductivity.

(b) Purpose

It is the purpose of this chapter—

(1) to provide a clear and comprehensive national mandate for the elimination of discrimination against individuals with disabilities;

(2) to provide clear, strong, consistent, enforceable standards addressing discrimination against individuals with disabilities;

(3) to ensure that the Federal Government plays a central role in enforcing the standards established in this Act on behalf of individuals with disabilities; and

(4) to invoke the sweep of congressional authority, including the power to enforce the fourteenth amendment and to regulate commerce, in order to address the major areas of discrimination faced day-to-day by people with disabilities.

(42 U.S.C. 12102) Sec. 3—Definitions

As used in this chapter:
(2) Disability.
The term disability means, with respect to an individual
(A) a physical or mental impairment that substantially limits one or more of the major life activities of such individual;
(B) a record of such an impairment; or
(C) being regarded as having such an impairment.

TITLE I. EMPLOYMENT

(42 U.S.C. 12111) Sec. 101—Definitions

As used in this title:
(3) Direct threat
The term direct threat means a significant risk to the health or safety of others that cannot be eliminated by reasonable accommodation.
(5) Employer
(A) In general
The term employer means a person engaged in an industry affecting commerce who has 15 or more employees for each working day in each of 20 or more calendar weeks in the current or preceding calendar year, and any agent of such person, except that, for two years following the effective date of this title, an employer means a person engaged in an industry affecting commerce who has 25 or more employees for each working day in each of 20 or more calendar weeks in the current or preceding year, and any agent of such person.
(9) Reasonable accommodation
The term reasonable accommodation may include—
(A) making existing facilities used by employees readily accessible to and usable by individuals with disabilities; and
(B) job restructuring, part-time or modified work schedules, reassignment to a vacant position, acquisition or modification of equipment or devices, appropriate adjustment or modifications of examinations, training materials or policies, the provision of qualified readers or interpreters, and other similar accommodations for individuals with disabilities.
(10) Undue hardship
(A) In general

The term undue hardship means an action requiring significant difficulty or expense, when considered in light of the factors set forth in subparagraph (B).

(B) Factors to be considered

In determining whether an accommodation would impose an undue hardship on a covered entity, factors to be considered include

(i) the nature and cost of the accommodation needed under this Act;

(ii) the overall financial resources of the facility or facilities involved in the provision of the reasonable accommodation; the number of persons employed at such facility; the effect on expenses and resources, or the impact otherwise of such accommodation upon the operation of the facility;

(iii) the overall financial resources of the covered entity; the overall size of the business of a covered entity with respect to the number of its employees; the number, type, and location of its facilities; and (iv) the type of operation or operations of the covered entity, including the composition, structure, and functions of the workforce of such entity; the geographic separateness, administrative, or fiscal relationship of the facility or facilities in question to the covered entity.

(42 U.S.C. 12112) Sec. 102—Discrimination

(a) General Rule

No covered entity shall discriminate against a qualified individual with a disability because of the disability of such individual in regard to job application procedures, the hiring, advancement, or discharge of employees, employee compensation, job training, and other terms, conditions, and privileges of employment.

(d) Medical Examinations and Inquiries

(1) In general

The prohibition against discrimination as referred to in subsection (a) shall include medical examinations and inquiries.

(2) Preemployment

(A) Prohibited examination or inquiry

Except as provided in paragraph (3), a covered entity shall not conduct a medical examination or make inquiries of a job applicant as to whether such applicant is an individual with a disability or as to the nature or severity of such disability.

(B) Acceptable inquiry
A covered entity may make preemployment inquiries into the ability of an applicant to perform job-related functions.

(42 U.S.C. 12114) Sec. 104—Illegal Use of Drugs and Alcohol

(a) Qualified Individual With a Disability
For purposes of this title, the term qualified individual with a disability shall not include any employee or applicant who is currently engaging in the illegal use of drugs, when the covered entity acts on the basis of such use.

(42 U.S.C. 12117) Sec. 107—Enforcement

(a) Powers, Remedies, and Procedures
The powers, remedies, and procedures set forth in sections 705, 706, 707, 709, and 710 of the Civil Rights Act of 1964 (42 U.S.C. 2000e-4, 2000e-5, 2000e-6, 2000e-8, and 2000e-9) shall be the powers, remedies, and procedures this title provides to the Commission, to the Attorney General, or to any person alleging discrimination on the basis of disability in violation of any provision of this Act, or regulations promulgated under section 106, concerning employment.

TITLE II. PUBLIC SERVICES

Subtitle A. Prohibition against Discrimination and Other Generally Applicable Provisions

(42 U.S.C. 12115) Sec. 201—Definitions

As used in this title:
(1) Public entity
The term public entity means
(A) any State or local government;
(B) any department, agency, special purpose district, or other instrumentality of a State or States or local government; and
(C) the National Railroad Passenger Corporation, and any commuter authority (as defined in section 103(8) of the Rail Passenger Service Act).
(2) Qualified individual with a disability
The term qualified individual with a disability means an individual with a disability who, with or without reasonable modifications to rules, poli-

cies, or practices, the removal of architectural, communication, or transportation barriers, or the provision of auxiliary aids and services, meets the essential eligibility requirements for the receipt of services or the participation in programs or activities provided by a public entity.

(42 U.S.C. 12132) Sec. 202—Discrimination

Subject to the provisions of this title, no qualified individual with a disability shall, by reason of such disability, be excluded from participation in or be denied the benefits of the services, programs, or activities of a public entity, or be subjected to discrimination by any such entity.

(42 U.S.C. 12132) Sec. 203—Enforcement

The remedies, procedures, and rights set forth in section 505 of the Rehabilitation Act of 1973 (29 U.S.C. 794a) shall be the remedies, procedures, and rights this title provides to any person alleging discrimination on the basis of disability in violation of section 202.

(42 U.S.C. 12141) Sec. 221—Definitions

As used in this part:
(2) Designated public transportation. The term designated public transportation means transportation (other than public school transportation) by bus, rail, or any other conveyance (other than transportation by aircraft or intercity or commuter rail transportation [as defined in section 241]) that provides the general public with general or special service (including charter service) on a regular and continuing basis.
(3) Fixed route system. The term fixed route system means a system of providing designated public transportation on which a vehicle is operated along a prescribed route according to a fixed schedule.

(42 U.S.C. 12142) Sec. 222—Public Entities Operating Fixed Route Systems

(a) Purchase and Lease of New Vehicles
It shall be considered discrimination for purposes of section 202 of this Act and section 504 of the Rehabilitation Act of 1973 (29 U.S.C. 794) for a public entity which operates a fixed route system to purchase or lease a new bus, a new rapid rail vehicle, a new light rail vehicle, or any other new vehicle to be used on such system, if the solicitation for such purchase or lease is made after

the 30th day following the effective date of this subsection and if such bus, rail vehicle, or other vehicle is not readily accessible to and usable by individuals with disabilities, including individuals who use wheelchairs.

(42 U.S.C. 12143) Sec. 223—Paratransit as a Complement to Fixed Route Service

(a) General Rule
It shall be considered discrimination for purposes of section 202 of this Act and section 504 of the Rehabilitation Act of 1973 (29 U.S.C. 794) for a public entity which operates a fixed route system (other than a system which provides solely commuter bus service) to fail to provide with respect to the operations of its fixed route system, in accordance with this section, paratransit and other special transportation services to individuals with disabilities, including individuals who use wheelchairs, that are sufficient to provide to such individuals a level of service (1) which is comparable to the level of designated public transportation services provided to individuals without disabilities using such system; or (2) in the case of response time, which is comparable, to the extent practicable, to the level of designated public transportation services provided to individuals without disabilities using such system.

Part II. Public Transportation by Intercity and Commuter Rail

(42 U.S.C. 12162) Sec. 242—Intercity and Commuter Rail Actions Considered Discriminatory

(a) Intercity Rail Transportation
   (1) One car per train rule. It shall be considered discrimination for purposes of section 202 of this Act and section 504 of the Rehabilitation Act of 1973 (29 U.S.C. 794) for a person who provides intercity rail transportation to fail to have at least one passenger car per train that is readily accessible to and usable by individuals with disabilities, including individuals who use wheelchairs, in accordance with regulations issued under section 244, as soon as practicable, but in no event later than 5 years after the date of enactment of this Act.
   (2) New intercity cars. General rule. Except as otherwise provided in this subsection with respect to individuals who use wheelchairs, it shall be considered discrimination for purposes of section 202 of this Act and section 504 of the Rehabilitation Act of 1973 (29 U.S.C. 794) for a person to purchase or lease any new rail passenger cars for use in intercity rail transportation, and for which a solicitation is made later than 30 days

after the effective date of this section, unless all such rail cars are readily accessible to and usable by individuals with disabilities, including individuals who use wheelchairs, as prescribed by the Secretary of Transportation in regulations issued under section 244.

TITLE III. PUBLIC ACCOMMODATIONS AND SERVICES OPERATED BY PRIVATE ENTITIES

(42 U.S.C. 12181) Sec. 301—Definitions

(2) Commercial facilities
The term commercial facilities means facilities
(A) that are intended for nonresidential use; and
(7) Public accommodation
The following private entities are considered public accommodations for purposes of this title, if the operations of such entities affect commerce:
   (A) an inn, hotel, motel, or other place of lodging, except for an establishment located within a building that contains not more than five rooms for rent or hire and that is actually occupied by the proprietor of such establishment as the residence of such proprietor;
   (B) a restaurant, bar, or other establishment serving food or drink;
   (C) a motion picture house, theater, concert hall, stadium, or other place of exhibition or entertainment;
   (D) an auditorium, convention center, lecture hall, or other place of public gathering;
   (E) a bakery, grocery store, clothing store, hardware store, shopping center, or other sales or rental establishment;
   (F) a laundromat, dry cleaner, bank, barber shop, beauty shop, travel service, shoe repair service, funeral parlor, gas station, office of an accountant or lawyer, pharmacy, insurance office, professional office of a health care provider, hospital, or other service establishment;
   (G) a terminal, depot, or other station used for specified public transportation;
   (H) a museum, library, gallery, or other place of public display or collection;
   (I) a park, zoo, amusement park, or other place of recreation;
   (J) a nursery, elementary, secondary, undergraduate, or postgraduate private school, or other place of education;
   (K) a day care center, senior citizen center, homeless shelter, food bank, adoption agency, or other social service center establishment; and

(L) a gymnasium, health spa, bowling alley, golf course, or other place of exercise or recreation.

(9) Readily achievable

The term readily achievable means easily accomplishable and able to be carried out without much difficulty or expense. In determining whether an action is readily achievable, factors to be considered include

(A) the nature and cost of the action needed under this Act;

(B) the overall financial resources of the facility or facilities involved in the action; the number of persons employed at such facility; the effect on expenses and resources, or the impact otherwise of such action upon the operation of the facility;

(C) the overall financial resources of the covered entity; the overall size of the business of a covered entity with respect to the number of its employees; the number, type, and location of its facilities; and

(D) the type of operation or operations of the covered entity, including the composition, structure, and functions of the workforce of such entity; the geographic separateness, administrative or fiscal relationship of the facility or facilities in question to the covered entity.

As used in this title:

(42 U.S.C. 12182) Sec. 302—Prohibition of Discrimination by Public Accommodations

(a) General Rule

No individual shall be discriminated against on the basis of disability in the full and equal enjoyment of the goods, services, facilities, privileges, advantages, or accommodations of any place of public accommodation by any person who owns, leases (or leases to), or operates a place of public accommodation.

(i) Denial of participation. It shall be discriminatory to subject an individual or class of individuals on the basis of a disability or disabilities of such individual or class, directly, or through contractual, licensing, or other arrangements, to a denial of the opportunity of the individual or class to participate in or benefit from the goods, services, facilities, privileges, advantages, or accommodations of an entity.

(ii) Participation in unequal benefit. It shall be discriminatory to afford an individual or class of individuals, on the basis of a disability or disabilities of such individual or class, directly, or through contractual, licensing, or other arrangements with the opportunity to participate in or benefit from a good, service, facility, privilege, advantage, or accommodation that is not equal to that afforded to other individuals.

(iii) Separate benefit. It shall be discriminatory to provide an individual or class of individuals, on the basis of a disability or disabilities of such individual or class, directly, or through contractual, licensing, or other arrangements with a good, service, facility, privilege, advantage, or accommodation that is different or separate from that provided to other individuals, unless such action is necessary to provide the individual or class of individuals with a good, service, facility, privilege, advantage, or accommodation, or other opportunity that is as effective as that provided to others.

(b) Integrated settings

Goods, services, facilities, privileges, advantages, and accommodations shall be afforded to an individual with a disability in the most integrated setting appropriate to the needs of the individual.

(c) Opportunity to participate

Notwithstanding the existence of separate or different programs or activities provided in accordance with this section, an individual with a disability shall not be denied the opportunity to participate in such programs or activities that are not separate or different.

(42 U.S.C. 12183) Sec. 303—New Construction and Alterations in Public Accommodations and Commercial Facilities

(1) a failure to design and construct facilities for first occupancy later than 30 months after the date of enactment of this Act that are readily accessible to and usable by individuals with disabilities, except where an entity can demonstrate that it is structurally impracticable to meet the requirements of such subsection in accordance with standards set forth or incorporated by reference in regulations issued under this title; and

(2) with respect to a facility or part thereof that is altered by, on behalf of, or for the use of an establishment in a manner that affects or could affect the usability of the facility or part thereof, a failure to make alterations in such a manner that, to the maximum extent feasible, the altered portions of the facility are readily accessible to and usable by individuals with disabilities, including individuals who use wheelchairs. Where the entity is undertaking an alteration that affects or could affect usability of or access to an area of the facility containing a primary function, the entity shall also make the alterations in such a manner that, to the maximum extent feasible, the path of travel to the altered area and the bathrooms, tele-

phones, and drinking fountains serving the altered area, are readily accessible to and usable by individuals with disabilities where such alterations to the path of travel or the bathrooms, telephones, and drinking fountains serving the altered area are not disproportionate to the overall alterations in terms of cost and scope (as determined under criteria established by the Attorney General).

(b) Elevator

Subsection (a) shall not be construed to require the installation of an elevator for facilities that are less than three stories or have less than 3,000 square feet per story unless the building is a shopping center, a shopping mall, or the professional office of a health care provider or unless the Attorney General determines that a particular category of such facilities requires the installation of elevators based on the usage of such facilities.

(42 U.S.C. 12184) Sec. 304—Prohibition of Discrimination in Specified Public Transportation Services Provided by Private Entities

(a) General Rule

No individual shall be discriminated against on the basis of disability in the full and equal enjoyment of specified public transportation services provided by a private entity that is primarily engaged in the business of transporting people and whose operations affect commerce.

NOTES

INTRODUCTION

1. The noted exceptions are *Bragdon v. Abbott*, 524 U.S. 624 (1998), and *Olmstead v. L.C. by Zimring*, 527 U.S. 581 (1999), where the Supreme Court ruled that it would be discriminatory for a state not to release people with disabilities from their institutional settings and into community-based treatment programs. See Michael L. Perlin, "'Their Promises of Paradise': Will *Olmstead v. L.C.* Resuscitate the Constitutional 'Least Restrictive Alternative' Principle in Mental Disability Law?" 37 *Houston Law Review* 999 (2000). Also see James Leonard, "The Shadows of Unconstitutionality: How the New Federalism May Affect the Antidiscrimination Mandate of the Americans with Disabilities Act," 52 *Alabama Law Review* 91 (2000): 144–46, for a good comparison with *Board of Trustees of the University of Alabama v. Garrett*, 1531 U.S. 356 (2001).

2. See Patricia J. Williams, *The Alchemy of Race and Rights* (Cambridge, Mass.: Harvard University Press, 1991); Derrick Bell, *Faces at the Bottom of the Well: The Permanence of Racism* (New York: Basic, 1992); Richard Delgado, *The Rodrigo Chronicles: Conversations about America and Race* (New York: New York University Press, 1995). For a critical view, see Daniel A. Farber and Suzanna Sherry, "Telling Stories Out of School: An Essay on Legal Narratives," 45 *Stanford Law Review* 807 (1993): 808.

3. Richard Delgado and Jean Stefanic, "Derrick Bell's Chronicle of the Space Traders: Would the U.S. Sacrifice People of Color If the Price Were Right?" 62 *University of Colorado Law Review* 321 (1991): 322.

4. Jenny Morris, "Impairment and Disability: Constructing an Ethics of Care That Promotes Human Rights," *Hypatia* 16 (2001): 5.

5. In October 2000, the Disability Rights and Education Defense Fund and the U.S. Social Security Administration held a conference about disability rights from an international perspective. See "From Principles to Practice: An International Disability Law and Policy Symposium," downloaded from http://www. dredf.org/symposium/index.html. Accessed August 2002.

6. Also, as Marta Russell explains, "The commodification of labor is a crucial contributing factor to the lack of economic advancement of disabled people." The economic system of capitalism in the United States "throws out" people with disabilities along with the sick, the aged, and the unemployed. Marta Russell, "What Disability Civil Rights Cannot Do: Employment and Political Economy," *Disability & Society* 17 (2003): 119.

7. This figure is from a Harris survey conducted in 2000. See Christine M. Tomko, "Note: The Economically Disadvantaged and the Americans with Disabilities Act: Why Economic Need Should Factor into the Mitigating Measures Disability Analysis," 52 *Case Western Reserve Law Review* 1033 (2002). According to the census figures, which have not been updated in summary form since 1997, 21 percent of all people with disabilities live in poverty, whereas for those with no disability, the number drops to 8.3 percent. See U.S. Census Bureau, 1997, downloaded from http://www.census.gov/hhes/www/disable/sipp/disab97/asc97.html. Accessed January 2003. Whom the Harris poll tracks as disabled is different, however, from whom the census includes. The Harris poll figures change with the type of poll taken, whereas the census figures are constant. By contrast, the definition of who is disabled under the ADA is cast broadly so that it includes people who have a major life activity substantially limited, in addition to those who have a history of an impairment or are regarded as having one.

8. See Chai Feldblum, "Definition of Disability under Federal Antidiscrimination Law: What Happened? Why? and What Can We Do about It?" 21 *Berkeley Journal of Employment and Labor Law* 91 (2000): 94. Also see Deborah A. Stone, *The Disabled State* (Philadelphia: Temple University Press, 1984).

9. Richard K. Scotch, "American Disability Policy in the Twentieth Century," in *The New Disability History: American Perspectives,* ed. Paul Longmore and Lauri Umansky (New York: New York University Press, 2001), 377–78. Also see David J. Rothman, *The Discovery of the Asylum: Social Order and Disorder in the New Republic* (Boston: Little, Brown, 1971).

10. Rothman, *Discovery of the Asylum,* xviii.

11. Alexis de Tocqueville, *Democracy in America,* trans. George Lawrence and J. P. Mayer (Garden City, N.Y.: Anchor, 1969).

12. See Rosemarie Garland Thomson, *Extraordinary Bodies: Figuring Physical Disability in American Culture and Literature* (New York: Columbia University Press, 1998), 42–43.

13. Ralph Waldo Emerson, "Self-Reliance," in *The Works of Ralph Waldo Emerson* (1847; reprint, New York: Tudor, 1938), 1:32, quoted in Thomson, *Extraordinary Bodies*, 41–42.

14. K. Walter Hickel, "Medicine, Bureaucracy, and Social Welfare: The Politics of Disability Compensation for American Veterans of World War I," in *The New Disability History: American Perspectives*, ed. Paul K. Longmore and Lauri Umansky (New York: New York University Press, 2001), 236–67.

15. See Peter David Blanck and Michael Millender, "Before Disability Civil Rights: Civil War Pensions and the Politics of Disability in America," 52 *Alabama Law Review* 1 (2000): 5. Also see Peter Blanck and Chen Song, "Civil War Pension Attorneys and Disability Politics," 35 *University of Michigan Journal of Law Reform* 137 (2001–2002), for another piece of the evolving perspective on disability, the Civil War pensions, and the Americans with Disabilities Act.

16. Theda Skocpol, *Protecting Soldiers and Mothers* (Cambridge, Mass.: Harvard University Press, 1992), 151.

17. Ibid., 241.

18. Thomson, *Extraordinary Bodies*, 42.

19. See Paul B. Bellamy, *A History of Workmen's Compensation, 1898–1915: From Courtroom to Boardroom* (New York: Garland, 1997).

20. Hickel, "Medicine, Bureaucracy, and Social Welfare," 239–41.

21. Ibid., 246.

22. See Douglas C. Baynton, "Disability and the Justification of Inequality in American History," in *The New Disability History: American Perspectives*, ed. Paul Longmore and Lauri Umansky (New York: New York University Press, 2001), 45.

23. See Rogers M. Smith, *Civic Ideals: Conflicting Views of Citizenship in U.S. History* (New Haven, Conn.: Yale University Press, 1997), and "Beyond Tocqueville, Myrdal, and Hartz: The Multiple Traditions in America," *American Political Science Review* 87 (1993): 549–66.

24. Ibid.

25. Ibid., 47.

26. Ibid.

27. See Jacobus Ten de Broek, "The Right to Live in the World: The Disabled in the Law of Torts," 54 *California Law Review* 841 (1966).

28. See Carolyn Gooding, *Disabling Laws, Enabling Acts* (London: Pluto, 1994), 22. After the Rehabilitation Act passed, disability rights for schoolchildren were included in the Education for All Handicapped Children Act of 1975, which was renamed the Individuals with Disabilities Education Act when it was amended in 1992. Finally, disability rights can be found in the Fair Housing Act Amendments of 1988.

29. See Edward D. Berkowitz, *Disabled Policy: America's Programs for the Handicapped* (New York: Cambridge University Press, 1987); Mary Lenz Walker, *Beyond Bureaucracy: Mary Elizabeth Switzer and Rehabilitation* (Lanham, Md.: University Press of America, 1985); and Ruth O'Brien, *Crippled Justice: The History of Modern Disability Policy in the Workplace* (Chicago, Ill.: University of Chicago, 2001).

30. See Senate Report, No. 1297, 93d Cong., 2d sess., 1974, p. 34.

31. See Richard K. Scotch, *From Goodwill to Civil Rights* (Philadelphia: Temple University Press, 1984). Also see K. Hull, *The Rights of Physically Handicapped People* (New York: Avon, 1979).

32. O'Brien, *Crippled Justice*, 125–28; and Paul K. Longmore, "Medical Decision Making and People with Disabilities: A Clash of Cultures," *Journal of Law, Medicine & Ethics* 23 (1995): 83.

33. Doris Z. Fleischer and Frieda Zames, "Disability Rights," *Social Policy* 28 (1998): 52; and Sharon Barnatt and Richard Scotch, *Disability Protests: Contentious Politics, 1970–1999* (Washington, D.C.: Gallaudet University Press, 2001), 165–66. Also See Doris Z. Fleischer and Frieda Zames, *The Disability Rights Movement: From Charity to Confrontation* (Philadelphia: Temple University Press, 2000); and Joseph P. Shapiro, *No Pity: People with Disabilities Forging a New Civil Rights Movement* (New York: Times Books, 1993).

34. For an overview of some of the ideas that were kicked around before and during the legislative process, see O'Brien, *Crippled Justice*, 168–71. Also see Robert L. Burgdorf, Jr., "The Americans with Disabilities Act: Analysis and Implications of a Second-Generation Civil Rights Statute," *Harvard Civil Rights/Civil Liberties Law Review* 26 (1991): 413–522.

35. See Feldblum, "Definition of Disability under Federal Antidiscrimination Law," 92.

36. The ambiguity of the regulations was clear in the Supreme Court decisions *Southeastern Community College v. Davis*, 442 U.S. 397 (1979), and *School Board of Nassau County, Florida, v. Arline*, 480 U.S. 273 (1987). Also see *Alexander v. Choate*, 469 U.S. 287 (1985), for the Court's confusing opinion on affirmative action. The Court decided that a reasonable accommodation was similar to affirmative action and then it reversed its opinion.

37. Between 1981 and 1988, discrimination against people with disabilities had become more pronounced. In 1988, only 23.4 percent of men with disabilities worked full time, down from 29.8 percent, and only 13.1 percent of women with disabilities worked, up from 11.4 percent. Salaries for men fell from 77 percent to 64 percent of what other workers made, and for women from 69 percent to 62 percent. Jeffrey O. Cooper, "Overcoming Barriers to Employment: The Meaning of Reasonable Accommodation and Undue Hardship in the Americans with Disabilities Act," 139 *University of Pennsylvania Law Review* 1424 (1993): 1425.

38. See Burgdorf, "Americans with Disabilities Act."

39. HIV was the only contentious issue that received much public attention. See Marta Russell, *Beyond Ramps: Disability at the End of the Social Contract* (Monroe, Maine: Common Courage Press, 1998), 112–15, for an illuminating discussion of the "Republican ploy" about civil rights.

40. See Mary Johnson, *Make Them Go Away: Clint Eastwood, Christopher Reeve and the Case against Disability Rights* (Louisville, Ky.: Advocado Press, 2003), xii, for an excellent account of the disability rights movement and opposition to the Americans with Disabilities Act.

41. See Shapiro, *No Pity*, 117–20.

42. See Russell, *Beyond Ramps*, 112. Also see Edward D. Berkowitz, "A Historical Preface to the Americans with Disabilities Act," *Journal of Policy History* 6 (1994): 112.

43. See O'Brien, *Crippled Justice*, 171–73; and Johnson, *Make Them Go Away*, 14–15, for discussions about how key legislators insisted that the enforcement mechanism be weakened. Also see Ruth O'Brien, "Duality and Division: The Development of American Labor Policy from the Wagner Act to the Civil Rights Act," *International Contributions to Labour Studies* (1994): 21–51, for a discussion about the different types of administrative agencies available to legislators.

44. See the appendix, which contains the major sections of the Americans with Disabilities Act, 1990, 104 Stat. 327, sec. 3, 41 U.S.C. 12102.

45. A fifth title, "miscellaneous provisions," includes, for instance, remedies for plaintiffs, retaliation, agency regulations, and means for alternative dispute resolutions. See James P. Colgate, "If You Build It, Can They Sue? Architects' Liability under Title III of the ADA," 68 *Fordham Law Review* 137 (1999): 141.

46. See *U.S. Airways v. Barnett*, 535 U.S. (2002), slip opinion, where the Supreme Court gave a limited perspective on what type of reassignment could be viewed as a reasonable accommodation.

47. See 1990, 104 Stat. 327, Title I, sec. 101, 42 U.S.C. 12111.

48. These public transportation provisions do not include aircraft or certain railroads since specific statutes about the airlines and the railroads prohibit their exclusion. See 1990, 104 Stat. 327, Title II, subtitle B, part I. In *U.S. Airways v. Barnett*, the Supreme Court introduced some new ideas that might qualify the notion of undue hardship. It made a reference to "reasonable in the run of cases" and "reasonable on its face." These phrases might well be addressed by the lower federal courts and could be used to qualify *undue hardship*. Nonetheless, the reasonableness requirement must be established before employers can rely on the undue hardship defense.

49. 1990, 104 Stat. 327, Title II, sec. 223C (4), 42 U.S.C. 12143.

50. The statute stipulates that "no qualified individual with a disability shall, by reason of such disability, be excluded from participation in or be denied the benefits of the services, programs, or activities of a public entity, or be subjected to discrimination by any such entity."

51. 1990, 104 Stat. 327, Title II, sec. 203, 42 U.S.C. 12132.

52. This provision for preventative relief is the same one that was allowed under section 504, which in turn had been modeled after Title VI of the Civil Rights Act. See Scotch, *From Goodwill to Civil Rights*, 52.

53. 1990, 104 Stat. 327, Title III, sec. 308(a)(2), 42 U.S.C. 12188.

54. 1990, 104 Stat. 327, Title II, sec. 308(b)(2)(C)(ii)(4), 42 U.S.C. 12188.

55. See Johnson, *Make Them Go Away*, 14–15, for a good overview of the differences between the original legislation proposed by Lowell Weicker in 1988 and the ADA.

56. All attorneys depend on fees, whether they accept contingency fees or have other payment arrangements. Contingency fees, which is where a private, for-profit attorney takes 25–40 percent of the damages awarded, do not work under

Title III because the ADA is a fee-shifting statute. That is, attorneys are only paid if their client—the plaintiff—prevails. This makes it unlikely that a private, for-profit attorney will take a case that only asks for injunctive relief. What is more, public-interest law organizations also depend on fees, which can account for 50 percent of an attorney's annual income, and therefore they too have difficulty taking these cases.

57. 1990, 104 Stat. 327, Title III, sec. 308(b)(2)(C)(ii)(4), 42 U.S.C. 12188.

58. The Supreme Court decision that initially narrowed section 504's scope was *Southeastern Community College v. Davis*. Also *Alexander v. Choate* proved to be a disappointment since it did not offer an expansive concept of what it meant to be "otherwise qualified" for a position.

59. The Senate report outlined the congressional intent underlying the term *qualified* for a position in the workplace. This provision differed from section 504 by getting rid of the word "otherwise" so as to clarify the issue about reasonable accommodations. A person is qualified not in spite of a physical or mental impairment, but after a reasonable accommodation has been made by an employer. Moreover, the means of judging someone's qualifications were determined not by examining every aspect of the job, but by scrutinizing its essential functions. The term *essential functions* was used so that people with disabilities would not be fired for failing to perform what the Senate report deemed to be marginal tasks or functions. Being qualified for state and local governmental services under Title II was not as stringent as it was under the employment provisions since it was not tied to essential functions. The recipients of the services simply had to show that they would benefit from them. What the term *reasonable accommodations* meant was explicated by the Senate report. Examples of workplace accommodations included job restructuring, part-time or modified work schedules, and reassignment to vacant positions. That reassignment had been included was significant since this meant that people with disabilities, like those resulting from workplace injuries, could request transfers out of positions where they could no longer perform the essential functions. Finally, Congress clarified what it meant by *undue hardship*. Both the House Judiciary Committee and the Senate report stipulated that a business would have to prove that it would be in financial peril. The complementary provision for state and local governmental services—undue administrative hardship—also had a high threshold. See Senate Report, No.116 to accompany S.933, the Americans with Disabilities Act, Committee on Labor and Human Resources, 101st Cong., 1st sess., p. 9; H.R. Conference Report, No. 558, 101st Cong., 2d sess., 1990. Many examples of reasonable accommodations also appeared in the statute. Also see Elizabeth Clark Morin, "ADA of 1990: Social Integration through Employment," 40 *Catholic University Law Review* 202 (1990).

60. Senate Report, No. 116, pp. 21–24.

61. These regulations were to be developed by July 26, 1991. See Burgdorf, "Americans with Disabilities Act," 463.

62. Michael Lewyn, "Thou Shalt Not Put a Stumbling Block before the Blind: The ADA and Public Transit for the Disabled," 52 *Hastings Law Journal* 1037 (2001): 1071.

63. Burgdorf, "Americans with Disabilities Act," 427.

64. See Russell, *Beyond Ramps*, 114, who argues that the Bush administration realized that "compliance" would be "largely voluntary."

65. *Karen Sutton and Kimberly Hinton v. United Airlines Inc.*, 527 U.S. 471 (1999), 479, 482.

66. Quoted in Russell, "What Disability Civil Rights Cannot Do," 119.

67. Feldblum, "Definition of Disability under Federal Antidiscrimination Law," 93.

68. See Ruth Colker, "The ADA: A Windfall for Defendants," 34 *Harvard Civil Rights/Civil Liberties Law Review* (1999): 99–163. The American Bar Association conducted a study of 700 Title I cases between 1992 and 1997 and found that employers won 92 percent of the time. Also see Ruth Colker, "Winning and Losing under the Americans with Disabilities Act," 62 *Ohio Law Journal* 239 (2001); and Jeffrey A. Van Detta and Dan R. Gallipeau, "Judges and Juries: Why Are So Many ADA Plaintiffs Losing Summary Judgment Motions, and Would They Fare Better before a Jury? A Response to Professor Colker," 19 *Review of Litigation* 505 (2000).

69. See Susan Gluck Mezey, Will Jordan, Catherine Thie, and Douglas Davis, "The Americans with Disabilities Act in Federal Court: Litigating against Public Entities," *Disability and Society* 17 (2002): 54. This article divides these cases into thirteen categories: physical access; zoning; credentials; prisons; benefits; law enforcement; athletics; school; health care; integration; exemptions; accommodations; and parking. Oddly, the most litigation is in prisons, which accounts for 74 percent of all of these decisions.

70. Ibid.

71. See *Pennsylvania Department of Corrections v. Yeskey*, 524 U.S. 206 (1998). Until the Supreme Court's ruling in favor of prisoners, most federal courts ruled that prisons were not covered under the ADA. Mezey et al., "Americans with Disabilities Act in Federal Court," 58.

72. Mezey et al., "Americans with Disabilities Act in Federal Court," 60–61.

73. O'Brien, *Crippled Justice*.

74. This is also the case with Title IV, the telecommunications provision. Just as in other cases involving compliance, the federal court judges have held that private parties can receive damages only if the reluctant party held back services with malicious intent. In the parts of the ADA that allow private parties to sue for damages, there is no stipulation that these damages must be awarded if there were animus against the person with a disability.

75. Interview with Sharon Miller, who was a disability rights litigator in the 1990s, November 3, 2002, Augusta, Maine.

76. Linda Greenhouse, "Court Had Rehnquist Initials Carved on Docket," *New York Times*, July 2, 2002, p. 1.

77. The 5–4 lineup about broke in *Nevada Dept. of Human Resources v. Hibbs* 538 U.S. slip opinion (2003) when Justice Stephen G. Breyer switched his position in favor of states rights under the Eleventh Amendment. Meanwhile, Chief Justice William Rehnquist and Sandra Day O'Connor also changed sides by upholding the federal government's authority. In the decision, Hibbs sued the state of Nevada

for firing him in violation of the Family and Medical Leave Act. Rehnquist wrote the majority opinion on "the other side of an issue that analysts had long predicted would define his legacy." Quoted from Frank J. Murray, "Justice Reverses Himself on Rights: Breyer Rules with Majority on Family Leave," *Washington Times*, June 2, 2003, A4.

78. See *Federal Maritime Commission v. South Carolina State Ports Authority*, 122 S.Ct. 1864 (2002), which rejected a private party's right to sue a state-run port; *Florida Prepaid Postsecondary Education Expense Board v. College Savings Bank*, 527 U.S. 627 (1999), for patent violations; *College Savings Bank v. Florida Prepaid Postsecondary Education Expense Board*, 527 U.S. 666 (1999), for trademark infringements; *Kimel v. Florida Board of Regents*, 528 U.S. 62 (2000), for age discrimination; and *Alden v. Maine*, 527 U.S. 706 (1999), for the Fair Labor Standards Act (FLSA) violations. The Court was building on the new federalism doctrine first established in *Seminole Tribe of Florida v. Florida*, 517 U.S. 441 (1996).

79. Linda Greenhouse, "5–4, Now and Forever; At the Court, Dissent over States' Rights Is Now War," *New York Times*, June 9, 2002.

80. Interview with Miller, November 3, 2002.

81. See *Kay Barnes v. Jeffrey Gorman*, 534 U.S. (2002), slip opinion. The Supreme Court overturned the Eighth Circuit Court of Appeals' decision, which awarded punitive damages. It did not rule on the question of whether the local police department was immune under the Eleventh Amendment. Meanwhile, the court of appeals had ruled that the Kansas City Police Board operated locally and could therefore not be considered an arm of the state with the payment coming from the state budget.

82. See Mezey et al., "Americans with Disabilities Act in Federal Court," 54. They note that seven lower court rulings have questioned Eleventh Amendment immunity to private damages under Title II.

83. Ibid.

84. Jaclyn A. Okin, "Has the Supreme Court Gone Too Far? An Analysis of *University of Alabama v. Garrett* and Its Impact on People with Disabilities," 9 *American University Journal of Gender, Social Policy & Law* 663 (2000): 689.

85. See *Medical Board of California v. Hason*, 02-479 on the Supreme Court docket, which was accepted for certiorari on November 18, 2002; scheduled for oral argument on March 25, 2003, and dismissed on March 3, 2003. Charles Lane, "On Second Thought . . . ," *Washington Post*, April 11, 2003, A25. Also see the lower federal court opinion, *Hason v. Medical Board of California*, 279 F. 3d 1167 (9th Cir. 2002).

86. See *Medical Board of California v. Hason*, No. 02-479 (2002 term).

87. See Charles Lane, "On Second Thought . . . ," A25.

88. Ibid.

89. See "Supreme Court Dismisses Title II Immunity Case," *Disability Compliance Bulletin* 25, no. 8 (May 1, 2003).

90. Quoted from Andy Sher, "High Court to Hear Tennessee Disability Rights Case," *Chattanooga Times Free Press*, June 24, 2003, A6. Also see Linda Greenhouse,

"The Supreme Court Roundup: Justices to Hear Case on Whether the Disabled Can Sue States on Access to Courtrooms," *New York Times*, June 24, 2003, A27. The case is *Tennessee v. Lane*, No. 02-1667.

91. Ruth Colker, "ADA Title III: A Fragile Compromise," 21 *Berkeley Journal of Employment and Labor Law* 377 (2000): 400; and O'Brien, *Crippled Justice*, 172.

92. Amy Hermanek, "Title III of the Americans with Disabilities Act: Implementation of Mediation Programs for More Effective Use of the Act," 12 *Law & Inequality Journal* 457 (1997): 469.

93. Mary Johnson, "Disabling a Civil Right," *Nation*, February 11, 2002, p. 20; the case is *Toyota Motor Manufacturing, Kentucky, v. Ella Williams*, 534 U.S. 184 (2002).

94. While not illegal, this type of extrajudicial activity has been frowned upon by some legal groups, like the American Bar Association's Ethics Committee. Interestingly, the American Bar Association has restricted all federal court judges, except Supreme Court judges, from accepting honoraria. See David M. O'Brien, *The Storm Center: The Supreme Court in American Politics* (New York: Norton, 1996), 120.

CHAPTER 3

1. E. Friedson, "Disability as Social Deviance," in *Sociology and Rehabilitation*, ed. M. B. Sussman (Washington, D.C.: American Sociological Society, 1965); and Henri-Jacques Stiker, *A History of Disability*, trans. William Sayers (Ann Arbor: University of Michigan Press, 1998).

2. *Sutton v. United Airlines Inc.*, 527 U.S. 471 (1999), 490–91.

3. I chose this term to replicate the idea that is behind the term *legally blind*. Placing the word *legally* in front of the term *disabled* highlights how this is an artificial, legal construct. This term is also used by people seeking Social Security Administration disability benefits.

4. Charles Lindner, "Supreme Court Upsetting a Rights Movement: The Supreme Court's ADA Employment Rulings Read as If They Were Drawn from the Pages of *Catch 22*," *Los Angeles Times*, June 2, 2002, p. M-2.

5. *Thalos v. Dillon Companies, Inc.*, 86 F. Supp. 2d 1079 (2000).

6. Lennard Davis, *Enforcing Normalcy: Disability, Deafness, and the Body* (New York: Verso, 1995), 11–12.

7. Ibid.

8. Erving Goffman, *Stigma: Notes on the Management of Spoiled Identity* (Englewood Cliffs, N.J.: Prentice-Hall, 1963), 48.

9. Benedicte Ingstad and Susan Reynolds Whyte, "Disability and Culture: An Overview," in their *Disability and Culture* (Berkeley: University of California Press, 1995).

10. Robert Murphy, *The Body Silent* (New York: Norton, 1990).

11. See Claude Levi-Strauss, *Structural Anthropology*, trans. Claire Johnson and Brooke Grundfest Schoepf (Garden City, N.Y.: Anchor, 1967), and *The Savage Mind* (Chicago, Ill.: University of Chicago Press, 1966).

12. Strauss, *Structural Anthropology*, 154.

13. Rosemarie Garland Thomson, *Extraordinary Bodies: Figuring Physical Disability in American Culture and Literature* (New York: Columbia University Press, 1997), 7–8.

14. Stiker, *History of Disability*, 5, 181, 188. Stiker differs from Davis in that he delineates a biological isotopy in which normal-abnormal are the binaries. In the modern era, the social isotopy of disability reigns in which the binary is characterized by the normal and the aberrant. Aberrations are incompatible with the organization of daily life and, while they cannot be corrected, the person can be adjusted.

15. The three-pronged definition of disability first appeared in the 1974 amendments to the Rehabilitation Act of 1973. HEW issued regulations in 1977 that further explicated the definition by defining the term *impairment* and observing that impairments are not limited to traditional disabilities.

16. A person who is "regarded as" having an impairment, like someone who has a mild limp or is rumored to have a mental illness yet has no such impairment, is also protected under the Americans with Disabilities Act. See Robert L. Burgdorf, Jr., "The Americans with Disabilities Act: Analysis and Implications of a Second-Generation Civil Rights Statute," 26 *Harvard Civil Rights/Civil Liberties Review* 413 (1991): 445–51.

17. The first case that involved the definition of a disability was *School Board of Nassau County, Florida, v. Arline*, 480 U.S. 273 (1987), where the Supreme Court ruled that a teacher with tuberculosis was protected from discrimination under the Rehabilitation Act. Relying on the three-pronged definition of a handicap recognized by the Department of Health, Education, and Welfare regulations in 1977 (which were added as a result of the 1974 amendments to the Rehabilitation Act and later included in the ADA), the majority decided that this disease was a disability. Although Arline's disease might not have affected a major life activity, which is the first prong of the definition, it fulfilled the second prong since she had a history of an impairment. At the same time, Arline's tuberculosis also satisfied the third prong of the definition—that she could be "regarded as" having a disability.

18. Chai Feldblum, a disability rights law professor who helped write the law, explained, "Congress felt comfortable relying on a definition that had fifteen years of experience behind it, and disability rights activists felt comfortable that the same individuals with the wide range of impairments who had been covered under existing disability antidiscrimination law would be covered under the ADA." See Feldblum, "Definition of Disability under Federal Antidiscrimination Law: What Happened? Why? and What Can We Do about It?" 21 *Berkeley Journal of Employment and Labor Law* 91 (2000): 92.

19. Simi Linton, *Claiming Disability: Knowledge and Identity* (New York: New York University Press, 1998), 33.

20. Ruth O'Brien, *Crippled Justice: The History of Modern Disability Policy in the Workplace* (Chicago, Ill.: University of Chicago Press, 2001), 176–88, 207–21.

21. *Sutton.*

22. This would not be true, however, of someone with a traditional disability, like a brilliant theoretical physicist who is blind.

23. *Bragdon v. Abbott*, 524 U.S. 624 (1998). See Patricia Nealon, "Court Sets Ruling on AIDS Bias," *Boston Globe*, November 27, 1997, A3. Justice Anthony Kennedy delivered the Court's opinion with Justices John Paul Stevens, David Souter, Ruth Bader Ginsburg, and Stephen Breyer joining. The minority was composed of Chief Justice William Rehnquist, who presented an opinion that dissented in part and concurred in part, with Justices Antonin Scalia and Clarence Thomas joining. Justice Sandra Day O'Connor was also part of the minority but wrote her own mixed opinion.

24. *Bragdon v. Abbott*, 641.

25. Ibid., 631.

26. Ibid., 657.

27. Rehnquist referred to Webster's Collegiate Dictionary and stated that the word *major* has two alternate meanings: first, "of comparative importance"; and second, "greater in quantity, number, or extent." Ibid., 659–60.

28. *Sutton*; *Albertson's, Inc. v. Kirkingburg*, 527 U.S. 555 (1999); and *Murphy v. United Parcel Service, Inc.*, 527 U.S. 516 (1999).

29. *Sutton*, 489–90.

30. Neither the EEOC, with its interpretative guidelines, nor the Department of Transportation's Architectural and Transportation Barriers Compliance Board's regulations recognized them. After the *Sutton* decision, they had to update their guidelines to consider mitigating measures.

31. *Sutton*, 479 and 482.

32. *Hendrick Hudson District Board of Education v. Rowley*, 458 U.S. 176 (1981), 200. The Supreme Court overruled the lower court, which had held that the plaintiff should receive an interpreter. Rehnquist wrote the opinion with Burger, Powell, Stevens, and O'Connor in agreement. Blackmun gave a concurring opinion. White wrote a dissenting opinion that Brennan and Marshall joined.

33. *Sutton*, 497.

34. Ibid., 511.

35. Ibid.

36. *Toyota Motor Manufacturing, Kentucky, v. Ella Williams*, 122 S. Ct. 681 (2002).

37. Unlike Williams, the twin sister pilots were not asking for any accommodation. Instead, they sued for nondiscriminatory treatment, which would have meant that United Airlines would not impose a restriction against people with impaired vision that could be fully corrected.

38. Ibid., 691; emphasis added.

39. Ibid., 694.

40. See *Sutton*, 482–87, 490, for the best explanation about the majority's concern that too many people would be considered legally disabled and the need for the Court to protect an employer's managerial discretion.

41. Sarina Maria Russotto, "Comments: Effects of Sutton Trilogy," 68 *Tennessee Law Review* 705 (2001): 723–24.

42. *Sutton*, 510.

43. *Gomez v. American Building Maintenance*, 940 F. Supp. 255 (1996).

44. See Hugh Davis Graham, *The Civil Rights Era: Origins and Development of National Policy* (New York: Oxford University Press, 1990), for an excellent legislative and legal history of both policies.

CHAPTER 7

1. Marta Russell, *Beyond Ramps: Disability at the End of the Social Contract* (Monroe, Maine: Common Courage Press, 1998), 160.

2. Henri-Jacques Stiker, *A History of Disability*, trans. William Sayers (Ann Arbor: University of Michigan Press, 1998), 112.

3. Daniel Wolinsky and Arthur L. Breakstone, "Reporting for the Rehabilitation and Sheltered Workshop," *Journal of Accountancy* (1975): 56–57.

4. See Mary Lenz Walker, *Beyond Bureaucracy: Mary Elizabeth Switzer and Rehabilitation* (Lanham, Md.: University Press of America, 1985), 132–35, 137, 255.

5. Stiker, *History of Disability*, 126.

6. Edward D. Berkowitz, *Disabled Policy: America's Programs for the Handicapped* (New York: Cambridge University Press, 1987), 155–59; and E. D. Berkowitz, "The Cost-Benefit Tradition in Vocational Rehabilitation," in *Measuring the Efficiency in Public Programs*, ed. Monroe Berkowitz (Philadelphia: Temple University Press), 12.

7. See Paul B. Bellamy, *A History of Workmen's Compensation, 1898–1915: From Courtroom to Boardroom* (New York: Garland, 1997).

8. See James Weinstein, *The Corporate Ideal in the Liberal State, 1900–1918* (Boston: Beacon, 1968).

9. Berkowitz, *Disabled Policy*, 159.

10. Deborah A. Stone, *The Disabled State* (Philadelphia: Temple University Press, 1984), sees it also as part of the creation of the American welfare state.

11. Stiker, *History of Disability*, 175.

12. *Karen Sutton and Kimberly Hinton v. United Airlines Inc.*, 527 U.S. 471 (1999).

13. What is more, of the 20 percent that make it into the courtroom and before a jury, 94 percent are decided in favor of employers. Ruth Colker, "The ADA: A Windfall for Defendants," 34 *Harvard Civil Rights/Civil Liberties Law Review* 99 (1999): 100–163. Also see Jeffrey A. Van Detta and Dan R. Gallipeau, "Judges and Juries: Why Are So Many ADA Plaintiffs Losing Summary Judgment Motions, and Would They Fare Better before a Jury? A Response to Professor Colker," 19 *Litigation Review* 505 (2000): 508–9.

14. *Sutton*; *Albertson's, Inc. v. Kirkinburg*, 527 U.S. 555 (1999); and *Vaughn L. Murphy v. United Parcel Service, Inc.*, 527 U.S. 516 (1999).

15. See Chai Feldblum, "Definition of Disability under Federal Antidiscrimination Law: What Happened? Why? and What Can We Do about It?" 21 *Berkeley Journal of Employment and Labor Law* 91 (2000): 93–94; and Ruth O'Brien, *Crippled Justice: The History of Modern Disability Policy in the Workplace* (Chicago, Ill.: University of Chicago Press, 2001), 200–203.

16. *Murphy v. United Parcel Service*, 516.

17. *Sutton*, 36.

18. Ibid., 28 and 30. Writing a separate concurring opinion, Ruth Bader Ginsburg also emphasized that the ADA was not intended to be so broad as to cover the 160 million people who wear glasses. Ginsburg concurred that the definition of a disability did not apply to this many people, who could no longer be considered "a discrete and insular minority," if that were the case. The ADA, she said, did not reach "the legions of people with correctable disabilities." Recognizing that the legislative authors had included this language in an attempt to equate the statute's protection with that under the Fourteenth Amendment, she dismissed the idea that this should be treated as a constitutional issue and underscored the term *minority* as evidence that the ADA did not include this many people.

19. Ibid., 33.

20. *Bragdon v. Abbott*, 524 U.S. 624 (1998). The First Circuit Court of Appeals of Boston ruled that people with HIV, even if they show no symptoms, do have a disability. See Patricia Nealon, "Court Sets Ruling on AIDS Bias," *Boston Globe*, November 27, 1997, A3. By contrast, the Fourth Circuit ruled that HIV was not a disability in *Ennis v. National Association of Business and Educational Radio, Inc.*, 53 F. 3d 55 (4th Cir. 1995), and *Runnebaum v. Nations Bank of Maryland*, 123 F. 3d 156 (4th Cir. 1997). Meanwhile, the First and Ninth Circuit courts ruled that it did constitute a disability. See *Gates v. Rowland*, 39 F. 3d 1439 (9th Cir. 1994), *United States v. Morvant*, Lexis 13074 (U.S. Dist. Lexis 1994), and *Howe v. Hull*, 873 F. Supp. 72 (U.S. Dist. 1994).

21. *Bragdon v. Abbott*, 639–41.

22. *Toyota Motor Manufacturing, Kentucky, v. Ella Williams*, 534 U.S. 184 (2002).

23. The majority decision in *Robert Barnett v. U.S. Airways*, 228 F 3d 1105 (2000), 1111, cites *Gustafson v. Alloyd Co.*, 513 U.S. 561 (1995), and *Smith v. Midland Brake, Inc.*, 180 F. 3d 1154 (1999).

24. *Barnett v. U.S. Airways*, 1111. The majority suggested that almost all circuits have held that an employer has a mandatory obligation to engage in the interactive process and that this obligation is triggered by either the employee's request or by the employer's recognition of need. See *Smith*; and *Fjellestad v. Pizza Hut of America, Inc.*, 188 F. 3d 944 (1999).

25. *Barnett v. U.S. Airways*, 1114.

26. Ibid.

27. Ibid.

28. The term *essential functions* was modified so that the employer's definition of these functions was given consideration. As Representative Steny H. Hoyer, a Democrat from Maryland, argued, "Consideration must be given to an employer's determination as to what job functions are essential." *Congressional Record*, 101st Cong., 1st sess., 1990, p. 136, E1840.

29. *Taylor v. Phoenixville School Dist.*, 184 F. 3d 296 (1999).

30. *Barnett v. U.S. Airways*, 1113.

31. *U.S. Airways v. Barnett*, 31.

32. Ibid., 10 (slip opinion).

33. Ibid., 13 (slip opinion).

34. Ibid., Souter's opinion, 4–5.

35. Jill S. Kingsbury, "Employment Law: 'Must We Talk about That Reasonable Accommodation?': The Eighth Circuit Says Yes, but Is the Answer Reasonable?" 65 *Missouri Law Review* 967 (2000).

36. The ADA provides "equal jobs or *benefits* to a qualified individual because of the known disability of an individual with whom the qualified individual is known to have a relationship or association" (emphasis added). 42 U.S.C., sec. 12112(b)(4). There is dispute in the federal courts about whether plaintiffs have standing to sue under the ADA to challenge the content of insurance policies under Title III. See *Doe v. Mutual of Omaha*, 179 F. 3d 557 (1999).

37. 29 U.S.C., sec. 2612(a)(1)D. The FLMA was passed in 1993. See Stacy A. Hickox, "Absenteeism under the Family Leave and Medical Act and the Americans with Disabilities Act," 50 *DePaul Law Review* 183 (2000).

38. If the two opinions conflict, the employee could see a third physician at the employer's expense. See 29 U.S.C., sec. 2613(d)(1) and (2) and *Foster v. Time Warner Entertainment Co.*, U.S. App. Lexis 10591 (2001).

39. The Department of Labor drafted regulations for implementing the FLMA, which stipulated that an employer can require a fitness-for-duty certification. These regulations, however, provide that the physician can simply state that the employee had the "ability to return to work." 29 C.F.R., sec. 825.310(c). Also see *Porter v. U.S. Alumoweld Co., Inc.*, 125 F. 3d 243 (1997), and *Albert V. Runyon*, 6 F. Supp. 2d 57 (1998).

40. If an employer is generous with this accommodation, it "does not necessarily bind" it "to *repeatedly* grant successive leaves." Quoted from *Amadio v. Ford Motor Co.*, 238 F. 3d 919 (2001). Also see *Vande Zande v. Wisconsin Department of Admin.*, 44 F. 3d 538 (1995).

41. *Wells v. District Lodge 751, International Association of Machinists and Aerospace Workers, AFL-CIO*, U.S. App. Lexis 3150 (2001).

42. There have also been some cases where employees have asked to use sick days in a more spontaneous way. See *Maziarka v. Mills Fleet Farm, Inc.*, 245 F. 3d 675 (2001). This case raises the issue of whether attendance is an essential function of the job. In *Maziarka*, the district court cited *Carr v. Reno*, 306 U.S. App. D.C. 217, 23 F. 3d 525 (1994); *Buckles v. First Data Resources Inc.*, 176 F. 3d 1098 (1999); and *Moore v. Payless Shoe Source, Inc.*, 187 F. 3d 845 (1999), and ruled that attendance cannot be so erratic that it makes the employee unqualified for the job. Also see *Vande Zande*.

43. Simon J. Williams, "Is Anybody There? Critical Realism, Chronic Illness and the Disability Debate," *Sociology of Health and Illness* 21 (1999): 797–820.

44. Ibid.; and M. R. Bury, "Social Constructionism and the Development of Medical Sociology," *Sociology of Health and Illness* 8 (1986): 137–69. For a conservative legal perspective about the need to return to the medical model, see Tony Maida, "How Judicial Myopia Is Jeopardizing the Protection of People with HIV/AIDS under the ADA," 27 *American Journal of Law and Medicine* 301 (2001).

45. Bury, "Social Constructionism and the Development of Medical Sociology"; and M. Kelly and D. Field, "Medical Sociology, Chronic Illness and the Body," *Sociology of Health and Illness* 18 (1996): 241–57.

46. See Heather Rae Watterson, "Genetic Discrimination in the Workplace and the Need for Federal Legislation," 4 *DePaul Journal of Health Care Law* 423 (2001).

47. See Robert Belton and Dianne Avery, *Employment Discrimination Law: Cases and Material on Equality in the Workplace*, 6th ed. (St. Paul, Minn.: West Group, 1999), for a thorough and clear explanation of the three stages.

48. 29 U.S.C., sec. 102(d)(2)(A) of the ADA, 42 U.S.C., sec. 12112(d)(2)(A).

49. 29 U.S.C., sec. 102(d)(2)(B) of the ADA, 42 U.S.C., sec. 12112(d)(2)(B).

50. If information is gathered during the exam that makes an employer determine that she does not want to hire a prospective employee, even though this condition is not what the exam was designed to determine, the employee is protected from discrimination for a "perceived disability." The burden shifts to the employer, who must demonstrate that the impairment will affect the person's job qualifications. See *EEOC v. Blue Cross/Blue Shield of Connecticut*, 30 F. Supp. 2d 296 (1998), and *Rowles v. Automated Production Systems, Inc.*, U.S. Lexis 21605 (1999).

51. Governmental officials can also be privy to this information in order to investigate compliance with the ADA.

52. Sec. 102(d)(4) of the ADA, 42 U.S.C., sec. 12112(d)(4). See *Norman Bloodsaw v. Lawrence Berkeley Lab.*, 135 F. 3d 1260 (1998). Also see Chai Feldblum, "Medical Examinations and Inquiries under the Americans with Disabilities Act: A View from the Inside," 64 *Temple Law Review* 521 (1991).

53. This standard was a legislative compromise with Title VII disparate impact jurisprudence cases in *Wards Cove Packing Co. v. Antonio*, 490 U.S. 642 (1989).

54. See *Porter*, which cited the EEOC, *Technical Manual on the Employment Provisions of the ADA*.

55. *Taylor v. Phoenixville School Dist.*, 184 F. 3d 296 (1999), 20 and 25.

56. *Chevron, U.S.A. v. Mario Echazabal*, 122 S. Ct. 2045 (2002).

57. Ibid., 2052.

58. Ibid., 2053.

59. Ibid., 2052.

60. Ibid.

61. Ibid.

62. Rick Baldoz, Charles Koeber, and Philip Kraft, "Making Sense of Work in the Twenty-First Century," in *The Critical Study of Work: Labor, Technology, and Global Production*, ed. Rick Baldoz, Charles Koeber, and Philip Kraft (Philadelphia: Temple University Press, 2001), 5; and see Juliet Schor, *The Overworked American* (New York: Basic, 1991).

63. Burgdorf reports that of the disabled people who have said they want to work, two-thirds of them have found employment. See Robert L. Burgdorf, Jr., "The Americans with Disabilities Act: Analysis and Implications of a Second-Generation Civil Rights Statute," 26 *Harvard Civil Rights/Civil Liberties Review* 413 (1991): 420–21. Also see Marta Russell, "What Disability Civil Rights Cannot Do: Employment and Political Economy," *Disability & Society* 17 (2002): 117–18.

64. See Russell, "What Disability Civil Rights Cannot Do," for analysis of this dilemma from a radical political economy approach.

CHAPTER 10

1. Simi Linton, *Claiming Disability: Knowledge and Identity* (New York: New York University Press, 1998), 18.

2. Leonard Kriegel, "Uncle Tom and Tiny Tim: Some Reflections on the Cripple as Negro," *American Scholar* 38 (1969): 412–30.

3. Linton, *Claiming Disability*, 9.

4. Paul Abberley, "The Spectre at the Feast: Disabled People and Social Theory," in *The Disability Reader: Social Science Perspectives*, ed. Tom Shakespeare (London: Casswell, 1998), 79.

5. Jenny Morris, "Impairment and Disability: Constructing an Ethics of Care That Promotes Human Rights," *Hypatia* 16 (2001): 1–16. Morris equates the word *disability* with racism or sexism, arguing that it should be used to define societal oppression. Instead, she substitutes the word *impairment.*

6. Mike Oliver, "A Sociology of Disability or a Disablist Sociology?" in *Disability and Society: Emerging Issues and Insights*, ed. Len Barton (London and New York: Longman, 1996), 20.

7. See Rob Imrie, "Oppression, Disability and Access in the Built Environment," in *The Disability Reader: Social Science Perspectives*, ed. Tom Shakespeare (London: Cassell, 1998).

8. Michael Lewyn, "Thou Shalt Not Put a Stumbling Block before the Blind: The ADA and Public Transit for the Disabled," 52 *Hastings Law Journal* 1037 (2001).

9. Section 16(a) of the Urban Mass Transportation Act, 49 U.S.C., enacted in 1970, states that "elderly and handicapped persons have the same right as other persons to utilize mass transportation facilities and services." Section 185(b) of the Federal-Aid Highway Act of 1973 also stipulated, "Projects receiving Federal financial assistance . . . shall be planned, designed, constructed, and operated to allow effective utilization by elderly and handicapped persons."

10. President Gerald Ford also issued Executive Order 11914, which ordered the Department of Health, Education, and Welfare (now Health and Human Services) to coordinate implementation of the policy of nondiscrimination in the Rehabilitation Act.

11. Lewyn, "Thou Shalt Not Put a Stumbling Block before the Blind," 1016.

12. *Americans Disabled for Accessible Public Transit (ADAPT) v. Lewis*, 211 U.S. App. D.C. 42 (1981). Because of this decision, which concluded that the regulations imposed "extremely heavy burdens on local transit authorities," the Department of Transportation issued regulations that were not final.

13. These regulations also contained a safe harbor provision.

14. Lewyn, "Thou Shalt Not Put a Stumbling Block before the Blind," 1064.

15. Sec. 222.

16. Sec. 223. See also Mary Johnson, *Make Them Go Away: Clint Eastwood, Christopher Reeve and the Case against Disability Rights* (Louisville, Ky.: Advocado Press, 2003), 85–94, for a good overview of the controversy about paratransit services.

17. Lewyn, "Thou Shalt Not Put a Stumbling Block before the Blind," 1071.

18. The definition of a disability is also discussed. A person who is disabled also has a disability for purposes of the ADA's public transit provisions, and all disabled persons are entitled to equal treatment regardless of the cause of their disability. See *Hamlyn v. Rock Island County Metropolitan Mass Transit District*, 964 F. Supp. 272 (1997). Also see Sharon Rennert, "All Aboard: Accessible Public Transportation for Disabled Persons," 63 *New York University Law Review* 360 (1988).

19. Another decision involved a commuter railroad's attempt to automate ticket sales. Here, the court decided that staffing considerations could not be considered an "alteration." Physical changes means those to a facility, not personnel. The court also underscored that the clerks had only worked until 1 p.m. anyway. See *Molloy v. Metropol TA*, 94 F. 3d 808 (1996).

20. *Hassan v. Slater*, 41 F. Supp. 2d 243 (1999).

21. Lewyn, "Thou Shalt Not Put a Stumbling Block before the Blind," 1072.

22. *James v. Peter Pan Transit Management*, U.S. Dist. Lexis 2565 (1999), and *Midgett v. Tri-Country Metropolitan Transportation District of Oregon*, 254 F. 3d 846, U.S. App. Lexis 14240 (2001).

23. *Cupolo v. Bay Area Rapid Transit*, 5 F. Supp. 2d 1078 (1997).

24. *Kinney v. Yerusalim*, 9 F. 3d 1067 (1993). Injunctive relief was awarded under 42 U.S.C., sec. 1983 (1988), for ADA violations.

25. *Sells v. New Jersey Transit Corp.*, 298 N.J. Super 640 (2000). Also see denial of application on the basis of impaired vision, mobility, and migraine headaches. *Pfister v. City of Madison*, 198 Wis. 2d (1995).

26. In one case, a disabled person was hurt after a driver left her at the end of a driveway instead of helping her into a relative's house. *O'Connor v. Metro*, 87 F. Supp. 2d 894 (1997).

27. Lewyn, "Thou Shalt Not Put a Stumbling Block before the Blind," 1041.

28. Ibid., 1036.

29. Ibid., 1087–88.

30. See Laura F. Rothstein, *Rights of Physically Handicapped Persons* (Colorado Springs, Colo.: Shepherd's McGraw-Hill, 1984; supp. 1987), cited in Paul K. Longmore, "Medical Decision Making and People with Disabilities: A Clash of Cultures," *Journal of Law, Medicine & Ethics* 23 (1995). What is more, thistactic of inflating the cost of accommodation is common. When the Fair Housing Act amendments passed in 1988, the National Association of Homebuilders fought the provisions mandating that all new housing be made accessible. They did so by conducting a study that indicated that accessibility would cost $50,000 per unit, whereas competing studies conducted by other groups, like the Niles Boulton Associates architectural firm, put the figure at $500 per unit. Another study came up with $440 per one-bedroom unit. See Mary Johnson, "Disabled Americans Push for Access," *Progressive* 55 (1991): 21–24.

31. Quoted in Fred Peika, "Bashing the Disabled," *Humanist* 56 (1996): 27.

CHAPTER 12

1. The prevailing medical perspective before the 1940s had doctors examining what caused, and how they could prevent or cure, a disability. See Glenn Gritzer and Arnold Arluke, *The Making of Rehabilitation: The Political Economy of Medical Specialization, 1890–1980* (Berkeley: University of California Press, 1985); and James I. Charlton, *Nothing about Us without Us: Disability Oppression and Empowerment* (Berkeley: University of California Press, 1998). For a perspective that attempts to strike a balance between the medical and the social models, see M. R. Bury, "Social Constructionism and the Development of Medical Sociology," *Sociology of Health and Illness* 8 (1986):137–69. Also see L. Crow, "Including All of Our Lives: Renewing the Social Model of Disability," in *Exploring the Divide: Illness and Disability*, ed. C. Barnes and G. Mercer (Leeds, England: Disability Press, 1996); and M. Kelly and D. Field, "Medical Sociology, Chronic Illness and the Body," *Sociology of Health and Illness* 18 (1996): 241–57.

2. See K. Walter Hickel, "Medicine, Bureaucracy, and Social Welfare: The Politics of Disability Compensation for American Veterans of World War I," in *The New Disability History: American Perspectives*, ed. Paul K. Longmore and Lauri Umansky (New York: New York University Press, 2001), 236–67.

3. See Paul Abberley, "The Spectre at the Feast: Disabled People and Social Theory," in *The Disability Reader: Social Science Perspectives*, ed. Tom Shakespeare (London: Casswell, 1998), 79; Simon Brisenden, "Independent Living and the Medical Model of Disability," in *The Disability Reader*, ed. Shakespeare, 24; and Paul K. Longmore, "Medical Decision Making and People with Disabilities: A Clash of Cultures," *Journal of Law, Medicine & Ethics* 23 (1995): 82–87.

4. Edward D. Berkowitz, "The Cost-Benefit Tradition in Vocational Rehabilitation," in *Measuring the Efficiency in Public Programs*, ed. Monroe Berkowitz (Philadelphia: Temple University Press), 12.

5. Henri-Jacques Stiker, *A History of Disability*, trans. William Sayers (Ann Arbor: University of Michigan Press, 1998), 165.

6. Ibid., 167.

7. Abberley, "The Spectre at the Feast," 79.

8. Brisenden, "Independent Living and the Medical Model of Disability," 23.

9. Edward D. Berkowitz, *Disabled Policy: America's Programs for the Handicapped* (New York: Cambridge University Press, 1987); and Ruth O'Brien, *Crippled Justice: The History of Modern Disability Policy in the Workplace* (Chicago, Ill.: University of Chicago Press, 2001).

10. Paul F. James, "The Education for All Handicapped Children Act of 1975: What's Left after Rowley?" 19 *Willamette Law Review* 721 (1983).

11. Brisenden, "Independent Living and the Medical Model of Disability," 21.

12. *Dennis Theriault v. Richard M. Flynn, Commissioner, New Hampshire Dept. of Safety*, 162 F. 3d 46 (1998). Following the same logic, another plaintiff submitted that the requirement of a medical certification, where others did not have to provide one, was unreasonable. See *Barbara Bailey v. Alan Anderson, Director of Motor Vehicles, Department of Revenue of the State of Kansas*, 79 F. Supp. 2d 1254 (2001).

13. 28 C.F.R., sec. 35.130(b)(6).

14. 28 C.F.R., pt. 35, app. A at 472–73 (1997).

15. See *Theriault; Strathie v. Department of Transportation*, 716 F. 2d 227 (1983); *Frederick Hatch v. Secretary of Maine and Maine Motor Vehicles Division*, 879 F. Supp. 147 (1995).

16. The judge cited *School Board of Nassau County, Florida, v. Arline*, 480 U.S. 273 (1987), and *Bragdon v. Abbott*, 54 U.S. 624 (1998).

17. *Stafford J. Coolbaugh v. State of La.*, U.S. App. Lexis 12713 (1998).

18. Overall, the case was about whether the reasonable accommodations that she required would change the fundamental nature of the certification program, which the school was not obliged to do. The college rejected Davis because, among other things, she would require individualized faculty supervision to finish her degree. *Southeastern Community College v. Davis*, 442 U.S. 397 (1979).

19. Pamela Hussey Simon, "Employment Discrimination: Analyzing Handicapped Discrimination Claims: The Right Tools for the Job," 62 *North Carolina Law Review* 561 (1984). Powell gave school officials and employers three reasons—no fundamental changes in programs, the person with a disability will not benefit, and the safety defense—for not providing accommodations.

20. *Southeastern Community College v. Davis*, 401–2.

21. *Arline;* and *Bragdon v. Abbott*.

22. Samuel R. Bagenstos, "The ADA as Risk Regulation," 101 *Columbia Law Review* 1479 (2001).

23. Ibid., 1481–82 and 1486–87. The author cites Linda Hamilton Krieger, "Backlash against the ADA: Interdisciplinary Perspectives and Implications for Social Justice Strategies," 21 *Berkeley Journal of Employment and Labor Law* 1 (2000).

24. Bagenstos, "The ADA as Risk Regulation," 1499.

25. Ibid., 1506–8. Bagenstos also presents the Oregon statewide health care plan as another example since it uses the term *quality-adjusted life years* to determine who will receive what type of care. The problem with this plan is that it denies care to those who are left with a physical impairment or a chronic illness after a procedure. The only thing that counts is how many lives the procedure saves while causing no disability.

26. Ibid., 1484.

27. See Timur Kuran and Cass R. Sunstein, "Availability Cascades and Risk Regulation," 51 *Stanford Law Review* 683 (1999). According to Bagenstos, Sunstein and Kuran have developed a technocratic perspective that is not politically conservative. They suggest that the following factors must be taken into account: first, the nature of the risk; second, if the risk is controllable; third, will the risk involve irretrievable losses; fourth, how are the social conditions generated and managed in terms of democratic control; fifth, will the dangers be distributed equally among citizens; sixth, is the risk process understood well by the public; seventh, will future generations encounter the same risk; and finally, how familiar are people with the risk.

28. *Albertson's, Inc. v. Kirkingburg*, 527 U.S. 555 (1999).

29. Ibid.

30. Ibid., 39–40.

31. Bagenstos, "The ADA as Risk Regulation," 1506–7.

32. A significant number of the Title III cases have been filed against the boards and associations that conduct standardized tests for job placement and admissions, like the Law School Admissions Test (LSAT). Between 1990 and 1993, the number of nonaccommodated students taking the LSAT declined, whereas the number requesting accommodations increased to 19.5 percent. See J. J. Knauff, "Dissing Disabilities: A Student's Duty to Mitigate Maladies," 85 *Brigham Young University Education and Law Journal* 103 (2001).

CHAPTER 15

1. Martha Albertson Fineman, *The Neutered Mother, the Sexual Family, and Other Twentieth-Century Tragedies* (New York: Routledge, 1995), 18–19.

2. The idea of sovereign immunity originated in England, where in feudal times, landowners maintained their own courts and could hear or refuse any case brought against them within their court. The Crown was not to interfere. This notion of control remained in place for centuries and became particularly important again just after England's revolutionary war. Addressing some of the concerns, Alexander Hamilton wrote in the *Federalist Papers* that no state should be amenable to any suit brought by an individual without the state's prior consent. Hamilton's idea became the foundation for the Eleventh Amendment, which preserves the sovereignty of states and reaffirms promises implicitly made in the Tenth Amendment, "which emphasizes that states retain all power not delegated specifically to the federal government." See Jaclyn A. Okin, "Has the Supreme Court Gone Too Far? An Analysis of *University of Alabama v. Garrett* and Its Impact on People with Disabilities," 9 *American University Journal of Gender, Social Policy and Law* 663 (2000): 691–93.

3. *Georgia v. Chisholm*, 2 Dall. 419 (U.S. 1793).

4. 1 Charles Warren, *The Supreme Court in United States History* 302 (1926), quoted in Bernard Schwartz, *A History of the Supreme Court* (New York: Oxford University Press, 1993), 21. For an article disputing what has been called the "profound shock theory," see James E. Pfander, "Rethinking the Supreme Court's Original Jurisdiction in State-Party Cases," 82 *California Law Review* 555 (1994).

5. The Tenth Amendment states, "The powers not delegated to the United States by the Constitution, nor prohibited by it to the States, are reserved to the States respectively, or to the people." Quoted in Edward S. Corwin, *The Constitution and What It Means Today*, revised by Harold W. Chase and Craig R. Ducat (Princeton, N.J.: Princeton University Press, 1978), 445.

6. Corwin, *The Constitution and What It Means Today*, 443–44.

7. *Collector v. Day*, 11 Wall. 113 (1871).

8. *Hammer v. Dagenhart*, 247 U.S. 251 (1918).

9. Corwin, *The Constitution and What It Means Today*, 445. The pivotal decision was *U.S. v. Darby*, 312 U.S. 100 (1941), which upheld the Fair Labor Standards

Act when Justice Stone wrote, "The power of Congress over interstate commerce is complete."

10. The Supremacy Clause, the Necessary and Proper Clause, the Spending Clause, and the Commerce Clause have all been interpreted to expand the jurisdiction of the national government. First, Marshall relied on the Supremacy Clause in *McCulloch v. Maryland*, 17 U.S. 316 (1819), arguing that only the national government is truly sovereign.

11. *Heart of Atlanta Motel, Inc. v. U.S.*, 379 U.S. 241 (1964).

12. In hindsight, other texts now explain Rehnquist's dissent in *National League of Cities v. Usery*, 426 U.S. 833 (1976), which articulated what became the majority's opinion twenty years later. See Sue Davis, *Justice Rehnquist and the Constitution* (Princeton, N.J.: Princeton University Press, 1989).

13. Alpheus Thomas Mason and Donald Grier Stephenson, Jr., *American Constitutional Law: Introductory Essays and Selected Cases*, 9th ed. (New York: Prentice-Hall, 1990), 129.

14. Ibid., 243.

15. See Theda Skocpol, "Bringing the State Back In: Strategies of Analysis in Current Research," in *Bringing the State Back In*, ed. P. Evans, D. Rueschemeyer, and Theda Skocpol (New York: Cambridge University Press, 1985), 3–33; and Stephen Skowronek, *Building a New American State: The Expansion of National Administrative Capacities, 1877–1920* (New York: Cambridge University Press, 1982), which explore this trend in American political development.

16. In 1976, Rehnquist did use the Tenth Amendment again as a check on federal power in *National League of Cities v. Usery*, which ruled that Congress could not extend the minimum wage and maximum hours provisions of the Fair Labor Standards Act to almost all employees of states and their subdivisions.

17. What one critic described as the Supreme Court's assault on congressional authority began with *Seminole Tribe of Florida v. Florida*, 517 U.S. 44 (1996), where the majority ruled that a state cannot be sued in federal court for a violation of the federal Indian Gaming Regulatory Act. In 1999 and 2000, the Supreme Court addressed the doctrine of the new federalism by limiting the enforcement of federal laws protecting patent rights in *Florida Prepaid Postsecondary Education Expense Board v. College Savings Bank and United States*, 527 U.S. 627 (1999). Also, in *Alden v. Maine*, 527 U.S. 706 (1999), the Court ruled that a state cannot be sued in its own court for violations of the Fair Labor Standards Act. The Age Discrimination in Employment Act was undermined with *Kimel v. Florida of Regents*, 528 U.S. 62 (2000). Finally, the Supreme Court asserted state immunity, thereby thwarting the ADA, in *Board of Trustees of the University of Alabama v. Garrett*, 1531 U.S. 356 (2001).

18. Mark Tushnet, "Federalism and the Supreme Court: The 1999 Term: What Is the Supreme Court's New Federalism?" 35 *Oklahoma City University Law Review* 927 (2000): 928.

19. From 1941 to 1996, the Supreme Court held that the Tenth Amendment was a "truism," as Justice Stone described in *U.S. v. Darby*.

20. Jack M. Balkin, "The Cloning Conundrum," *New York Times*, January 30, 2001, p. A27.

21. Marc D. Falkoff, "Abrogating State Sovereign Immunity in Legislative Courts," 101 *Columbia Law Review* 852 (2001).

22. See Cass Sunstein, "A Narrowed Right to Challenge the States," *New York Times*, May 31, 2002. Sunstein wrote this op-ed piece in response to the Supreme Court's latest 5–4 decision about federalism. See *Federal Maritime Committee v. South Carolina State Ports Authority*, 122 S. Ct. 1864 (2002).

23. *Atascadero State Hospital v. Scanlon*, 473 U.S. 234 (1985).

24. The state sovereignty critics are not only on the Supreme Court bench. While Justice David Souter provided strong historical refutation of the majority's defense of state sovereignty immunity, he did so without engaging with the Court's rationale about political accountability. See Scott Freuhwald, "If Men Were Angels: The New Judicial Activism in Theory and Practice," 83 *Marquette Law Review* 485 (1999); Ellen D. Katz, "State Judges, State Officers, and Federal Commands after *Seminole Tribe* and *Printz*," 1998 *Wisconsin Law Review* 1465 (1998); Frank B. Cross, "Realism about Federalism," 74 *New York University Law Review* 1304 (1999); and Daniel J. Meltzer, "State Sovereign Immunity: Five Authors in Search of a Theory," 75 *Notre Dame Law Review* 1011 (2000).

25. Falkoff, "Abrogating State Sovereign Immunity in Legislative Courts," 854.

26. Balkin, "The Cloning Conundrum," A27.

27. William J. Rich, "Privileges or Immunities: The Missing Link in Establishing Congressional Power to Abrogate State Eleventh Amendment Immunity," 28 *Hastings Law Quarterly* 235 (Winter 2001): 235–28.

28. In *City of Boerne v. Flores*, 521 U.S. 507 (1997), the Court limited the scope of section 5 and held that Congress had not validly enforced the Fourteenth Amendment when it passed the Religious Freedom Restoration Act (RFRA) of 1993.

29. *Florida Prepaid*, 861; *Education Expense Board v. College Savings Bank*, 527 U.S. 627 (1999).

30. Falkoff, "Abrogating State Sovereign Immunity in Legislative Courts," 861.

31. The disability rights movement was particularly encouraged about this prospect in 1974 when a judge in North Dakota in a state court applied a "compelling state interest" test to a statute about public education. The judge used this test to show that a statute discriminated against disabled people for reasons that had nothing to do with their actual limitations. *In re G.H.*, 218 N.W. 2d 441 (N.D. 1974). The rationale was based on the federal district court in *Fialkowski v. Shapp*, 405 F. Supp. 946 (E.D. Pa. 1975). See James R. Baugh, "The Federal Legislation on Equal Educational Opportunity for the Handicapped," 15 *Idaho Law Review* 71 (1978).

32. *Brown v. Board of Education*, 347 U.S. 483 (1954).

33. Eric T. Sharpe, "A House Is Not a Home: *City of Cleburne v. Cleburne Living Center*," 6 *Pace Law Review* 274 (1986): 274–77; *Reed v. Reed*, 404 U.S. 71 (1971). The Supreme Court ruled that a classification based on sex was subject to scrutiny. See *Frontiero v. Richardson*, 411 U.S. 677 (1973). Justice William J. Brennan joined

William O. Douglas, Byron R. White, and Thurgood Marshall and found support in *Reed* to designate sex as inherently suspect. Brennan thought sex was like race and national origin in that it was immutable. It was not followed in *Stanton v. Stanton*, 421 U.S. 7 (1975), since there the Court found nothing rational in requiring child support for males until the age of twenty-one and for females only until eighteen.

34. Sharpe, "A House Is Not a Home," 273.

35. See *Levy v. Louisiana*, 391 U.S. 68 (1968); *Kramer v. Union Free School District*, 395 U.S. 621 (1961); and *Avery v. Midland County*, 390 U.S. 474 (1968).

36. Sharpe, "A House Is Not a Home," 283.

37. *Halderman v. Pennhurst* 446 F. Supp. 1295 (1978) at 1321–22; and *Medora v. Colautti*, 602 F. 2d 1149 (1979) at 1152. In 1981, the Court ruled in *Pennhurst State School and Hospital v. Halderman*, 451 U.S. 1 (1981), that the bill of rights in the Developmental Disabilities Act (DDA) had not given persons with disabilities any constitutional guarantees. While Terri Lee Halderman, a child with mental retardation, lived in less than ideal conditions, the Court held that she had no substantive right to better conditions in this state-operated school and hospital. This decision came on top of *Youngberg v. Romeo*, 457 U.S. 307 (1982), a case that balanced the so-called demands of an organized society against disabled people when the mother of a thirty-three-year-old, who had the mental capacity of an eighteen-month-old, failed in her suit against an institution that she thought maltreated her son.

38. *City of Cleburne, Texas, v. Cleburne Living Center, Inc.*, 473 U.S. 432 (1985). Justice Byron White delivered the opinion that Chief Justice Warren Burger, Lewis F. Powell, Jr., William H. Rehnquist, John Paul Stevens, and Sandra Day O'Connor joined. Thurgood Marshall concurred and dissented in part with William J. Brennan, Jr., and Harry A. Blackmun joining him.

39. The lone dissenting voice in *Pennhurst*, Justice White first argued that the mentally retarded were vulnerable to discrimination. He also thought they lacked the political power to change their situation through the political process. Yet, White did not concede that disabled people satisfied the powerlessness category. As he saw it, the mentally retarded profited from legislation that recognized them as a group.

40. *Board of Trustees of the University of Alabama v. Garrett*, 531 U.S. 356 (2001). Chief Justice William H. Rehnquist wrote the majority opinion and was joined by Antonin Scalia and Clarence Thomas. Justice Anthony Kennedy wrote a concurring opinion, which Sandra Day O'Connor joined. Patricia Garrett, a registered nurse at the University of Alabama, returned to work after undergoing a lumpectomy, radiation treatment, and chemotherapy. The hospital told her that she could not return to her previous position as a director and transferred her to a lower-paying managerial position. Milton Ash, a security guard for the Alabama Department of Youth Services, claimed that his employer ignored two requests that he made for reasonable accommodations, and that retaliation ensued because of these requests.

41. Justice Ruth Bader Ginsburg wrote the opinion. The three dissenters were Rehnquist, Scalia, and Thomas.

42. Quoted from David G. Savage, "Justices Reject 'Unnecessary Segregation' of Mentally Disabled at State Hospitals," *Los Angeles Times*, June 23, 1999, p. A10.

43. Mark A. Johnson, "Note: *Board of Trustees of the University of Alabama v. Garrett*: A Flawed Standard Yields a Predictable Result," 60 *Maryland Law Review* 393 (2001).

44. Justice Breyer wrote the dissent with Souter, Ginsburg, and Stevens joining him.

45. *Garrett*, 377.

46. Johnson, "Note: *Board of Trustees of the University of Alabama v. Garrett*," 384.

47. *Garrett*, 385.

48. See *Olmstead v. L.C. by Zimring*, 527 U.S. 581 (1999).

49. James Leonard, "The Shadows of Unconstitutionality: How the New Federalism May Affect the Antidiscrimination Mandate of the Americans with Disabilities Act," 52 *Alabama Law Review* 91 (2000): 144–46.

50. Ibid., 92.

51. Okin, "Has the Supreme Court Gone Too Far?" 689.

52. Ibid. According to Okin, the *Garrett* decision resembled other cases in that the Court argued that the section 5 test is flawed and should be more deferential to Congress's unique institutional role in enforcing the Fourteenth Amendment's guarantees.

53. Tushnet, "Federalism and the Supreme Court," 927.

54. To follow this interpretation of federalism means that the Court has over-turned *Wickard v. Filburn*, 317 U.S. 111 (1942), which made virtually nothing fall out of the reach of the Commerce Clause. See Tushnet, "Federalism and the Supreme Court," 930.

55. Balkin also accuses the high court of "doctrinal duplicity" given the *George W. Bush and Richard Cheney v. Albert Gore, Jr.* (531 U.S. 98 [2000]), decision, which many critics say violated the federalism doctrine that the court had been building. See Balkin, "The Cloning Conundrum."

56. Falkoff, "Abrogating State Sovereign Immunity in Legislative Courts," 855.

57. Ibid., 856. The Supreme Court has consistently upheld Congress's right to create legislative tribunals, though it has imposed limits on this authority. See the 1855 decision in *Murray's Lessee v. Hoboken Land & Improvement Co.*, 59 U.S. 272 (18 How.), where it was ruled that Congress can create non–Article III tribunals for the adjudication of public rights, which are defined as "those which arise between the government and persons subject to its authority in connection with the performance of the constitutional functions of the executive or legislative departments." There is no question, for instance, that the secretary of labor can bring suit against a state for violations of the Fair Labor Standards Act. See Ruth O'Brien, "'A Sweatshop of the Whole Nation': The Fair Labor Standards Act and the Failure of Regulatory Unionism," *Studies in American Political Development* 15 (2001): 33–52.

58. *Garrett*, 388.

59. Falkoff, "Abrogating State Sovereign Immunity in Legislative Courts," 852.

60. Corwin, *The Constitution and What It Means Today*, 229.

61. The most significant questions raised about suability do not revolve around situations like O'Brien's, where the federal official makes reference to official immunity. Rather, they are decisions where such an officer goes beyond the scope of his lawful authority. Frankfurter boiled it down to this: "The federal courts are not barred from adjudicating a claim against a governmental agent who invokes statutory authority for his action if the constitutional power to give him such a claim of immunity is itself challenged." *Larson v. Domestic & Foreign Corp.*, 337 U.S. 682 (1949), 709–10. Also see *United States v. Lee*, 106 U.S. 196, 207–8 (1882), which held that ejection proceedings could be brought against an army officer.

CHAPTER 17

1. See Leslie Francis and Anita Silvers, "Disability Rights Today," *Human Rights: Journal of the Section of Individual Rights and Responsibilities* 27 (2000): 3–7.

2. This title became enforceable on January 26, 1992. For businesses with ten or fewer employees and gross receipts of $500,000 or less, it was enforced one year later. The provision does not include places of worship, religious organizations, or private clubs. The U.S. Equal Employment Opportunity Commission and U.S. Department of Justice, *The Americans with Disabilities Act Handbook* (Washington, D.C.: Government Printing Office, 1991), 2.

3. Robert J. Burgdorf, Jr., "The Americans with Disabilities Act: Analysis and Implications of a Second-Generation Civil Rights Statute," 26 *Harvard Civil Rights/Civil Liberties Review* 493 (1991).

4. John J. Sarno, "The Americans with Disabilities Act: Federal Mandate to Create an Integrated Society," *Seton Hall Legislative Journal* 17 (1993): 409.

5. Amy Hermanek, "Title III of the Americans with Disabilities Act: Implementation of Mediation Programs for More Effective Use of the Act," 12 *Law and Inequality Journal* 457 (1994): 462.

6. Equal Employment Opportunity Commission and U.S. Department of Justice, *Americans with Disabilities Act Handbook*, III-34 of Title III, sec. 36.104.

7. Other factors are the number of people employed, the impact of such action upon the operation of the facility, the overall financial resources of the covered entity, the overall size of a covered entity with respect to the number of employees and the number, type, and location of its facilities, geographic separateness, and the administrative or fiscal relationship of the facility or facilities in question. *Colorado Cross Disability Coalition v. Kevin W. Williams*, 264 F. 3d 999 (2001). Also see *First Bank National Association v. FDIC*, 79 F. 3d 362 (1996).

8. James P. Colgate, "If You Build It, Can They Sue? Architects' Liability under Title III of the ADA," 68 *Fordham Law Review* 137 (1999): 148.

9. Ibid., 138.

10. Ibid., 162.

11. Ibid., 150.

12. See *U.S. v. Ellerbe Becket, Inc.*, 976 F. Supp. 1262 (1997).

13. See *Doukas v. Metropolitan Life Insurance Co.*, 950 F. Supp. (1996), which stipulated that insurance is included, whereas the Seventh Circuit ruled the opposite in *Doe v. Mutual of Omaha Insurance Co.*, 179 F. 3d 557 (1999). Also see Jesse A. Langer, "Note: Combating Discriminatory Insurance Practices: Title III of the Americans with Disabilities Act," 6 *Connecticut Insurance Law Journal* 435 (1999–2000); and Kristin Kay Romero, "Casenote: Defending Discrimination in *Doe v. Mutual of Omaha Insurance Co.*: Determining if a Health Insurance Policy's Aids Benefit Cap Violates the ADA," 9 *George Mason Law Review* 179 (2000).

14. *Bragdon v. Abbott*, 524 U.S. 624 (1998).

15. Ibid.

16. *Paralyzed Veterans of America v. Ellerbe Becket Architects and Engineers, P.C.*, 950 F. Supp. 393 (1996), and *Independent Living Resources v. Oregon Arena Corp.*, 982 F. Supp. 698 (1997). Also see Adam A. Milani, "Oh, Say, Can I See—and Who Do I Sue If I Can't? Wheelchair Users, Sightlines over Standing Spectators, and Architect Liability under the Americans with Disabilities Act," 3 *Florida Law Review* 523 (2000).

17. Ruth Colker, "ADA Title III: A Fragile Compromise," 21 *Berkeley Journal of Employment and Labor Law* 377 (2000): 380.

18. Ibid., 378–81.

19. Ibid. According to Colker, Title III represented a "fragile compromise." In return for a broad list of covered entities, civil rights advocates agreed to a limited set of remedies under the ADA.

20. Ibid., 400.

21. Ibid., 401.

22. See Amy Hermanek, "Title III of the Americans with Disabilities Act," 468–69. She cites newspaper articles from different parts of the country, including Peter S. Greenburg, "Disabilities Act Still Virtually Toothless," *Cleveland* (Ohio) *Plain Dealer*, May 16, 1993, p. 81; and Alexander Reid, "Disabilities Act Widely Ignored: Many Communities Reported Not Complying," *Boston Globe*, February 21, 1993, p. 1.

23. Hermanek, "Title III of the Americans with Disabilities Act," 469.

24. See *Gladys Haney v. Sunnydale Town Ctr.*, No. CV 762408 (1997).

25. One plaintiff she cites did receive a large award of $512,000 against a doctor and a hospital for their failure to admit him to the hospital in violation of the ADA. These awards reflect compensation. Colker, "ADA Title III: A Fragile Compromise," 402.

26. Hermanek, "Title III of the Americans with Disabilities Act," 469–70.

27. Colker, "ADA Title III: A Fragile Compromise," 405–6.

28. *PGA Tour Inc. v. Casey Martin*, 532 U.S. 661 (2001); but see *Olinger v. U.S. Golf Association*, 205 F. 3d 1001 (2000), for a ruling that came to the exact opposite conclusion.

29. Ibid. The prevalence of this view became apparent as reporters solicited the PGA golfers' views about Martin's accommodation request. Tiger Woods, the golf sensation of 1997, uttered a statement that reflected this type of animosity: "As a friend, I'd love to see him have a cart. But from a playing standpoint, is it an advantage? It could be. If it's 100 degrees in Memphis, does it help to ride?" A press poll showed that twenty-four of thirty-eight golfers insisted that the rules should not be changed to accommodate Martin's request for a golf cart. Only five players thought Martin should be allowed to use the cart, while the other nine players remained undecided.

30. Thomas Heath, "Disabled Golfer's Suit against PGA Tour Goes to Trial," *Washington Post*, February 2, 1998, A1.

31. Athelia Knight, "Politicians Tee Off for Martin; With Trial Next Week, Dole, Sen. Harkin Show Support," *Washington Post*, January 29, 1998, C9.

32. Joe Gordon, "Golf: Martin Begins to Drive; Ready to Play in Tournament," *Boston Herald*, March 4, 1998, 72.

33. See Ruth O'Brien, *Crippled Justice: The History of Modern Disability Policy in the Workplace* (Chicago, Ill.: University of Chicago Press, 2001), for this argument about employment discrimination; and Susan Gluck Mezey, Will Jordan, Catherine Thie, and Douglas Davis, "The Americans with Disabilities Act in Federal Court: Litigating against Public Entities," *Disability and Society* 17 (2002): 60–61, which presents a similar argument for discrimination under Titles II and III.

34. See *U.S. v. Virginia*, 518 U.S. 515 (1996). Also see Edward Schiappa, "What Is Golf? Pragmatic Essentializing and Definitional Argument in *PGA Tour, Inc. v. Martin*," *Argumentation and Advocacy* 38 (2001): 18–27, for an interesting argument about essentialism and the determination of the fundamental nature of the program under the ADA.

AFTERWORD

1. See Rosemarie Garland Thomson, *Extraordinary Bodies: Figuring Physical Disability in American Culture and Literature* (New York: Columbia University Press, 1997). Also see Leonard Kriegel, "The Wolf in the Pit in the Zoo," *Social Policy* 13 (1982): 16–23; Paul Longmore, "Screening Stereotypes: Images of Disabled People," *Social Policy* 16 (1985): 31–38; and Diane Price Herndl, *Invalid Women: Figuring Feminine Illness in American Fiction and Culture, 1840–1940* (Chapel Hill: University of North Carolina Press, 1996).

2. See Jenny Morris, "Impairment and Disability: Constructing an Ethics of Care That Promotes Human Rights," *Hypatia* 16 (2001): 6.

3. See Larry M. Preston, "Theorizing Difference: Voices from the Margins," *American Political Science Review* 89 (1995): 943.

4. Quoted in ibid. See Toni Morrison, "Interviews," in *Toni Morrison*, ed. Henry Louis Gates and K. A. Appiah (New York: Amistad, 1993), 372.

5. Mary Johnson, *Make Them Go Away: Clint Eastwood, Christopher Reeve and the Case against Disability Rights* (Louisville, Ky.: Advocado Press, 2003), xii.

6. See Linda Hamilton Krieger, ed., *Backlash against the ADA* (Ann Arbor: University of Michigan Press, 2003). Some of the contributors to this volume who are disability rights activists, lawyers, and scholars are Lennard J. Davis, Mathew Diller, Harlan Hahn, Linda Hamilton Krieger, Vicki A. Laden, Stephen L. Percy, Marta Russell, and Gregory Schwartz.

BIBLIOGRAPHIC ESSAY

Books and articles on disability rights are now being written at a ferocious pace. Two university presses, University of Michigan and New York University, recently launched disability book series. Approximately thirteen journals with disability in the title exist. And, as of the spring of 2003, a Lexus-Nexus search on the Americans with Disabilities Act (ADA) produced more than 5,000 law review articles published since 1991.

Two factors account for this fast-emerging and ever-expanding field. Scholars in both the social sciences and humanities recognize that the ADA is one of the most significant pieces of social legislation enacted in a generation. Between the mid-1970s and 1990, little social policy legislation passed that had such a great impact on the American polity. What is more, the ADA has faced resistance in the federal courts.

Second, disability studies programs were being put in place when the ADA was passed. Following the interdisciplinary studies program model—like those about women, African Americans, and gays and lesbians—disability studies scholars, many of whom had been part of the disability rights movement, had already won their academic battles and slogged through university curriculum committee paperwork to establish their programs.

This bibliographic essay makes no attempt at being current or comprehensive. Instead, it reviews some of the recent work on disability as well as the standard books and articles about it. The essay provides a representative overview of the field of disability rights and an understanding of disability studies.

To begin with, memoirs offer readers a way of visualizing how disability affects people's lives and the lives of those around them. Most of the recent memoirs included in the canon of disability studies are not tales of triumph like Helen Keller's autobiography. Memoirs used in disability studies often write against this type of narrative. For elegantly written memoirs by some of our contributors, which are alternately humorous and profound, see John Hockenberry, *Moving Violations: A Memoir: War Zones, Wheelchairs, and Declarations of Independence* (New York: Hyperion, 1995); Leonard Kriegel, *Flying Solo: Reimaging Manhood, Courage and Loss* (Boston: Beacon, 1998); and Stephen Kuusisto, *Planet of the Blind: A Memoir* (New York: Delta, 1998). Other notable memoirs are Lucy Grealy, *Autobiography of a Face* (Boston: Houghton Mifflin, 1994); Nancy Mairs, *Waist-High in the World: A Life among the Nondisabled* (Boston: Beacon, 1996); and Kenny Fries, *Body, Remember: A Memoir* (New York: Dutton, 1997). Fries also has edited an excellent volume, *Staring Back: The Disability Experience from the Inside Out* (New York: Plume, 1997), which includes memoirs, fiction, essays, poetry, and plays.

For a good overview of disability issues in the United States, readers should consult Joseph Shapiro, *No Pity: People with Disabilities Forging a New Civil Rights Movement* (New York: Times Books, 1993). Marta Russell's punchy book *Beyond Ramps: Disability at the End of the Social Contract* (Monroe, Maine: Common Courage Press, 1998) presents an activist's account of the ADA's passage and disability rights. Mary Johnson, the editor of the *Ragged Edge*, the leading disability rights magazine, has written a pointed and lively book titled *Make Them Go Away: Clint Eastwood, Christopher Reeve and the Case against Disability Rights* (Louisville, Ky.: Advocado Press, 2003). A scholarly account of the movement is Doris Z. Fleischer and Frieda Zames, *The Disability Rights Movement: From Charity to Confrontation* (Philadelphia: Temple University Press, 2000). Sharon Barnatt and Richard Scotch have compiled some key articles and original documents in *Disability Protests: Contentious Politics, 1970–1999* (Washington, D.C.: Gallaudet University Press, 2001).

Of the ground-breaking works that present the big picture in theoretical terms, Henri-Jacques Stiker's *A History of Disability,* translated by William Sayers (Ann Arbor: University of Michigan Press, 1998) is the most compelling. Covering deafness, Lennard J. Davis's *Enforcing Normalcy: Disability, Deafness, and the Body* (New York: Verso, 1995) connects disability to normalcy in a way that teases out larger theoretical issues. For works that place disability rights in context with other important theoretical approaches, or "isms," see Michelle Fine and Adrienne Asch, eds., *Women with Disabilities: Essays in Psychology, Culture, and Politics* (Philadelphia: Temple University Press, 1988); Iris Marion Young, *Justice and the Politics of Difference* (Princeton, N.J.: Princeton University Press, 1990); Anita Silvers, "Reconciling Equality to Difference: Caring (f)or Justice for People with Disabilities," *Hypatia* 10 (1995): 30–55; Susan Wendell, *The Rejected Body: Feminist*

Philosophical Reflections on Disability (New York: Routledge, 1996); Shelley Tremain, "On the Government of Disability," *Social Theory and Disability* 27 (2001): 617–36; Jenny Morris, "Impairment and Disability: Constructing an Ethics of Care That Promotes Human Rights," *Hypatia* 16 (2001): 1–16; Mairian Corker and Tom Shakespeare, eds., *Disability/Postmodernity: Embodying Disability Theory* (London: Continuum, 2002); and Ruth O'Brien, "Other Voices at the Workplace: Gender, Disability and an Alternative Ethic of Care," *SIGNS: Journal of Women in Culture and Society* (forthcoming, 2004).

A rich body of work examines disability in culture, including Erving Goffman, *Stigma: Notes on the Management of a Spoiled Identity* (Englewood Cliffs, N.J.: Prentice-Hall, 1963); Robert Bogdan, *Freak Show: Presenting Human Oddities for Amusement and Profit* (Chicago, Ill.: University of Chicago Press, 1988); Robert Murphy, *The Body Silent* (New York: Norton, 1990); and Rosemarie Garland Thomson, *Freakery: Cultural Spectacles of the Extraordinary Body* (New York: New York University Press, 1996) and *Extraordinary Bodies: Figuring Physical Disability in American Culture and Literature* (New York: Columbia University Press, 1997). A short but eye-opening introduction to how different cultures treat disability is Benedicte Ingstad and Susan Reynolds Whyte's essay in *Disability and Culture* (Berkeley: University of California Press, 1995). *Disability in Different Cultures: Reflections on Local Concepts*, edited by Brigitte Holzer, Arthur Vreede, and Gabriele Weigt and translated by Pat Skorge, Mary Kenney, and Eva Schulte-Noole (Bielefeld, Germany: Transcript Verlag, 2001), is a useful reader.

Several disability studies readers do a thorough job of representing the whole gamut of literature. See the readers edited by Len Barton, *Disability and Society: Emerging Issues and Insights* (London and New York: Longman, 1996); Lennard J. Davis, *The Disability Studies Reader* (New York: Routledge, 1997); Tom Shakespeare, *The Disability Reader: Social Science Perspectives* (London: Casswell, 1998); and Colin Barnes, Geoff Mercer, and Tom Shakespeare, *Exploring Disability: A Sociological Perspective* (London: Polity 1999). A classic essay that helped launch the field by equating disability rights with minority rights is Leonard Kriegel, "Uncle Tom and Tiny Tim: Some Reflections on the Cripple as Negro," *American Scholar* 38 (1969): 412–30. Simi Linton has written disability studies' first historiography, *Claiming Disability: Knowledge and Identity* (New York: New York University Press, 1998); and David Pfeiffer and K. Yoshida have presented a valuable article titled "Teaching Disability Studies in Canada and the USA," *Disability and Society* 10 (1995): 47–95.

One of the central themes in disability studies focuses on juxtaposing the medical model and the rights model of disability. Some of the articles that provide a commendable overview are Harlan Hahn, "Civil Rights for Disabled Americans: The Foundation of a Political Agenda," 181–203, in *Images of the Disabled, Disabling Images*, edited by Alan Gartner and Tom Joe (New York: Praeger, 1987); Douglas Bilker, "The Myth of Clinical Judgment," *Journal of Social Issues* 44 (1988): 127–40; and Paul K. Longmore, "Medical Decision Making and People with Disabilities: A Clash of Cultures," *Journal of Law, Medicine and Ethics* 23 (1995): 82–87. James I. Charlton, *Nothing about Us without Us: Disability Oppression and Empow-*

erment (Berkeley: University of California Press, 1998), has transformed the societal model into a human rights model. Other literature in medical sociology reconciles the medical and the rights models by focusing on illness and "bringing the body back in." See M. R. Bury, "Social Constructionism and the Development of Medical Sociology," *Sociology of Health and Illness* 8 (1986):137–69; L. Crow, "Including All of Our Lives: Renewing the Social Model of Disability," in *Exploring the Divide: Illness and Disability*, edited by C. Barnes and G. Mercer (Leeds, England: Disability Press, 1996); and M. Kelly and D. Field, "Medical Sociology, Chronic Illness and the Body," *Sociology of Health and Illness* 18 (1996): 241–57.

Paul K. Longmore, one of disability studies' founders, and Lauri Umansky have compiled a superb reader entitled *The New Disability History: American Perspectives* (New York: New York University Press, 2001). Longmore also has a book of historical articles and essays, *Why I Burned My Book and Other Essays on Disability* (Philadelphia: Temple University Press, 2003). Also see ground-breaking historical works by Hugh G. Gallagher, *FDR's Splendid Deception* (New York: Dodd Mead, 1985); and Nora Groce, *Everyone Here Spoke Sign Language: Hereditary Deafness on Martha's Vineyard* (Cambridge, Mass.: Harvard University Press, 1985). An excellent history of medicine is Paul Starr, *The Social Transformation of American Medicine: The Rise of a Sovereign Profession and the Making of a Vast Industry* (New York: Basic, 1982). For histories of mental illness, see Gerald N. Grob, *The Mad among Us: A History of the Care of America's Mentally Ill* (Cambridge, Mass.: Harvard University Press, 1994); and David J. Rothman, *The Discovery of the Asylum: Social Order and Disorder in the New Republic* (Boston: Little, Brown, 1971) and *Conscience and Convenience: The Asylum and Its Alternative in Progressive America* (Boston: Little Brown, 1980). Vital work on the nineteenth century is Peter David Blanck and Michael Millender, "Before Disability Civil Rights: Civil War Pensions and the Politics of Disability in America," 52 *Alabama Law Review* 1 (2000).

Excellent books about the history of disability policy include Deborah A. Stone, *The Disabled State* (Philadelphia: Temple University Press, 1984); Richard K. Scotch, *From Goodwill to Civil Rights* (Philadelphia: Temple University Press, 1984); Edward D. Berkowitz, *Disabled Policy: America's Programs for the Handicapped* (New York: Cambridge University Press, 1987); and Stephen L. Percy, *Disability, Civil Rights, and Public Policy: The Politics of Implementation* (Tuscaloosa: University of Alabama Press, 1989). The history of rehabilitation can be found in Mary E. MacDonald, *Federal Grants for Vocational Rehabilitation* (New York: Arno, 1980); Edward D. Berkowitz, *Rehabilitation: The Federal Government's Response to Disability, 1935–1954* (New York: Arno, 1980); and Mary Lenz Walker, *Beyond Bureaucracy: Mary Elizabeth Switzer and Rehabilitation* (Lanham, Md.: University Press of America, 1985). Despite the seemingly narrow subject of "rehabilitation history," Berkowitz and Walker, in particular, provide a comprehensive understanding of the political, societal, and legal contexts from which the twentieth century notion of disability emerged. More recent is Ruth O'Brien, *Crippled Justice: The History of Modern Disability Policy in the Workplace* (Chicago, Ill.: University of Chicago Press, 2001), which traces the history of rehabilitation, the passage of section 504 and the ADA, and the Supreme Court's reluctance to enforce disability rights.

Given the number of ADA cases that the federal courts have interpreted, law review articles are being penned at a fast pace. A first-rate theoretical discussion of disability law is Martha Minow's *Making All the Difference: Inclusion, Exclusion and American Law* (Ithaca, N.Y.: Cornell University Press, 1990). Good overviews of the whole statute are presented by Bonnie P. Tucker, "The Americans with Disabilities Act: An Overview," 1989 *University of Illinois Law Review* 923 (1989); Robert L. Burgdorf, Jr., "The Americans with Disabilities Act: Analysis and Implications of a Second-Generation Civil Rights Statute," 26 *Harvard Civil Rights/Civil Liberties Review* 413 (1991); and Chai Feldblum, "Definition of Disability under Federal Antidiscrimination Law: What Happened? Why? and What Can We Do about It?" 21 *Berkeley Journal of Employment and Labor Law* 91 (2000).

For Title I employment law, readers would be advised to consult Arlene B. Mayerson, "Restoring Regard for the 'Regarded as' Prong: Giving Effect to Congressional Intent," 42 *Villanova Law Review* 587 (1997); and Steven S. Locke, "The Incredible Shrinking Protected Class: Redefining the Scope of Disability under the Americans with Disabilities Act," 68 *University of Colorado Law Review* 107 (1997). Ruth Colker's "The ADA: A Windfall for Defendants," 34 *Harvard Civil Rights/Civil Liberties Law Review* 99 (1999), presents a valuable set of statistics about the Title I employment cases.

A relatively smaller number of articles cover Title II governmental services provisions and Title III public accommodations provisions since the federal courts have rendered fewer decisions than under Title I. For an overview of litigation under these two titles, see Ruth Colker, "ADA Title III: A Fragile Compromise," 21 *Berkeley Journal of Employment and Labor Law* 377 (2000); Michael Lewyn, "Thou Shalt Not Put a Stumbling Block before the Blind: The ADA and Public Transit for the Disabled," 52 *Hastings Law Journal* 1037 (2001); and Pamela Brandwein, "Constitutional Doctrine as Parting Tool: The Struggle for 'Relevant' Evidence in *University of Alabama v. Garrett*," 35 *University of Michigan Journal of Law Reform* 37 (2001). Readers who prefer social science treatments of the statute should refer to Edward D. Berkowitz, "A Historical Preface to the Americans with Disabilities Act," *Journal of Policy History* 6 (1994): 96–119; Leslie A. Francis and Anita Silvers, *Americans with Disabilities* (London: Routledge, 2000); and Susan Gluck Mezey, Will Jordan, Catherine Thie, and Douglas Davis, "The Americans with Disabilities Act in Federal Court: Litigating against Public Entities," *Disability and Society* 17 (2002): 49–64.

INDEX